X-15 DIARY

The Story of America's First Space Ship
———— By RICHARD TREGASKIS

FOREWORD BY SCOTT CROSSFIELD

University of Nebraska Press
Lincoln and London

Library of Congress Cataloging-in-Publication Data
Tregaskis, Richard, 1916–1973.
X-15 diary: the story of America's first space ship / by Richard Tregaskis;
foreword by Scott Crossfield.
p. cm.
Originally published: New York: Dutton, 1961.
Includes bibliographical references and index.
ISBN 0-8032-9456-5 (pbk.: alk. paper)
1. X-15 (Rocket aircraft) 2. Aerodynamics, Hypersonic—Research—United
States. I. Title.
TL789.8.U6T74 2004
629.133'38—dc22   2004007734

This Bison Books edition follows the original in beginning chapter 1 on arabic
page 17; no material has been omitted.

Foreword

He came, he saw, he chronicled. Richard Tregaskis's style of journalistic research has created his brand icon of Americana. His diaries open to the readers' view the realities of the story: the scene, the players, and the drama of the earthy details that are the real essence of the structure of historic events that arise from the limitless connection of small parts.

Tregaskis was among us at the birthing of the X-15 Research Airplane operation that created a major technological steppingstone to space. He was with us for two years watching, questioning, probing into the smallest detail of our every step. He was very sensitive to the idea of stress and tension in all who were engaged in the frustrating tasks of bringing together the many pieces of an invention of man's fertile but less than precise imagination. I think that being a gentle and humane man he never fully understood that those traits were not in any way dominant in the flight-test population.

Dick Tregaskis was everywhere we turned filling out his tale, and when we were idle he was all over the country or buried in literature to become fully cognizant of our assessment of successful progress. He could penetrate the barrier of the laconic and the true thoughts of the private person. *X-15 Diary: The Story of America's First Space Station* is among the preferred references for those who wish to know the X-15 story in-depth and with understanding.

I commend this volume of Tregaskis lore to those who want to live with all the actors that Tregaskis came to know by name and as intimate friends in order to draw out the elements of developing history. The "trouble-plagued X-15" was not. It was, as Tregaskis taught, a difficult but very rewarding small step in the human endeavor.

THIS BOOK is an attempt to present verbal photographs of hundreds of men and women at work on one of our important space projects. There are thousands more involved in our other space efforts, just as demanding and exacting, and many as dangerous too. To the men and women I name and follow at their work, and to the faceless thousands trying just as hard on other sectors of the War Against Space, this book is respectfully dedicated.

Contents

Photographs

AT NOON on the concrete plain beside the hangars of Edwards Air Force Base, a group of men in coveralls are rolling out a slim, sleek, black dart of a missile. It has stub wings, and rocket tubes at the square rear end mark its power supply. Large white lettering on its bulging side reads, "U.S. AIR FORCE." It rides on a yellow rubber-tired cart or dolly. The dolly bears owner identification, "NASA," standing for National Aeronautics and Space Administration—appropriate since many of the research vehicles sent out into space are handled and launched by NASA.

The smooth black hull is almost entirely two cylindrical tanks, one mounted behind the other. The forward tank will be filled with liquid oxygen, lox, a rocket oxidizer, and the rear one with water alcohol. Other smaller tanks within the hull will be pumped full of the other gases needed for rocket flights: helium to start the fuel flowing; hydrogen peroxide to generate the power the missile will need for its control systems; nitrogen which, coupled with compact air-conditioning equipment, will supply an atmosphere in which delicate instruments can keep on functioning, despite the hundred-below emptiness in which the missile will fly.

All these characteristics are to be expected in a missile-like vehicle that will be probing the outskirts of space. But there are a few differences about this one. One difference is the small hump on top of the hull just behind the needle-like nose probe. That hump has narrow, dark blue glass windows, and controls inside, much like those on a conventional airplane. It is a cockpit. And inside the cockpit, air conditioning not alone for the sake of instrumentation, but also to keep a man alive.

On the bottom side of the fuselage, below the nose, another difference from the usual missile is visible: dual rubber-tired wheels on sturdy struts, now extended to share with the yellow dolly the job of supporting the bird.

Farther aft on the bottom of the fuselage, beneath the tail, are two trap doors which can be extended to form heavy landing skids. Altogether, the nose wheels and skids are somewhat like the landing gear on a conventional airplane. For this is a missile in many senses of the word, but in another way it is something very different, a vehicle designed to carry a *man* into space and bring him back safe to earth. It is the X-15, our first space ship (though NASA prefers to call it the last of a line of research airplanes), being wheeled out for a preflight check on the day before a big mission—the mission on which a man will try to fly higher into space than any man on our side of the Iron Curtain (or on the other side, as far as we know) has ever been.

But first, before the flight can start, there are twenty hours of exacting preparations to be made. And they are only the last of an infinity of efforts, months and years of effort, of blood, sweat, and tears which made this flight possible. A record-seeking flight into space is only the spectacular foam on top of a wave that has traveled thousands of miles before it can break on the beach of the Unknown. A space mission is like a battle—it can happen only because of untold sagas of self-sacrifice and heroic devotion which preceded it and now make it possible. And that battle, like the wave breaking on the beach, is only a temporary advancement until the next wave or the next battle on the way to eventual victory, or defeat.

This flight, millions of people are hoping, will go well beyond the world's altitude record established on September 7, 1956, by Captain Iven C. Kincheloe, Jr., in an early high-altitude airplane, the X-2.

For a few seconds in his historic flight, Captain Kincheloe, in the now-archaic rocket plane X-2, had been unable to control his aircraft. He had hit the fringe of space, the edge of the vacuum. As he climbed above 100,000 feet and headed for his world record of 126,200 feet, he was above the atmosphere, at 23.9 miles straight up, the first man to escape the sea of air which surrounds the earth. So his conventional control surfaces, ailerons, rudder, and elevators, had no air against which they could work. Kinch, in his uncomfortable, old-fashioned MC-4 pressure suit, cramped into his tiny cockpit, was tossed end for end with his plane. Like the plane, he was buffeted and beaten up as it flipped, spun, and rolled, out of control.

He had to wait an interminable thirty seconds until the craft had fallen back into the earth's atmosphere and the air grew thick enough so his controls could take effect.

Space is usually defined as the area beyond the earth's atmosphere, and the earth's atmosphere is virtually nonexistent from 100,000 feet up. Tongues of weak atmosphere may extend beyond that level, but practically, at the 100,000-foot level, the void is beginning, the Wild Black Yonder where there are no air particles to reflect the sunlight and carry sound. At Kincheloe's altitude there would be no more than a cupful of air in a cubic mile. So, in a sense, for a few seconds he was the first space man. (NASA disagrees, says that space begins at 100 miles out. Harrison Storms, chief engineer at North American Aircraft's Los Angeles division, which built the X-15, believes it starts at 90,000 feet or 17 miles.)

The X-15, the big black rocket, was designed to go beyond that. One year after the Kincheloe record, construction was started on the X-15. Planning for the craft had actually begun way back in 1952, since, as technology advances in the Space Age, lead time for planning and building a missile increases immensely. That lead time, however, was accelerated after Kincheloe's record flight in the X-2.

Kinch, the blond, handsome, dedicated Air Force pilot of whom it was once said that he had been sent from Central Casting for the part of Number-One Space Pilot, was to have been the ranking Air Force jockey for the X-15. He didn't live long enough for the job. On July 26, 1958, aged thirty, he was killed when his hot fighter plane, an F-104 not unlike a missile, lost its engine on take-off from Edwards. He tried to roll his nine-ton mount onto its back so that he could eject and take to his silk. But he got just halfway over. His ejection seat blasted him clear of the plane, but his parachute opened only partially and he fell to his death.

Of Kincheloe we will write more later because he was one of the royal family of the Space Age, a sort of Flash Gordon who commanded everyone's respect. But when he died, others were standing in line for the honor and the danger of flying his X-15.

When the first of the three X-15s was completed and pushed onto the hardstand outside the North American Aviation factory at Los Angeles International Airport, 100 miles to the south of Edwards Air Force Base, in October 1958, there were eight selected test pilots waiting to fly it.

The first of the fliers was the North American test pilot, Scott Crossfield, backed up by another company test jockey, Alvin S.

White. Their job was to prove to the Air Force and NASA the air-worthiness and dependability of the craft. The other six pilots waiting in line came from the Air Force, NASA, and the United States Navy. All these agencies had contributed to the X-15 program.

There was a good deal for the company pilots to prove, in the course of their acceptance trials, because the X-15 was our first flying craft to have controls, instruments, and a shape designed to take a pilot out into the edge of space and come back to a controlled landing on earth.

The X-15 was the first man-carrying machine to have what are called reaction controls: in its nose and its stub wing were eight small rocket jets which could be fired to alter its attitude in space, where there is no air for conventional control surfaces to bite on. These reaction or ballistic controls were the first to be designed into a man-carrying aircraft. Something similar had been added to one of the early X-1 rocket planes, in a preliminary move to test the X-15 rocket controls. But the plane didn't have enough power to climb into thin air where the controls could be tested effectively.

The X-15 was the first ship to be designed and built around such space controls. And many other items in the X-15 marked it as our first space ship; for instance, its flight instruments, for the first time designed to measure speed and altitude where there would be no air. Before X-15, airplane instruments had taken their readings from pressure gauges that estimated speed and height over the earth. The X-15, borrowing from the know-how acquired by the men who built missiles, employed a gyroscope system which could give accurate measurements of speed and altitude in the void of space.

And since the X-15 had to bring the pilot back from space to a safe landing on earth, it had to have controls which would function in air as well as those designed for space. So it was given stub wings, each one only nine feet long, and a so-called "rolling tail," to provide the pilot with control in atmosphere. The tail surfaces, almost as wide as the wings, combined the functions of elevators and ailerons. And besides embodying a new configuration, the new space beast was built of new materials, especially employed to research the problem of overheating as the vehicle hit the atmosphere at great speed after it came back from the penetration of space. Whether such a craft and its lineal descendants are restricted to flights into space surrounding earth, or whether they become space taxis designed to land on Mars, Venus, or other planets, the problem of aerodynamic heating as they hit atmosphere at high speed will always have to be encountered, for the planets of our solar system all have atmospheres of some sort around them, and any vehicle entering those atmospheres is apt to be arriving at the tremendous speeds that can be generated in space, where there is no atmospheric resistance. There is a never-ending quest for materials and shapes which will resist the great heat a space ship will meet under such conditions—3,000 or 4,000 degrees Fahrenheit or more. And many of the Air Force and NASA engineers believe the most important research objective of the X-15 is to explore this problem.

Fortunately, this craft is here, visible, watchable, and measurable for a reporter to observe before, during, and after its assault on the world's altitude record.

There was no such good luck in the time when something similarly important happened in Spain in 1492, as a sailing captain known as Christoforo Colombo readied three small carracks for a voyage into the earthly unknown. There were no journalists available at the Spanish seaport town of Palos in August of that year, as Columbus and his ninety officers and men started out to prove the world was round, and eventually to find the new land then christened "Cipango," later renamed America.

Since all involved in that voyage were men of action, with no disinterested correspondents present to cover the battle Colombus was about to undertake, we are left with very little information about his fleet.

Hence today the most popular sailing ship model in the world, Columbus's flagship *Santa Maria,* is almost the most inexact. No one knows what she looked like. And the figures on her dimensions and tonnage are only approximate. She could have been anywhere between 100 and 130 tons burden, she might have been 100 feet long, or 125.

But nowadays we are much better fixed for facts as men send our first space ship into the edges of the Infinite which we will be exploring for the next few hundreds of years. That is why as early as February of 1959 I started living with this big black beast of a rocket— or, to be exact, three rockets.

These were the X-15s, three sister ships almost identical, the first vehicles to probe the Wild Black Yonder. The Wild Black Yonder is the infinity of space amid which we live, a tiny planet aware enough of itself to want to find out what is out there in the universe, what trillions of living creatures may people the trillions upon trillions of miles in the void, the trillions of planetary systems that circle uncounted oceans of stars. There are estimated to be at least 40 billion stars in our own galaxy, and at least 10 billion other galaxies in space. Harlow Shapley, the eminent Harvard astronomer, has estimated there may be as many as 100 million stars with planetary systems wherein life could be found. Such is the staggering new frontier we are beginning to touch.

The X-15 program is our first step in that direction. In catching up with the project, I felt the same excitement I had known when, as a war correspondent, I boarded a ship or a plane heading for a beachhead where an unknown enemy waited, in one of the many armed conflicts which have plagued our time. This campaign against space, as I rapidly found out, has the same kind of dedicated, self-sacrificing, heroic men and women involved in it. But the dedication and sacrifice and heroism are for a nobler goal than war, the opening of a breath-taking new age of cosmic exploration.

1 The First Flights

FEBRUARY 26, 1959. With Dick Barton, from the Public Relations Department of North American Aviation, and Raun Robinson, one of the two assistant chief engineers on X-15, I went down to the West High Bay section of the factory to get my first look at the X-15.

It's a big, light, open factory bay, with two X-15s lined up in tandem. The one closest to the airfield is much farther on, constructionwise, than the other. It looks just about finished, where the other one still has the appearance of a skeleton, as if the basic structure were still being put together. These are Birds Nos. 2 and 3. Bird No. 1, the first of the three in the $121.5 million program, has already been taken (by truck) up to Edwards Air Force Base, where pretty soon it will make its first flight under the wing of a B-52 mother ship.

Bird No. 2—the one closest to the field here in the West Bay— will be ready for its first public roll-out tomorrow, Dick Barton said. In a week or two it will probably be trucked up to Edwards.

Bird No. 2 looks very impressive—sleek, black, powerful—a missile with stubby little wings and a cockpit on top of the nose. When we came into the bay the cockpit canopy was up and a group of technicians in sports shirts clustered around that part. The canopy was being raised and lowered. One man held a flashlight so he could check something in the relative darkness when the canopy was lowered. The slit eyes of the cockpit windows are made of dark blue glass, to keep the glare of space to a minimum.

We went to the cockpit and climbed up the work ladder beside it. The plane seems very solid, sleek, and well finished. The metal of the exterior is largely Inconel X, a high nickel-steel alloy especially resistant to heat.

"Most of it is tanks," Dick said, and pointed to the middle of the ship's body. There, under the slick black surface, are the two huge tanks, in tandem, that make up most of the fuselage. They will hold 1,200 gallons of water alcohol, the fuel, and 1,000 gallons of liquid oxygen or lox, the oxidizer needed to burn it. There are other, smaller tanks, for hydrogen peroxide, helium, and nitrogen—all the gases needed to make the various systems of the bird work.

We looked into the cockpit. There is a huge aluminum brace set up as a kind of semicircle behind the head of the pilot.

"That'll hold his head if there is buffeting," Dick said.

We looked at the steel seat, which can be blown clear of the aircraft by an explosive charge if the pilot has trouble.

"The seat is the pilot's office," Dick said. "He'll stay with it, even if he ejects. He won't leave it until he's well into atmosphere."

He pointed out the metal wings that flanked the chair. "If the pilot bails, the wings will fold out and give him some stability so he won't tumble so much." I looked into the big gap behind the cockpit, an empty compartment with scores of switches set up on one wall. Raun Robinson indicated a large black box of instrumentation sitting beside it on the factory floor.

"About 400 pounds of instruments will be put into the compartment," he said. "Some will connect with the instrument panel, some will send dope to the ground." (The total weight of the instrumentation in various compartments is 1,300 pounds.)

He took me around to one of the stubby little wings and pointed out a kind of grid pattern of holes in the lower side of the black surface.

"These taps are for pressure," he said. And Barton explained that this is a research aircraft, that the main purpose of it is to explore the close reaches of space, so there are 790 taps on it to record temperature and pressure.

We stopped at the nose, a solid-feeling cone of black metal. Raun said: "It's a heat sink. It'll soak up the heat of re-entry." He explained that the heat here would get up as high as 1,200°, depending on how fast the bird is flying when it comes back into atmosphere. Some other parts of the bird, the belly and the underside of the wing, will get nearly as hot as the nose—that is, if it comes back into atmosphere in the proper attitude, nose down. But if something goes wrong with the space controls and it re-enters upside down, or tumbling, lots of the other parts are going to get excessively heated. "If that should happen, the pilot'll be in plenty bad trouble," Dick Barton said.

I asked Dick about the reason for painting the ship black. I'd heard that black paint was supposed to emit more of the re-entry heat than a white color. The engineers have a fancy word for this. They call it high emissivity.

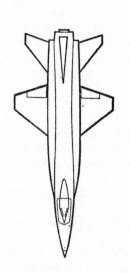

X-15
Three View
SPECIFICATIONS

LENGTH.. 50 FT

WING SPAN............................. 22 FT

HEIGHT...................................... 13 FT

WING AREA .... 200 SQ FT

SWEEP $^c/_4$ .... 25°

WEIGHT AT LAUNCHING..............
...................31,275 LBS

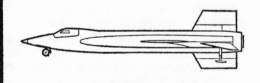

The early aircraft in our Air Force series of rocket planes were painted for visibility in light colors like the light orange of the X-1 in which Captain (now Lieutenant Colonel) Chuck Yeager first broke the sound barrier in 1947. But the engineers on X-15, confronted with more outer skin heating than ever before, wanted a paint which would give off a maximum of the ship's heat as it hit atmosphere at high speed. They had the answer after heat-chamber tests. [Paul F. Bikle, director of the NASA facility at Edwards Air Force Base, points out that black generally has better emissivity, and that the X-15 was also painted black to provide a uniform color over the materials of various colors in the structure, thus giving a minimum of temperature differences.]

FEBRUARY 27. Today was the time for roll-out of Bird No. 2. A bright, clear, warm morning. On the smooth concrete expanse outside the West High Bay Barton and I saw a knot of men and women gathered around the bird. The bird, even in the sunlight, has a sinister look about it—that slick, black body with the two bulges (side tunnels) like muscles along its flanks, the nose as sharp as a mosquito's. It's as sinister as a mosquito would be if the mosquito weighed sixteen tons and had the horsepower of the *Queen Mary,* and carried a man on its back.

Beside the X-15, this morning, sat the big metal mass of the ejection seat. It had been taken out of the cockpit area, and blinds hung up inside the cockpit to mask it from rubbernecks. Some of the stuff inside is still, apparently, on the classified list—although *Newsweek* magazine has already printed a photograph of the supposedly secret instrument panel, the one with the stable-platform (gyro) gauges on it. As in a war, there's always an officious type who hasn't the correct word about what is or isn't on the secret list.

Near the ejection seat stood a man in the Silver Suit—the Air Force calls it MC-2—which the pilots lined up to fly the X-15 will wear. The man in the suit today was not a pilot, but Rex Martin, a technician from North America's Human Factors Department, demonstrating the equipment. The people gathered around the X-15 were stockholders, Dick Barton said. Most of them were men, middle-aged or older, wearing business suits, quite formal for the bright Los Angeles sun. A company guide was answering questions.

"How many men will be in it?" one youngish woman wanted to know.

"One man," said the guide, poker-faced.

The guide moved to the ejection seat, a formidable pillar of metal —gray steel, with convolutions of tubing and wiring twined through the mass of it.

"Unfortunately we can't show you the cockpit," the guide said. "There are some classified things in it. This is the ejection seat." He pointed to the heavy planes of metal, like wings, which were folded up beside the flanks of the steel chair.

"These guide wings come out to avoid tumbling," he said.

There was a pause, a silence. "Because he has a long way to fall," he went on. He pointed out the steel ankle straps that extend automatically to protect the pilot's legs if he has to eject.

"Does he have a chute?" a well-dressed, middle-aged man asked.

"Yes." A nervous titter ran through the crowd, and the man reproached the guide: "You didn't say anything about it."

"An aneroid pulls out the chute at 15,000 feet," the guide went on. "It opens automatically in case he should be unconscious."

Again there was a silence. The stockholders seemed ill at ease in the presence of this space ship, the first rocket ship ever built by North American, also the company's first creature of pure science.

An elderly woman, standing between me and the ejection seat, pointed to that complicated mass.

"My, isn't that an intricate thing," she said to me.

I agreed while the head guide was saying: "If you will break into smaller groups, the hosts will answer questions."

One stockholder pointed to the man in the Silver Suit, and asked the guide as the group began to drift apart:

"Is that the suit the pilot will be wearing?"

"Yes. He can tell you about it." The stockholder walked toward the silver-suited Martin and I tagged along with him.

Martin looked warm. He was not wearing the helmet and beads of sweat stood on his forehead, even though the air-conditioning system of the suit was working; I could hear the hissing of the ventilating nitrogen gas from the rubber tube ends that projected from his circular collar. I was asking how many layers of cloth there are under the outer envelope of flexible aluminum, when another company employee came bustling up.

"What authority do you have to make notes on this?" he asked me. "The suit is classified."

I explained that I was writing a book about the X-15 and this was part of the job. I pointed out that the other people here were also looking at the suit.

"Yes, but you're making notes," he said, scandalized.

Barton came to my rescue, pacified the self-appointed intelligence agent, and explained to me that certain things about the suit—such as the number of layers and how they are fashioned underneath—are on the secret list.

The theory, I know, is that the suit, which will be the working garb of our first space man, may have some features the Russians might be able to use when they send men into space. The pretext for censorship is that the Russians, if they knew about it, might be able to make some military use of the space suit.

That's the theory, but I doubt its validity. Ever since the beginning of the Space Age, when the Russians fired Sputnik I into orbit on October 4, 1957, there have been repeated reminders that we'd have reason to copy the Russians rather than vice versa.

I was miffed by this first bout with security on the X-15 project, but Barton changed the subject by introducing me to a neat, rather stubby man standing nearby. He was Al White, the company back-up pilot, assigned to the X-15. The first company test pilot, Scott Crossfield, wasn't here today.

White seemed serious, thoughtful, and engaging. Barton explained that besides being the company back-up pilot on the X-15, White was also the first pilot on the B-70, the 2,000-mile-an-hour bomber North American is building behind veils of secrecy.

Neither White nor Crossfield will make any of the X-15 flights to record altitudes and speeds, Dick said. Those will be reserved for Air Force and NASA pilots. The company pilots will have the job of demonstrating that the ship is flyable and its various complicated systems workable.

I asked White what was the most immediate worry in testing the X-15. He said: "The landing—because Scott [Crossfield] won't know about it until he does it. Once he's in, he'll know it can be done."

White said the landing speed is pretty hot—about 180 knots, which translates to 212 miles an hour. With its tiny wings, the X-15 isn't exactly built for a comfortable kind of landing. White pointed out the landing skids, two steel skis that fold down beneath the tail to provide main gear. There is also a nose gear of two rubber-tired wheels.

"That first time," White said, "we'll know. She'll just be in and she'll be down." He didn't say what I suppose must be on his mind: that the engineers could assert the plane was landable, but that nobody could be sure until a test pilot had done it. No matter how good a ship is theoretically, how many times it can be attested with a slipstick or on paper, there always is a time when it must prove it can, in fact, fly. The test pilot is like a soldier in the field: no matter how enthusiastic the scientists are about a weapon in the laboratory, unforeseen difficulties always develop in combat use, and the soldier's life or death depends on how serious the difficulties are.

I asked White what the biggest over-all worry will be after the X-15 has been over the hurdle of the first landing.

"Re-entry," he said without hesitation. "When you cut loose from the B-52 [the mother ship which will carry the X-15 up to launch altitude], you have to choose your angle of attack. If the angle is too steep, you'll come in too fast and you could burn up from re-entry heat when you hit atmosphere, because you'll be coming down at the same angle as going up. If it's 45° going up, you'll be coming down at 45."

That, he explained, was what they meant by the ballistic curve of the X-15 flight. Like an artillery shell, the X-15 will have power only at the first stage of the flight. Then it will arc up and back like a shell—just as the curve of the artillery projectile depends on the angle of the barrel when the gun is fired.

An elderly stockholder had been listening in and blinking at Al through his bifocals. "Will the plane be out of control, then?" he asked, his eyes bugging.

"Well, the pilot has to select his angle of attack," Al said. "Naturally, he wouldn't go straight up. If he did, he'd come straight down and burn up. He'd buy the farm."

It was refreshing to hear the old RAF slang for being killed—which had seeped into our American pilot language during World War II. Refreshing, that is, to hear the possibility of death phrased with such candor and intimacy.

I asked Al about the reaction controls, the small rocket jets in the nose and wings which are supposed to give the pilot the power of changing the attitude of the X-15 during the ballistic phase of its flight. They can't alter the curve of the flight itself, but they can theoretically trim the plane so that it will stay upright over the curve—and so it won't be entering atmosphere upside down when it comes back from space.

"They've never been tried before in space," Al said soberly. "They had some small ones on the X-1B [the X-1B was a modification of the early rocket plane, X-1, which first broke the sound barrier]. But they didn't have the power to get up there where the controls could be tested in thin air—so they had to simulate space conditions by flying at less dynamic pressure—slower speed at lower altitude. But it didn't work out."

White came back to one of the favorite themes of test pilots: that sometime, in the ultimate, a man has to take it up and fly it. "It's one thing to fly the simulator," he said, meaning the ground-based mockup of the X-15 in which pilots can make imitation flights through the use of a roomful of electronic calculators. "But you really don't know till you fly it."

MARCH 9. The first flight of the X-15 is scheduled for tomorrow. It'll be a captive flight—i.e., the X-15 will stay attached to the wing of the mother ship B-52—to check out some of the systems.

I had tried to set up a place on the North American ferry plane that will carry some engineers up to Edwards for the flight. But Earl Blount, the public-relations chief at the aircraft company, said there were no places available—every seat was taken and there was a waiting list among the engineers.

So I set out to drive up. The road is one of the noble highways that abound in California, a smooth ribbon winding through the rugged brown San Gabriel Mountains north of Los Angeles to the Mojave Desert.

Edwards Air Force Base is a collection of big bare buildings in a big bare wasteland. It isn't completely a wasteland, since the dry lake beds of the Edwards vicinity make ideal natural landing fields for hot military planes and rocket ships of the X-1, X-2, and X-15 ilk. Such fast birds characteristically need plenty of runway space for their landing—the rocket ships especially, since they always have to make glide landings, their power always spent in the first few minutes of the flight. Hence the Air Force Flight Test Center and the corresponding facility of NASA (National Aeronautics and Space Administration) have been installed here; also the civilian contractors concerned, such aircraft firms as Douglas, Convair, North American, and Lockheed.

I drove around the northern edge of the Edwards Air Force Base reservation, miles and miles of road unreeling across the desolate plain, with high mountains rising in the distance. There is a sparse covering of mesquite, sage, a scattering of stubby little joshua trees. I saw a couple of dust storms sweeping across the desert—rushing local winds that drag a trail of tan-colored dust with them.

The Edwards buildings are scattered from hell to breakfast—big hunks of hangars plunked down in the middle of nowhere.

I found a relatively dense arrangement of buildings near the flagpole that marks the headquarters of Edwards Air Force Base, Air Research, and Development Command.

At Headquarters I checked in with the Air Force Public Information Office. Colonel Charlie Brown, the head man, filled me in about tomorrow's flight.

Brown, a debonair, pleasant man, took me to a big wall map of Edwards. He pointed out the long strip of the main paved runway, 15,000 feet long, where the B-52 with the X-15 attached under one wing will take off.

He said the B-52 pilot, Captain Charles Bock, called tomorrow's flight a "fairly sporty course." There are a lot of unknowns such as the stability of the X-15/B-52 combination on take-off, landing, and in flight; also a long list of X-15 systems to be checked, such as instruments, the fuel jettison system, the landing gear, and the auxiliary power units.

Brown said that the B-52 crew had made simulated runs with extra fuel and of course the pylon, the structure which will support the X-15 under the right wing, but without the X-15.

"They tried a lower vertical test last week. [The X-15 lower tail fin has to be dropped before landing can be attempted.] There were propellant servicing tests—crew familiarization. But—" he shrugged in deference to the test pilot's axiom that an aircraft is never proved till actually flown. The burden of that proof tomorrow, as in many later flights, will be in the hands of the company pilot, Scott Crossfield.

MARCH 10. I was up at five-thirty and drove down to Headquarters from the Air Force barracks building where I stayed the night. Somewhere among the huge hangar structures ranged along the edge of the field, I knew, the X-15 was in the midst of the fueling operation. Long before this it must have been mated to the B-52, attached to the pylon under the wing.

But I had been told that nobody from the press is to be allowed anywhere near the bird at this juncture. I felt lucky enough to be in the vicinity. I should be able to work my way closer as the program progresses.

At Colonel Brown's office I met two other journalists who were to cover the first air lift of the X-15. They were from *Life*—Ralph Crane, the photographer, and a text man, Jim Goode.

We were the only representatives of the press. The North American and Air Force people aren't making any noise about the program at this stage. In fact, today they'd rather be left completely alone and cover today's events, I gathered, by issuing an announcement after the flight—the anti-democratic method but immediately more efficient for the people involved in the job.

With Lieutenant John Kirkley of the PIO office, we piled into an Air Force station wagon and headed for the runway where the B-52/ X-15 combination will take off. At seven-thirty we pulled up to a security gate where a line of vehicles was being cleared for entrance to the runway vicinity.

Airman Dick Johnston, of Westfield, New York, our driver, wheeled us near the 15,000-foot marker at the northeastern end of Runway Four. Kirkley and the rest of us had some discussion about the best place to locate. Crane wanted to set up his camera somewhere near the spot where the big bird would lift off. Also, there was the possibility that the plane might have trouble—might get out of balance with the extra load or have a power failure or other malfunction and clobber itself on take-off. This might seem a ghoulish consideration, but as reporters we must not miss the event if it should happen.

The safe thing was to choose the end of the runway: whatever was going to happen would probably have occurred by then. We could follow it with binoculars and Crane could catch it with his 300-mm lens and rapid-sequence camera.

So we settled down at the 15,000 marker and waited. Across the field, near the big North American hangar structure, we could see the tall orange tail of the B-52 sitting still. As we might have expected in such an important operation, there was a delay.

The sun grew hot over the bareness of the desert, and Jim Goode uninhibitedly stripped off his shirt. I followed suit and felt somewhat abashed when a cavalcade of blue Air Force sedans showed up at the 13,000-foot marker. A group of men in uniform climbed out. Some had the braid of field officers on their caps.

"The general has had his coffee," said someone in our little group.

Now, at nine-twenty, the big, jagged orange tail of the B-52 could be seen moving over the curve of the field, in the distance. It was taxiing toward the south end of the runway. In short order two rakish-tailed chase planes, which will escort the flight as trouble-shooters and camera planes, had blasted into the air—a good sign that take-off would be soon.

"How do these people always know when it's going to be?" Goode grumbled, meaning the general. We'd been waiting for an hour and a half.

We agreed, but nobody said so, because by now the tall B-52 tail had taken its place at the far end of the runway, and we knew the moment was near.

A huge, square-fronted red fire truck had rumbled up near us to take emergency position at the end of the runway. I could hear the radio cackling: "Edwards taxi to 24 . . ." and then a lot of unintelligible gobbledegook.

The B-52 was moving. Through the binoculars I watched the tall orange mast of the tail edging through a pool of thin, eddying black smoke that would be the mark of water injection as the throttles were jammed forward for take-off, hitting maximum power.

Now the wide span of the B-52 was rising above the *curve of the earth* refracted in a mirage. The shape came at us through the smoke cloud, gaining speed. The small black blob of the X-15 (weighing about eight tons with today's partial load of fuel) was almost invisible under the right wing.

It seemed to be a trifling load for the 150-ton B-52. The big plane lifted smoothly, and was clear of the ground only halfway down the runway. By the time it roared over our heads, it must have been 400 feet up. It climbed easily, spiraling into a clean blue sky.

Another chase plane, a hornet-like F-104, screamed down the runway, the afterburner blatting out an extra impact of noise as he hit max power to catch the big bomber. He flipped up into the sky, becoming a dot in seconds.

This would be Bob White, the first X-15 test pilot for the Air Force, flying chase. He'd be a safety man watching over the new bird. Today's flight would be the beginning of a warm up, leading eventually to the day when he'll take the X-15 controls and go after the world records for altitude and speed, for the glory and progress of the Air Force. [Paul Bikle, the director of the NASA facility at Edwards, adds the following later note: "White (USAF) and Walker (NASA) are the two primary X-15 research pilots. They are alternating on the flights. Flights are for research progress and *not* for the glory of USAF or any other participating organization."]

Today—if an emergency should come up, like an explosion or fire—and Scott Crossfield should have to cut loose from the mother ship, White would follow him down, and give him check readings in altitude, course, and speed as he brought the rocket ship to a glide landing. And if the flight followed the prescribed course with no accident, White would be the X-15's closest window in the sky, flashing radio reports to ground control and to Crossfield, checking angles at which the people in the B-52 mother ship might not be able to see.

The other two chase planes—F-100s—would also give aerial checks on the behavior of the X-15/B-52 combination. And each of the F-100s, two-seater models, carried an Air Force movie cameraman. The fliers were Al White, the company back-up pilot whom I had met at the roll-out of Bird No. 2; and Captain James W. Wood of Air Force.

The sky was quiet. Even our red fire truck with its raucous radio had moved, and we had no clue to what was going on in the blue.

We saw the long white plume of a vapor trail curving across the sky to the north, turning toward the west. It was the wide white highway in the sky tracked by the B-52 high up. Faint baby contrails dragged below and behind, laid by the chase planes that followed like sucker fish after a shark.

Now, as the entourage swept around toward the west, one of the contrails was lagging well behind, and all of them seemed to be growing fainter. Then the whole formation faded into the blue. I couldn't pick out anything, even with my 10-power binoculars. We asked Kirkley to try to check on what was happening up there.

Kirkley asked Airman Johnston, the driver, to call the Edwards tower to get some information. Johnston tried to call on the two-way radio in the station wagon, and reported to Kirkley, Goode, Crane, and me: "The tower has a secret service phone and you can't get to them."

"It figures," Goode commented bitterly.

Later, I got hold of the tape recording of the X-15 radio conversation of that day. At about that time Crossfield had tested the reaction of his control surfaces, while Bill Berkowitz, the launch officer, checked by watching the X-15 on the screen of the B-52's television camera.

The B-52 crew practiced the procedures of launching the X-15, then Crossfield's radio and his power system went out momentarily. Captain Bock, the B-52 pilot, reported to Q. C. Harvey, the test conductor, at ground control:

"Okay, Q. C., we are going to abort this one."

"Affirmative," Q. C. Harvey said. "Give me a second here, will you? I'd rather not go through any gyrations with him out of communication."

A few moments later Harvey told the B-52: "Okay, we'll consider it an abort and come back in for a landing, Chuck."

"Roger," Bock replied. "I'm starting very slowly now. I'm going to make it a gradual letdown."

So the B-52 was descending gently toward the base, but they had not suffered any major trouble yet. [That was still to come.]

It was ten-forty when the contrails appeared again, circling in a wide sweep, and soon after they were low enough so that the planes were dots we could see, and the contrails, which appear only at higher altitude, had disappeared.

[It was only later that I found out that at this point in the mission there was a narrow brush with tragedy. The B-52 was at 15,000 and circling toward a landing, when the cockpit of the X-15 suddenly filled with smoke. The tape of the radio communications became unintelligible. One of the last audible sentences was Crossfield saying: "The cockpit is full of smoke." The story had to be pieced together from the memories of the crew.

Crossfield and the B-52 crew feared that fire had broken out in the rocket ship. With the X-15 sitting under the huge wing fuel tanks of the B-52, one misguided tongue of flame could have taken the X-15, the mother ship, Crossfield, and the four B-52 crewmen all to kingdom come.

Crossfield told me months later that the question of being jettisoned and making an emergency landing with the X-15 on fire flipped through his mind at this point with more than ordinary urgency. If he had cut loose, with the steep gliding angle of the missile-like X-15, he might not have been able to pick the right landing spot on the lake bed. Starting from 15,000 feet, he'd have had time to make only one half-circle and he'd have been on the deck. And of course the fire might have blown the X-15 apart before he landed.

An alternative would have been to cut loose, then eject himself from X-15, and the plane would have been wrecked on its first mission. I'm sure that the proud Crossfield would never have permitted this. He said: "It's a matter of professional integrity, if you please, to get it home—that's what I'm paid for."

But the moment was one of great danger. Crossfield told me: "I didn't know if it was a big fire or a small one. You know I was right there under the big tanks. I had a standing agreement with Bock: there's only one of me and four of them, so he was to drop me if it came to a question. I think I said to Bock at that time: 'Don't hesitate to cut me loose.' No, I can remember better: I said, 'If you're gonna cut me loose, give me warning.' "]

But Crossfield's radio was fading fitfully, and Bock and the others couldn't hear him. Bock didn't cut him loose. A quick check by the B-52 and the chase planes showed no external signs of fire in the X-15. And Scott had no fire warning light in his instrument panel.

So Bock greased the big bomber into a landing as quickly as he could, with the mystery of the smoke in the cockpit boldly put into abeyance.

"It might be a low pass," John Kirkley said as Bock's B-52 came lower. But it was a landing. I saw the wide wing of the B-52 coming in and the multiple knobs of the landing gear were extended. The chase planes fanned out wide behind the bomber as it swept in.

I looked for the X-15 with my binoculars. It seemed very tiny and indistinct in this light, as much white as black.

Now a new, loud, thrumming sound came into the sky and we saw a light-colored flying-banana helicopter come into view. It hovered over the north end of the runway, beating the air as the B-52 swept gracefully in for a landing. In the chopper would be the North American flight surgeon, Dr. Toby Freedman, and others ready for emergency work if there was trouble.

The chopper was setting down as the B-52 lumbered to a stop, and a motor cavalcade of two ambulances with big red crosses, trucks, a mobile crane, green North American station wagons, blue Air Force sedans, and the North American mobile control dashed after it.

We jumped into our station wagon and joined the parade. Kirkley didn't want to obtrude the press too close to the center of activity—he had his orders—so we skirted the knot of vehicles and cluster of men which had agglomerated around the wide-winged B-52.

Through my field glasses I watched the B-52 and its captive black rocket, from the tail. The bomber's wing slanted down on the right side because of the weight of the X-15. On the opposite side, the wheeled outrigger near the B-52's wing tip hung several feet above the ground, in the air.

A fire truck with flashing red eye on top had moved very close. The North American van, with public-address speaker and an anomometer on its roof, stopped close by. I could see men gathered around the bullet shape of the X-15, many of them apparently rubbernecking, because they were motionless. Several men, probably technicians, clambered up and down the steel stepladder that had been wheeled next to the X-15 cockpit. The traffic was so heavy that

I wondered how Crossfield could get down. The cockpit canopy was raised but I couldn't see the man in the silver suit.

(Later information: the smoke had cleared from the cockpit when Crossfield shut off his auxiliary power units. When the technicians dug into the innards of the ship, they found the weird cause of the smoke: a generator in the A.P.U. system had overheated and thrown some of its blades, and the resultant smoke had been passed through the cockpit ventilating system through the ducts which demisted the windshield—just as an automobile defroster might fill up the car, if the engine compartment was full of smoke. That small accident might well have cost the Air Force the first X-15, and perhaps also a very valuable test pilot—could have, except for some cool thinking on the part of Crossfield and the B-52 crewmen.)

Crane and Goode were anxious to stop by the Air Force photo lab to see what aerial pictures the service photogs might have made of today's flight. I went along because it was plain we weren't going to get any closer to the X-15: Air Police and North American Company police had formed a cordon around the aircraft. Without special identity badges we'd never get by them.

From our distance we could conclude that the mission, the first flight of the X-15, was probably a success. At least nobody was carrying Crossfield off on a stretcher and the B-52/X-15 combination was safely back on the ground, apparently without damage.

We went by the photo lab, looked at the first pictures of the first take-off, and I tried by phone to arrange to see Crossfield. No dice. Crossfield was holding his distance from the press.

I did, however, make a date to see Bob White, the Air Force captain who with NASA pilot Joe Walker is scheduled to make the X-15 flights to record altitudes and speeds.

White was still wearing a flight suit when I saw him in an Air Force office. He of course had been through a long morning as pilot of the leading chase plane, the swift 104.

We sat and talked for a few moments. White is a handsome man, about average height, with bright, clear eyes and curly hair, and a quick, rather tight smile. You'd estimate he was thirty-one or thirty-two—he's actually thirty-five. He's younger than Crossfield or Joe Walker, who are both pushing forty, and Al White, who *is* forty. I asked about the advanced ages of the leading X-15 pilots, who, one might expect, would be younger. Captain White smiled and said:

"Sure, the ideal requirements would be a guy in his twenties, with a master's degree in engineering and so many thousand hours of jet time, and rocket experience, but there's a limit. It takes quite a lot of time to get that background."

White started flying early, during World War II. He was commissioned a second lieutenant, he told me, when he was nineteen, had a combat career flying fighters out of England with the Eighth Air Force. His missions were mostly ground strafing. He got his degree in electrical engineering at New York University, studying under the GI Bill. He went back to active duty to fly fighters again in the Korean War; and after that war became an Air Force test pilot. White test-flew many of the century-class jets, the Air Force's hottest fighter airplanes, and was appointed back-up pilot to Captain Iven C. Kincheloe, when Kinch was selected to fly the X-15.

When Kinch, who still holds the world's altitude record [126,200 feet or just a shade under 24 miles], was killed flying his 104 in July of 1958, Bob White moved up to the position of first Air Force pilot on the X-15.

White summed up his job as a test pilot on our first space craft: "We do it and come back home and demonstrate that a man can do it—rather than leaving it to unmanned vehicles." That was a bare summary of the X-15 mission, but it was accurate.

Besides Bob White, Joe Walker, Scott Crossfield, and Al White there are four other pilots waiting in line for a crack at flying X-15. The others are Captain Bob Rushworth, the Air Force pilot backing up Captain White; Joe Walker's back-ups at NASA, Jack McKay and Neil Armstrong; and a Navy pilot, Lieutenant Commander Forrest S. Petersen.

It's quite a lineup, all these eager beavers waiting for a chance at the first space ship. Men have been this eager ever since the United States rocket planes began, with X-1 in 1947. Once a magazine writer asked Kincheloe why he risked his neck flying rocket ships for a captain's pay when he could have had many a cushy job as a civilian test pilot with an airplane manufacturer. Kinch said, according to Vic Boesen, the magazine writer in question:

"I got into it because I wanted to. If I didn't, fifteen other guys were waiting to do it."

Evidently the X-15 pilotage assignment, at least in Kinch's mind, was more than a job—it was a much-coveted honor. The dashing Kincheloe, who looked somewhat like Flash Gordon and was physically and mentally the man to fly the X-15, expected a long career piloting the bird. He told my friend Boesen: "I don't intend to get

killed in this business." He had one child, another one on the way
when he augered in.

The other X-15 pilots are also family men. I counted up the children the eight men have: twenty-two. Jack McKay is the leader with
six. Scott Crossfield has five, Bob White has two. [White didn't tell
me then, but his wife was pregnant with their third child, Maureen,
born seven months after our first interview.]

After talking with Bob White, I went to a projection room at the
film lab to look at some footage made at the time of the death of
one of the most famous of the rocket pilots, Captain Milburn G. Apt.
He, too, was a family man, with two children. On September 7, 1956,
Captain Apt flew the X-2 to a world's speed record of 2,094 mph,
which still stands, and a few minutes later he was killed as the plane
spun down out of control and he ejected. He never freed himself from
his escape capsule.

Part of the film I saw was made by an automatic sequence camera
set up behind Apt in the cockpit of the X-2 on the day of the fatal
accident. The plane was the second and last X-2. The first had been
lost in an aerial explosion in 1953, taking the Bell Aircraft test pilot,
Skip Ziegler, and Frank Wolko, a scanner in the B-29 mother ship,
to their deaths. The rapid-sequence film taken on Apt's record and
fatal flight was a series of still exposures made at one-second intervals, so the effect was one of jerky motion.

Gene Lemmon, a civilian in charge of Air Force film production at
Edwards, explained that the short subject I was about to see was in
fact a training film on how to stay alive at Mach 2 (1,300 mph at
50,000 feet) and beyond. It included some animation and some clips
taken by an automatic movie camera set in the X-1B when it went
out of control with Major (then Captain) Arthur "Kit" Murray in
the pilot's seat.

"The film shows inertia coupling in operation," Lemmon said.
"All of the test pilots have seen it [the film] at least once."

Inertia coupling is what happens when a high-speed aircraft loses
stability at high altitude where the air is thin. The rocket planes have
been prone to it, their long bodies and small wings and small control
surfaces seem to dispose them toward it.

The effect is that the plane rolls, yaws, and tumbles end for end,
completely out of control. This happened to Apt, and it had also
nearly killed Chuck Yeager (first to break the sound barrier), to
Murray, and to Joe Walker, rocket pilots all. It had also happened

to Kincheloe on the day he set the world's altitude record, twenty days before Apt was killed.

The practical answer to inertia coupling, according to Lemmon, seems to be to wait until the bird has flipped down 40,000 or 50,000 feet where the atmosphere is thicker, so the control surfaces can take effect. A very light hand on the control stick, therefore, is standard procedure, as both a preventive and a curative measure. [Bikle, the NASA chief at Edwards, adds the following note: "Better to say here that dense atmosphere at lower altitudes slows down A/C to Mach No. where A/C has adequate stability to recover." I am passing on this note for whatever it may be worth to the reader.]

Lemmon told me: "As Jim Carson, the Air Force test pilot on the 107, said it: 'As I passed through Mach 2 I didn't move a thing but my eyeballs.' "

The motion-picture section was dramatic: the movie taken from Murray's plane, from roughly the pilot's point of view, showed the mountains and sky rotating dizzily. It was as if you were in a barrel kicked out of a high-flying bomber; black-and-white pictures of earth and sky flipping and turning around you fast.

The tumbling of these photographs seemed to go on and on, but I knew it was all a matter of a few seconds. In that time Murray had pinwheeled down the sky from about 80,000 feet to 40,000 feet— eight miles straight down. In the thicker air, the aerodynamic stability of the plane began to take effect and he got the ship under control and landed.

The pictures of Apt's flight were the most horrifying, because you knew that he didn't survive the ordeal. You saw his white-helmeted head and upper body from the rear as he moved violently from side to side, caught by the gasping stop motion of the camera. One second he was upright, the next he had moved jerkily in an arc to the left, the next his round helmet and his upper body were halfway to the wall of the cockpit. His restraining straps help him partially, but amid the whirring of the film, the sharp edge of white light from the projector, you could imagine the brutal beating the g-forces were giving him.

Then the film was over, the projector went off, and the room lights were snapped on. Lemmon had seen this film countless times, but it still seemed to awe him. He was silent. So was I, thinking of all the men who risked and sometimes gave their lives so the X-15 and its successors in space could be developed, from the Chinese soldiers in the thirteenth century who set up the first rocket brigade at Kaifeng to defend their city, to Max Valier in 1930, the first casualty of liquid-rocket research, and Kit Murray and Mil Apt nowadays and Scott Crossfield this morning.

I checked at the PIO office and saw the first newspaper story on today's flight. It was in the Antelope Valley *Ledger-Gazette,* a local journal:

"Man's effort to probe and eventually conquer outer space was launched this morning when the North American X-15 made its first flight at Edwards Air Force Base as a 'passenger' under the wing of a modified B-52 bomber."

The Los Angeles papers we saw still ran their predate story written early today. The Los Angeles *Mirror-News* article by Don Dwiggins said:

"Scott Crossfield, North American Company test pilot, poised today to take man's first step toward space—inside rocket ship X-15, world's first manned space craft."

By hanging around Edwards today we were able to appreciate some of the inner convolutions of the flight.

MARCH 11. I drove down to the NASA hangar this morning. The NASA building is the farthest from the green headquarters structure and the flagpole. It's past the graveyard where parts of wrecked and junked planes are kept, and this fact and its detachment seem to make it even more bleak than is standard for Edwards.

I checked in with Marion Kent, who handles administration for this *nouveau-riche* agency, suddenly wealthy because of a half-billion-dollar-a-year budget, which in turn stemmed from public dismay that we have lagged so far behind the Russians in space conquest.

President Eisenhower created the National Aeronautics and Space Administration from an existing outfit called NACA (the National Advisory Committee for Aeronautics) in August 1958. NACA had been a small low-budget government research bureau before the dawn of the Space Age, October 4, 1957, when the Russians fired Sputnik I into orbit and covered us with national confusion, and goaded us further with Sputnik II (better known as Muttnik) four weeks later.

Kent is a mild-mannered, polite, and serious man who in these early stages of NASA's organizational life had been assigned the collateral duty of caring for such journalistic types as may visit the place. I asked him about the NASA pilots lined up to fly the X-15: which of them has the greatest amount of experience in flying rocket ships? He said Joe Walker and Jack McKay were fairly close in rocket time, but he thought McKay had the lead. I asked if I could see one or both of them, and he said he'd arrange a meeting with McKay today. Walker had gone to the Chance-Vought Aircraft Company to get some time in an advanced space-flight simulator there.

On the way to meet McKay, I asked Kent about the space controls on X-15—the reaction or ballistic rocket tubes which are for the first time built into a ship, to lend control in the vacuum of the Wild Black Yonder. These controls are interesting to me because they are among the great unknowns of space-ship design: we have never been in space, so we can't know exactly how the controls will work, even though the engineers assure us they will function perfectly. The idea of steering yourself in space with directed rocket blasts is a new one, although it will eventually be the standard way of controlling rocket ships on space voyages.

Kent told me the first such device he knew about was on the Iron Cross, a device conceived by NACA to test this kind of reaction control on the ground. It was only a crude mockup to measure the responsiveness of the rocket jets.

"The Iron Cross was a mess of I-beams," Kent said. "We later put that same system on the X-1B and the tankage went bad. We didn't restore it for economic reasons. Something like it is now being put on an F-104."

He said I could look at the Iron Cross and the 104 today: both gadgets are in the building.

Kent said one thing that bothers him about the X-15 is the rate of descent—which is an immediate matter now because the first drop and glide flight will be coming up soon.

We met Jack McKay at NASA's new cafeteria, and sat over coffee. Jack, like the other X-15 pilots, is about average size. He's chunky in build, and if his coloring were dark, you'd say he is beetle-browed. But his bushy eyebrows are blond, which adds a strangely querulous note to his otherwise aggressive face. His features are craggy and today his mood seemed to be one of relaxed good humor.

(Later, an engineer told me about McKay: "He's just a damn good Joe. He'll fly anything. He's the kind of test pilot that'll fly for you all day long. He doesn't like to criticize the airplane. If it'll fly, he'll fly it—and maybe enjoy it. Then he goes home, and maybe has a few on the way.")

McKay is the X-15 pilot with the largest number of children—six. But I didn't ask him about his family. Instead, I inquired about Captain Mil Apt and the way the high-speed rocket pilots get into inertia coupling or tumbling. The film on the subject was still vivid in my memory: Apt's last flight as recorded by the rapid-sequence camera. McKay had seen the film, too, studied it carefully.

"Apt was getting a dihedral effect," McKay said, meaning the strange reversal of controls that sometimes hits high-speed planes at high altitudes. "He was trying to correct with his stick but it just got worse."

I remembered how Apt's white-helmeted head slammed around the cockpit, his arm moving the control stick way over to his left.

"He bailed at 40,000 feet—too high," Jack McKay explained. (Apt had to blast the capsule nose of the X-2 free of the rest of the ship, before he could pull his parachute ripcord. He never got clear of the capsule.) "The airplane at that altitude," McKay continued, "had enough stability to recover—even that airplane and even in an inverted spin. But he wasn't thinking very clearly. It knocked him around a lot. They found a blood clot behind his left eye."

McKay led us down to the hangar level, and we looked at the Iron Cross. It was only two heavy steel girders arranged in an X shape, with a pilot's chair and instrument panel mounted on one end of one of the beams. A mass of tubing and cables ran out to the ends of the other beams—the plumbing for the rocket jets which boost the extremities up or down.

The gadget was not operable as we saw it, sitting on the hangar floor. It would have to be moved out onto a tripod so there would be more clearance as it turned. But we could see the effect: earthbound, a pilot riding the Iron Cross can try out the kind of controls he'd be using in space—although in space they'd be much more responsive because there'd be no air to inhibit them. The device gives a kind of skeletal preview of space flight.

"Your first impression is: it's a Tinker toy," Jack said. "But it helps give you an idea." In a few seconds the craggy-faced regular guy with the ready sense of humor became the engineer (he got his aeronautical engineering degree from Virginia Polytechnic) and I was lost in his complicated exposition of quantitative and qualitative evaluation, high and low dynamic pressure, Q (which I have learned is engineering shorthand for the forces of air striking a moving object), and those unpleasant g-forces.

We walked over to the 104 Lockheed jet fighter which is being equipped with rocket controls somewhat like those of the Iron Cross. The idea is that the X-15 men, flying this 104, will be able to try something like space flight by piloting the 104 at maximum altitude. Jet power can't take a plane into space the way rocket propulsion can, but perhaps at 80,000 or 90,000 feet a reasonable facsimile of space can be achieved so that the reaction controls can be tried more realistically.

Jack showed me the shining steel rockets that will be the high-altitude controls fixed in the wing tips and nose of the 104, to blast those parts up or down at the pilot's will. I made a mental note to get a closer look at the similar controls in wings and nose of the X-15. The big difference in X-15 is that the controls will have a real test in space.

We watched technicians as they prepared a wingtip for one of the shining, highly-machined rocket tubes. A technician showed the spot at the extreme end of the wing where the aluminum panel had been removed and the reaction-control tube will fit.

Jack and Marion Kent led me from the hangar to the plotting room where NASA technicians will follow the X-15 flights through tele-metering and radar equipment. The rooms were spotted with chart boards and oscillographs designed to record temperature, pressure, and other readings sent back automatically from X-15 during flights.

We stopped to talk to a radar expert beside a complicated plotting scope which is supposed to fix the position of the X-15 at any moment during a mission. NASA has a new, elaborate beacon just installed for the purpose. The expert on hand at the moment was Al Wolf.

Ken asked Wolf, for my benefit: "How do you track it?"

Wolf grinned. "We have a helluva time."

It came out that the radar beam and telemetering equipment hadn't worked too well on the first flight yesterday. (Later, NASA had so much trouble with the complex new beacon that they went back to the old, dependable model they'd used in testing the earlier Xs. And the wrinkles and bugs in the new telemetering equipment, after initial difficulties, were ironed out and it began to work fine.)

I went by Kent's office to meet Walt Williams, head of the NASA outfit at Edwards (properly called the High Speed Flight Station, later rechristened Flight Research Center).

Williams is a round-faced, bull-necked man with impatient hazel eyes. He's a veteran of nineteen years' service with NACA before it became NASA. X-15 is really his baby, because he was involved

from the early planning of the project onward, and is now head of the
X-15 Committee. That committee is the joint Air Force-NASA-Navy
group which will make the decisions as to which pilot will be flying
what missions. In effect, Williams will be boss of the schedule.

I asked him whether the Russians have anything of the X-15 type,
any controllable rocket ship which can take man into the fringe of
space.

He was cautious in his answer: "Judging from their movie on
space travel, they have a similar vehicle. It has more sweepback."
But he qualified even that opinion: "That's only what I read in the
papers."

THURSDAY, MARCH 12. I called Earl Blount at North American today
and asked about the next flight of X-15. He said there will be at
least one more captive flight before the ship is cut loose for its first
glide-landing attempt. Maybe the next captive mission will be next
week.

He said good-humoredly: "The engineers tell me they'll be sure
this time that every part is okay and working."

I asked Blount if I could talk to some of the engineers about the
problems they've had so far with the X-15. He said he'd try to set
up an interview with Harrison Storms, the North American engineer
who is the daddy of X-15. Also with the two company X-15 pilots—
Scott Crossfield and Al White.

MONDAY, MARCH 16. This morning at the North American plant I
met the over-all guiding genius of the X-15, Harrison "Stormy"
Storms, who is also the company's chief engineer at the Los Angeles
division. He is a slim, small man who seems young—forty-three—to
have reached his exalted status at North American. But a minute's
conversation with him reveals the sharp mentality behind the long,
thin jaw and brown eyes. He speaks a racy, slangish American, but
with an amazing precision for someone trained not in word symbols
but in the other language of thought, mathematics.

I asked what the biggest problem in flying the X-15 is going to be,
and he answered quickly: "The landing. Any time you lay yourself
open to dead-stick landings, you've got problems. Navigation is the
first problem. You've got to hit the lake [bed] after the powered part
of the flight, and you have to be there with altitude enough for a
circle before landing. "You've got to hit the lake area at 25,000

feet. At that altitude, one circle and you're on the ground in the X-15."

I remarked that the X-15, with its tiny little wings, had a remarkably steep gliding angle, the ratio of forward travel to downward travel while gliding. I asked what the gliding angle of the X-15 is, and he said three or four to one, meaning three or four lengths forward to one down. That is really a violent gliding angle, the steepest I've heard of. Even the 104s, with their elementary nubbins of wings, have a gliding angle of six or seven to one. But then there's never been a man-carrying ship with the missile-like speed of the X-15, either.

"What has a steeper angle than the X-15?" I asked.

"A stone," Stormy answered solemnly.

We talked about the 104s with which the X-15 pilots have been practicing landings. With power off, and landing gear and partial nose flaps down, the 104 roughly duplicates the landing characteristics of the X-15, the engineers estimate. By making landings with the 104s in this so-called "dirty configuration," the pilots can practice something very close to X-15 landings long before they get into the black beast's cockpit to fly.

Soon Storms got around to a subject close to his heart: the possibilities of the X-15 as an orbiting vehicle—one which could not only arc out into space for a few minutes, but could generate enough speed to escape some of the earth's gravitational pull and go into orbit around it.

Dynasoar, the Air Force's secret man-carrying space ship, is going to be designed to orbit a couple of years from now, and orbiting is the object of Project Mercury, the compartment-in-space, funnel-shaped vehicle which has already been built by the McDonnell Aircraft Company. That "tin can," it has been announced by NASA, will carry an astronaut into space and into a brief orbit—and this prediction may or may not come true. The Mercury capsule, it is planned, will be boosted into space on the nose of an Atlas rocket; with shorter flights with smaller boosters being made to lesser altitudes first. But the Mercury capsule is short on controllability, and many test pilots view its chances of success with skepticism. Dynasoar, by contrast, will be a controllable aerodynamic ship, capable of landing like an airplane, instead of being brought back to earth by parachute, as is the plan with the Mercury capsule. But Dynasoar is a long way off; and meanwhile Stormy and many other experts think the X-15 could be modified so that it could quickly become an orbiting, controllable vehicle.

The Air Force once—two and a half years ago—considered this possible extension of the X-15 project. It was to be called the X-15B. The decision was negative. The X-15B is still held in abeyance. This is too bad, since the Russians are apparently preparing to orbit a man soon, and if we had decided on the orbiting X-15B, when it was proposed, we could be in the final stages of building the B model right now, Storms said.

"It could have been done," he said, "and it still can. Two years would be required to build it. It would have to have a booster to get it up to speed. That could take the form of an Atlas or B-70 [the B-70 is the 2,000-mile-an-hour bomber design of which North American is fashioning a prototype]."

"What we'd have to do is get 25,600 feet per second [17,500 miles an hour]. I couldn't care less about how I do it, as long as the speed is there."

Stormy was not at all worried about the problems of safely putting a man into the void in an orbiting space ship. "You'll have to supply everything for the pilot, since there's no air and periods of no gravity, and a high range of temperature and g-forces, but that can be done.

"It's like walking into the ocean," he said. "You get your toes wet, and you go in a little more until pretty soon you're in deep water. It's getting a little damp before you go all the way around the earth. You're in the deep end of the pool."

I asked Stormy for a definition of space—precise definitions varying considerably even in the best-informed engineers.

"I'd say space starts at 90,000 feet. The air is getting pretty thin there. You have about 98 or 99 per cent of it under you and you're worrying about where it will be gone. You have to be above 200,000 feet to be sure."

I asked Storms about a part of the X-15 that fascinates me: the rocket controls in wing and nose, which are supposed to keep the ship flying in the right attitude as it arcs briefly into space, out of the air. Would those controls work?

"Sure, they'll work," he said. "All you have to do is to try them in atmosphere, subtract the Q [atmosphere], and you know they'll work." In other words, it's a mathematical proposition to check out the rocket controls by flying the ship in earth's atmosphere, then subtracting the air pressure which would not exist out in space.

He gave a random example: "It [the vacuum of space] just changes the force [of the rocket jet] from say 10 pounds to 12 pounds."

He meant that a control jet which had a force of 10 pounds at sea level would have a force of 12 pounds in space, where there would be no air for it to push against. It's as simple as that in theory, anyhow; though I am distrustful, like the test pilots, of theoretical calculations, until they are proved in practice.

I asked Stormy about the schedule of X-15 flights, and the approximate timetable for the first powered flight. He said he'd estimate the first flight would be in June. But that will be with the small engine now in the No. 1 bird. That engine is actually the old X-1 power plant multiplied by two: two X-1 engines are mounted in the tail of Bird No. 1, one above the other. This combination should give about 16,000 pounds of thrust, not very much where high-powered rocket engines are concerned—only about a thousand pounds more thrust than the rocket engine of the X-2. The really sensational performance will be with the big engine, the XLR-99, which is supposed to have been delivered before this, but is still in the development and testing stage back at the Reaction Motors factory in New Jersey. That big engine, said Stormy, now is promised for July. Meanwhile, the smaller power plant will be flying soon; and with it the X-15 will have the capability of breaking the world speed and altitude records set by the X-2

At lunchtime I at long last met Scott Crossfield, the No. 1 company test pilot. I say at long last, because I've been trying to arrange to meet him for several weeks.

Crossfield is shy about meeting the press. As far as I can gather, he would prefer to be left alone, to do his job without having to explain it to laymen.

However, Dick Barton, of North American public relations, prevailed on the pilot to come to lunch with us. And Al White, the X-15 back-up pilot, who has a greater interest in his responsibility of keeping the public informed, came along without protest.

One of the first things Crossfield said—and he said it assertively as if he wanted to get the record straight—was the following: "We do not plan to make the ultimate determination of the capability of the X-15." By that, Dick Barton explained, Crossfield meant that he and Al White would demonstrate only that the ships would fly as promised—that the record flights would be up to Air Force and NASA pilots. Crossfield wanted to make that clear because it had already been misrepresented in the public prints that he would be the first man into space; whereas he was only a company test pilot demonstrating the acceptability of the aircraft to the purchaser, the Air Force.

He went on categorically, as if he were still making a formal statement: "The X-15 is the first qualified airplane of its kind ever to be built. No other can withstand the forces and temperature the X-15 will."

I hoped we could get onto a more relaxed conversational footing. We went to a café near the airport, where a lot of aircraft people eat lunch. Crossfield drove us in his slightly beat-up 1955 Ford. On the way I saw how quick his reflexes are. It was at the first intersection, the right-angle meeting of heavy traffic streams at Sepulveda and Imperial boulevards.

The problem was to make a left turn, and the complicating factor was that a car was blocking our path as it came from the direction opposite.

If I had been driving, I would have waited for the other car to pass. But Crossfield whipped his car into a left turn, and we were into the turn before I saw what he had apparently spotted a fraction of a second earlier: the other car was flashing for a right turn, and that turn would take him safely out of our way. I guess that kind of rapid perception can be a matter of life and death to someone in Crossfield's job.

At the restaurant I had a chance to size up Crossfield a bit, mentally and physically. He is about average height, a little slimmer than average. His face and eyes, today at least, seemed drawn, although his wide cheekbones would naturally create that look.

He has aquiline, finely cut features, well-spaced eyes, dark, slick hair, and a sallow complexion. His general mien seems to be critical, appraising, and confident.

We were soon in a violent argument about whether the Germans were mainly responsible for our present-day rocket and missile progress. I had been saying in passing that the Peenemunde alumni, the great German scientists who developed the V-2 at the World War II base on the Baltic Sea, were basically responsible for subsequent rocket progress on both sides of the Iron Curtain; that the Russians and our own scientists built on the German know-how, and even brought German scientists to help out, as on our side Wernher von Braun and General Walter Dornberger, respectively the great engineering and administrative minds of the German V-2 program.

"You're just absolutely wrong," Crossfield broke in vehemently.

Somewhat goaded, I also mentioned that the X-15 is very close to being a V-2 with a man in it. The X-15 has just about the same weight, size, and performance, and was designed to reach the same altitude and speed.

"There's no connection," Crossfield said positively, and a spirited argument followed, in which I had further proof that he is a man of very firm convictions.

Dick Barton, a conciliatory type, skillfully changed the subject, and we were soon talking about World War II, in which both Crossfield and White were fighter pilots, Crossfield with the Navy, White with the Army Air Forces.

But we soon drifted back to Crossfield's favorite topic, the X-15 and its associated problems. Scott, who generally seemed quite tense (I didn't know then about his recent trouble on the first flight), voiced the idea that the space medics overestimate the dangers of space travel and underestimate the capability of the human physique to accommodate to them.

"If we listened to the space medics . . . we'd never get off the ground," he said. "They have a morbid evaluation of the hazards."

He spoke about the violent ranges of temperatures and bodily stresses the X-15 pilots will encounter. But, he said, if you give a normal man "a temperature somewhere between a Legionnaire in the Sahara and the farmer in Minnesota" and "an atmosphere between sea level and 35,000 feet," he will make it. He said almost all of the air conditioning of the X-15 is for the benefit of the measuring devices and instruments, not the pilot. "The man uses less than one quarter of the environmental control . . . he has an evaporative cooler, the sweat mechanism. I've made it to 160 degrees in the heat chamber with just perspiration as protection."

Crossfield seemed sensitive about his age, which some of the younger fliers believe to be somewhat advanced for the pilot of the first space ship. He is thirty-six, and will be thirty-seven in October. Al White is forty, and will be forty-one in December.

"Al and I are considered freaks because we are able to do the things we do at our age," Crossfield said. "But you can't minimize the value of will." He went on to say that once, at the big Navy centrifuge at Johnsville, Pennsylvania, his g-suit went out of action, but he was able to take nine g's before he went out cold—"just because I wanted to."

Al agreed: "Drive is a big factor."

Scott went on: "History is full of cases of 4Fs who did remarkable things with big physical handicaps: like Teddy Roosevelt, Disraeli, and Wiley Post with one eye."

I asked Scott what is going to be the biggest problem on the first glide flight of the X-15, which should be in the next month or so.

"The landing," he said without hesitation. "After 10,000 feet you can't make a circle, only a 180, and you're on the deck."

I asked him about the rate of descent of the X-15 in a glide.

"Auto rotation in a helicopter is a lot tougher." In this maneuver a helicopter can descend as fast as 80 feet per second, with power off and rotor blades flat. (But he was kidding me; the sink rate of the X-15 is faster—100 to 150 feet per second.)

Crossfield smiled his tight, bright smile. "But we can make it."

FRIDAY, MARCH 20. Today, at the North American factory, I caught up with a few of the 125 engineers who have worked and are working on the X-15 project. The first was Earl Sikes, a mild, gentle-voiced man of about forty. He said modestly that he is only one of 50 senior engineers assigned to the X-15. There are also about 50 regular grade engineers and 25 juniors. The seniors are superior in experience and usually in education.

Sikes told me about some of the thorny problems his cohorts had to face designing and building the X-15. One of the toughest was making parts out of heat-resistant, lightweight new metals, some of which had never been worked before. Some strange methods had to be devised to handle these virgin materials.

The main objective, said Sikes, was to use a metal that could resist temperatures ranging from 300 degrees below zero to 1,200 above. The liquid oxygen and helium gases used in the ship range from 200 to 300 below, and the heat of re-entry, as the X-15 plunges back into atmosphere after its jaunt into space, could go up as high as 1,200 degrees Fahrenheit, when the friction of the air at such great speed would burn up an ordinary metal such as steel or aluminum.

Another limiting factor in the choice of metals is weight, since the lighter the weight, the better the performance. "The nightmare for everybody is weight," Sikes said.

He quoted the engineering rule I had heard before: "Every pound saved adds a half foot per second in speed." Or, in more understandable terms, every pound saved adds a third of a mile per hour in speed. Sykes said the engineers had shaved a tiny thickness from certain unstressed parts of the tankage and saved 20 pounds, which added 60 feet per second, or just short of seven miles an hour. And slab-grinding the surface of the main tanks, so they would be an even thickness all over, saved 300 pounds, yielding 102 miles per hour in velocity. Of such mundane arithmetic is space-ship performance made: you add the increments of weight saved and come up with your predicted speed—and the speed in turn is translatable into higher altitude, since how high you are able to climb depends on how much speed you can build as you zoom out of the atmosphere and arc over into space. Breaking altitude records depends on lighter weight and higher power working together.

The original plan of the North American engineers was to use titanium for the main X-15 tanks—those huge, boiler-like containers that hold the rocket fuel and the oxidizer—a total of 18,000 pounds (2,400 gallons). But titanium proved very difficult to shape and weld, so the engineers shifted to a nickel-steel alloy called Inconel X. It's about the weight of steel but much more heat-resistant than steel. The name comes from International Nickel Corporation, the maker.

Sikes said the fabricators had lots of trouble working Inconel X and titanium, especially with welding. He mentioned that X rays were used to inspect the welds, and surgical techniques—white gloves, purified water, strong cleansing agents, and even plastic envelopes much like surgical tents were used in attempts to keep the welds clean.

"We had a lot of trouble with contamination," he said. "We got porosity in the welds. We had to reweld again and again. We had trouble especially in titanium. We used white gloves, and the joint was cleaned with high-energy cleaner. Then we wiped it with surgical gauze. We used a surgical tent like a big oxygen tent, like a big plastic bag, around the weld. We blew out the air and put in an inert gas, argon. Then the welding was done through holes in the bag. The welder's hands went into gloves in the bag. This helped, because the titanium would otherwise pick up hydrogen in the air, and that makes the weld brittle."

The technicians and workmen had labored six months with the infuriating job of mending bad welds, until they evolved the surgical technique, the technique centering in the 10-foot transparent envelope. But even this and the other sanitary procedures didn't produce the kind of smooth-welding result the engineers demanded in the eight-foot-long liquid helium tanks. Those tanks finally were sent out to another firm where a high-pressure welding machine successfully did the job.

The surgical welding method did work well in making the main big tanks of Inconel X. Those tanks are respectively eleven feet and nine feet long and four feet in diameter. One ranged behind the other, they make up the main body of the X-15, with the pilot's "office" ahead of them and the engines behind. These big tanks are doughnut shaped as you look at them from the front or back of the airplane. The "hole in the doughnut" is filled with the helium tanks which gave so much trouble in the making. These long, slim tanks, eight feet long and fourteen inches in diameter, contain the 300-degrees-below helium which is used to push the lox and fuel toward the engine at the rear. There the turbo pump, a compact machine very much like a fire pump, will shoot the liquids into the combustion chamber.

With all the piping and tanks which have to be put together into a compact package there are considerable plumbing problems, and the engineers and workmen become, in effect, plumbers with airplane skills, with a liberal admixture of each. The use of new, untried light metals makes the job extra difficult.

Sikes pointed out that almost all of the joints in an airplane are riveted, but the body of the X-15, borrowing from missiles, is almost all welded. Missiles are held together with welds rather than rivets and other fasteners, to get smoother joints and more strength. The plumbing in the X-15, like the stainless steel pipes that carry helium under high pressure, was generally hard to weld. New brazing techniques had to be invented to fasten the sleeve and tube ends.

I asked Barton if later I could go over to the West High Bay section of the factory, where Birds No. 2 and No. 3 are still being worked on, and see some of the fancy equipment the fabricators used in their plumbing chores. He said yes, some of it, anyhow. Most of the spectacular equipment by now has been disassembled and the parts put to work somewhere else in the factory. But he'd check up on it, and the next time I came down to the plant I could probably see some of it, and maybe talk to some of the workmen and artisans who did the job.

This afternoon I went in to talk briefly to the general manager of the North American plant, a sinewy, rather taciturn man named Ralph Ruud, and he gave me a brief but pointed indoctrination on the mission of X-15.

"A missile is only an intermediate stage," he said. "The reason for it all is to get a man aboard—because you can't equal the thinking qualities of a man with any machine. A man has 10 billion to 12 billion binaries or neurons working for him in his brain—that is, binary decision elements. It's a very compact mechanism. If you had 6,000 IBM machines of the 609 style—a whole Empire State Building full of thinking machines—you still couldn't equal the human brain. . . .

But when I asked Ruud what he considered was the biggest problem in flying the X-15, he said something very surprising—surprising in that at first examination it seemed to conflict with his views about the superiority of the human organism over a thinking machine.

"The toughest problem," he said, deliberating over his phrasing, "is to make the pilots stay on their planned programs and not let their human reactions take over."

He meant, I knew, that the test pilots must carry out the instructions of the engineers, and not let their instincts take over in an emergency. He illustrated the point.

"Al Blackburn [a North American test pilot and currently president of the Experimental Test Pilots Society] was testing the ZEL [ZEL stands for Zero Length Launch, it is an F-100 mounted on a track like a catapult. With a rocket boost of some 100,000 pounds thrust, it leaps directly into the air with no take-off run.] He knew with that tremendous thrust he shouldn't pull back on the stick. But when he felt that momentum, he instinctively pulled back on the stick—a habit that came from years of flying. He said he could have cut his hand off."

An expert experimental test pilot will follow out the special instructions of the engineers for the aircraft involved, Ruud said, instead of going by instincts built on years of flying experience on other aircraft. Even in an emergency, he'll follow the patterns the engineers dictate.

What Ruud was saying about human instincts didn't really conflict with the point he'd made about the superiority of the human brain over a calculating machine, for he was careful to point out that our brain is superior to our lower emotional and instinctive facilities— that the reasoning faculties are more valuable than the autonomic nervous system we share with the lesser animals. His praise was for the cerebellum, our upper brain, the infinitely complicated but also unbelievably compact thinking apparatus of man which may never be equalled artificially, no matter how long our species exists.

"We want to get men into space. We want to get experience in the maintenance of human beings in space . . . we'll let the man grow up with the project."

TUESDAY, MARCH 24. This morning I went to the West High Bay section of the factory, where the second X-15 is nearly completed and the third is progressing behind it. The second bird, with the white letters 66671 on its tail, looks ready to fly. But Bird No. 3, 66672, still looks skeletal—and there is a gaping black hole in its tail. Someday that hole will be filled by the first of the big engines, the powerful XLR-99. But it's six months late now.

With Dick Barton I looked around for the plastic envelopes that had been used for some of the delicate welding jobs on X-15. Gene Ricketts, the foreman who runs experimental assembly, was our guide.

We soon found the 10-foot plastic envelope. It was not being used now, but you could see how the welder put his arms into the shoulder-length gloves to make a joint inside the purified atmosphere of the transparent container.

Ricketts said: "In some small pieces even the oil in the pores of your fingers could be critical." He showed us some of the X rays used to check porosity in the welds. To me, the images looked only like blocks of gray with different degrees of lightness. Ricketts said it was a specialized art to read this kind of X ray.

"Besides the white gloves, we tried other ways of getting better welds," Ricketts told us. "We tried filing for edge preparation: you draw the file in a certain way to avoid trapping lint or air bubbles. We found the contamination in the welds came from nitrogen and oxygen in the air as well as the parent material [the metal]. We found we had to have a completely inert atmosphere around the work—with the surgical tent, we had to spend a couple of hours to purge the inside and put the argon gas in.

"On one titanium pressure vessel we had faulty material. We changed to Inconel—we added 150 pounds." Ricketts' face looked woebegone as he recalled the weight-to-performance rule I'd been hearing from the people who built the X-15—one half foot per second lost for every pound of weight added. Thus the addition of 150 pounds in the pressure tank meant 51 miles an hour less speed for X-15, and therefore less altitude.

Barton and I walked over to the cockpit area of Bird No. 2. This is the ship we saw rolled out for the stockholders nearly a month ago. It appeared to be completed then, but a lot of complicated instrumentation had still to be installed. Today a group of workmen were clustered around the cockpit, several of them busy with bundles of wires that led to the compartment behind the pilot, the instrument bay.

Barton introduced me to one of the shirt-sleeved technicians for a fill-in on the work at hand. He was Roy "Shorty" Holland, a grave, polite, pleasant man who is the lead man on X-15 propulsion systems.

I asked him about the impressive collection of electronic "black boxes" and attendant bundles of wiring in the instrumentation bay. I pointed to one tight bundle of wires inside a fabric skin about as big around as a full-grown python. It was open on one end and we could see the hundreds of wires which make it up.

"Temperature pick-up wires," he explained. "Most of this stuff is telemetering—for sending the dope back to the ground automatically." He pointed to an instrument box. "These are pressure transducers, temperature gauges, and strain gauges." A transducer is a gadget that re-creates a power stimulus for transmission to the ground.

I asked Shorty about the fabrication troubles the work force seemed to have with X-15 from beginning to end.

"Yeah—more meaty problems than any other aircraft before," he said. "Because in the X-15 we had to intermingle missile systems and techniques with aircraft techniques that were very different. It's a hybrid; maybe that's why it's so interesting."

Another checkered-shirt worker chimed in. He was Bob Karicofe, a final-assembly foreman.

"One thing we got from missiles is the bladder system," he said. "To squeeze out liquids and gases where there's no gravity. You know about the bladders?"

I had heard about the system of plastic bladders used on X-15, as in missiles, to force liquids such as hydrogen peroxide to flow even when there is no gravity. Missiles have used that kind of pressure system since the V-2. Probably such bladder systems will be a standard part of space-ship equipment in the future—that is, if they check out as being dependable enough in the X-15.

Karicofe was going on: "The X-15 isn't a one-shot affair like a missile, it has to come back and fly over and over again. We've got to solve a lot of problems that don't matter with a missile—as long as it can get up there."

He and Shorty went back to work over the complex machinery of the cockpit. They seemed to have the same fascinated interest as the X-15 pilots and engineers, and in fact everybody who is involved in this project. It's understandable, because everyone knows the lessons learned from X-15 will affect the design and performance of space ships for generations to come. That's one reason it's such a stimulating adventure.

WEDNESDAY, MARCH 25. I called Colonel Brown at Edwards Air Force Base to check on the date of the next flight. He said the mission, originally scheduled for Friday the twenty-seventh had slipped back a little because of some unexpected engineering troubles. It looks now as if it will be Tuesday the thirty-first. If so, this will be the second flight of the Blackbird (the No. 1 Bird), and like the first flight it will be a "captive" mission: i.e., the bird will be kept attached to the wing of the mother ship—except, of course, in the case of some unforeseen emergency, such as the trouble with smoke on the first mission that nearly led to an unscheduled launch.

MONDAY, MARCH 30. This morning I drove to Edwards to get ready for the second flight of the X-15, which was originally scheduled for last Tuesday, but has slipped over to Tuesday, tomorrow. Most of the trouble, I understand, has been with the radio system. The X-15 originally got its radio power from the mother ship; but an independent system had to be worked out against the day it will be launched. There's been a lot of trouble with noise and interference in the independent system, so Charlie Brown was telling me at PIO headquarters.

This time I've managed to secure a North American Company check list, a step-by-step program of every move to be made during the mission. It's 68 pages long!

The check list is groaningly detailed. In the fashion of the armed services, every single move and measurement is spelled out so that only a yes or no decision is required, so that minimum intelligence is involved, and also so it will be easy for an inspector to check up in case a mistake has been made.

Not only the parts of the list which have to do with such simple things as checking equipment aboard ("Ladders six feet two each, five-gal drinking water and cups, snakebite kit") but even the items that concerned Crossfield's highly skilled maneuvers during the flight, were set up along the chimpanzee yes-no system of reasoning. That way there should at least be less chance of error, even though the effect on the pilot's ego must be devastating. Under Section 6:

> "APU (Auxiliary Power Unit) Source and Pressure:
> APU Switch To On.
> No. 2 hydraulic gauge for pressure build up.
> Verify No. 1 and No. 2 generator lights are on.
> Check electrical load drop off.
> 6.9   Verify No. 1 A/C generator lights are on.
> Check electrical load drop off.
> 6.13   Verify D.C. Bus. voltage 28 volts.

6.14   Strain gauge battery voltage.
Turn generator switches off. No. 1 and No. 2 APU."

I thumbed through the blue-covered book, relieved that my job is only to observe, not to carry any of the operating weight of this endlessly detailed operation.

TUESDAY, MARCH 31. I got up in the dark and was picked up at the barracks building by Lieutenant Kirkley and another member of the press, Cornell Capa. Our Air Force sedan took us to the hard-stand area where the X-15 was being prepared for Flight No. 2.

This was my first chance to watch the preparation for a flight. In a rambling array of floodlights and searchlights blazing through the first dawn light the fat B-52 mother ship was the nucleus around which most of the working figures agglomerated. A cordon of uniformed company police patrolled a ring of rope that kept bystanders at respectful distance.

The slick black shape of the X-15 was in place under the bomber's wing—had been since four o'clock yesterday afternoon. Now a hydrogen peroxide tank cart, a sort of overgrown peanut wagon in appearance, had been rolled up to the bird and a group of men in fireproof hooded suits were gathered around it. A rushing sound as of a small waterfall seemed to come from somewhere near. I saw that someone had laid out a string of big fire hoses and they were playing gently, spreading a low-velocity current of water along the concrete hardstand underfoot. The point being to forestall an explosion; or, rather, to forestall a *premature* explosion, since all of the fuel gases and liquids in the X-15's complicated plumbing are supposed to burn with explosive force sometime during a mission. That is the function of all the explosives; yet the timing must always be right, and the explosion must occur in the right measure.

The scene as the fuelers did their work was positively Martian. The hooded figures in their stiff fireproof suits moved deliberately among the pipes, amid a dense fog which rose from the concrete. It was condensation from one of the sub-zero gases being administered to the bird. As the fog grew thicker the scene reminded me of something from a Sherlock Holmes novel, grave-robbing ghouls on the misty moor digging among the spirits of the dead.

The fuels being loaded into the bird today were only a small part of what it will carry on a powered flight; the full load of hydrogen peroxide, which will be needed on all the flights, because the X-15's auxiliary power units (APUs) depend on it. Without the APUs the ship could not fly. It depends on the APU system for flaps and control surfaces, hydraulic-booster systems, main landing gear, etc. There are two duplicate APU systems so that one will be sure of working, and they work on a principle worked out long ago by the German V-2 engineers: peroxide is passed through a silver catalyst bed—like air breathed through the stick-type cigarette lighter—and the resulting chemical reaction liberates heat and therefore power.

Today the two big main tanks, for 1,400 gallons of water alcohol and 1,000 gallons of liquid oxygen respectively, were not to be filled. A small sample of simulated fuel—actually only 20 gallons of water—was loaded instead. The idea of this was that Crossfield would jettison it to test his dumping mechanism. It was dyed green so that observers could follow the pattern of the dumping. Importance of the jettison system: it is vital for any rocket ship to be able to get rid of its combustible cargo in a few seconds, in case of an emergency.

For today's flight plan only one high-explosive substance had been loaded into the ship; that was the hydrogen peroxide required for every flight. But the hydrogen peroxide is plenty dangerous. From the days of V-2 onward many a bad explosion has been triggered by H_2O_2. Now, with the H_2O_2 fueling about done, I noted that a towering red Air Force fire truck still stood by, a blinking red beacon atop the cab indicating that it was ready for an emergency.

As the fueling with the inert gases, cold helium and nitrogen, went on, I noted a North American flight-test engineer standing by, watching with an appraising, cautious eye. He was Cooper Lindley. Slightly as I know him, I would say he is a sort of prototype of the engineer, what you would expect an engineer to be: tall, lean, inquiring, thoughtful, analytical, with a sardonic sense of humor.

Lindley had been working here at the mating area since four this morning, and he had labored late last night. He was one of a half-dozen engineers overseeing the mating, the fuelling, the thousands of check list items which must be run down before the flight can begin. The mating actually took place at four in the afternoon, yesterday, and now the preflight preparations had reached page 28 in the check list. Take-off is on page 35—if it is to happen. I detected a dubious look in Lindley's eye.

"Murphy's law," he muttered. "Anything that can go wrong will go wrong."

By now the morning sun was warm on the Edwards hard stand, the fueling carts had been moved away. But the work stand still stood beside the X-15 cockpit, technicians in checkered shirts still clustered around the open cockpit canopy. There was no sign of Scott Crossfield and his silver suit. I looked at my watch. It was after eight—and the take-off had been scheduled for eight.

"Slipped again," Lindley said with a shrug, and he added that the cause of the slippage this time was in the APU system. "Put off another day."

"You expect trouble with the generators tomorrow again?" I asked, trying to pass off the disappointment good-naturedly.

"We don't expect to have trouble with anything," he said. "As far as we're concerned, that bird is perfect just before the flight. We work on it and get it out, but there are things you can't foresee."

He said it takes four days to prepare the ship for a flight. "Things come up and there's sometimes time to straighten them out. We had a sound at 2,400 cycles on the radio last night—a troublesome sound. But we had time to work on it. That was fixed, it would have been all right, except for the APU."

I said jokingly that I had always thought science was infallible —a matter of balanced equations and controlled experiments, and Lindley, still serious, answered:

"Probability is the working method of science. Six out of ten times you might make something a certainty. You just try and try again. When you finally have something simple, it's probably the result of much trial and error—trial and error, that is, within certain parameters or zones of possibility. We don't just try anything, we try things within certain areas of promise."

I said I was surprised to hear a scientist admitting that science worked by trial and error like the more mundane fields of human endeavor.

"That's certainly true of engineering," Lindley said. "It might not be so true of less practical science."

I took advantage of the chance to ask Lindley, now that he was relatively relaxed, about the first mission of X-15, which as we know now nearly landed in disaster and loss of life and equipment.

"Crossfield landed in emergency procedure," he said, speaking of the fire scare when the X-15 cockpit had filled with smoke. "He knew he was having trouble with one of his APUs. He didn't know which one, so he cut 'em both off and blanked out his radio. He was working on the same emergency procedure as he will later on when he'll have his tanks full of water alcohol and lox."

Lindley didn't say it, but by now I knew that if the X-15 had caught fire on that first flight, it would probably have detonated the big fuel tanks in the B-52 wing right over it. The resulting explosion would have been enough to dispose of the B-52, the X-15, the four crewmen of the B-52, and Scott Crossfield.

I asked Lindley about the plan for the flight after today's abort.

"We expect to be back here at the same old stand tomorrow morning, in business," he said. "We'll see you then."

WEDNESDAY, APRIL 1. When I came on the scene at the mating area this morning, about the same point in the check list had been reached. Batteries of lights with rattling generators illuminated the fat silver bomber and her black dart bird with the cockpit canopy propped up like the empty paper of a cupcake. Men in mackinaws thronged around the work ladders. Uniformed company cops oversaw the cordon around the work area.

I recognized Cooper Lindley's polite but slightly acid voice on the public-address bullhorn, coming from the direction of the North American control wagon:

"Power on, please, for the B-52. . . . Verify, please, Freddie, if you have power on. . . . Okay, thank you very much."

The time was five thirty-five. A Hot Papa wearing a hood and plastic fireproof suit was pushing the H_2O_2 cart toward the X-15. The technicians moved away from the area as the firehoses began to spray water onto the concrete and the Hot Papa began to fiddle with his plumbing. He and two assistants worked over the H_2O_2 and two other tank carts carrying helium and nitrogen. The eerie graveyard mist of condensed gases rose and began to swirl around the hooded men.

A North American photographer standing next to me explained about the Hot Papa. "He's the honcho for loadin' these things." I asked about the fog swirling around the Hot Papa and his assistants.

"It's only vaporization—it's not the gas you see. The temperature is so cold it makes the air vaporize. The helium, liquid nitrogen, they're all below zero. The helium is down to minus 320. If there's any leakage, the air vaporizes around the leak."

A tidy, compact man in a sports jacket was in the control van and talking into the mike connected to the speaker on the roof of the vehicle:

"Fifteen minutes from now we should be in a position for crew ingress and start."

The tidy man was Q. C. Harvey, the North American test conductor. Harvey, a B-29 flight engineer during World War II, had
got his feet wet as a rocket engineer for Bell Aircraft during the X-1
program. He is an old hand by now at the business of testing manned
rockets. Right now he is the head man, the field commander, of the
flight-test program for X-15. The fate of the whole X-15 program
will hinge on the rightness of his on-the-spot decisions during the
first phase, the North American testing phase, of the program. Then,
after the ship has been proved to be flyable, the NASA and Air Force
testing chiefs will take over Q. C.'s job for the research flights which
may incidentally break the world altitude and speed records.

A big, chunky, tousle-haired young man in a flying suit hove up
next to me as I watched the fueling operation. I had noticed him
hurrying about, talking to the engineers and technicians. Now, when
he stopped for a minute, I asked him what his job is in today's mission.

"I'm Bill Berkowitz," he said. "I fly the launch panel." He was the
so-called launch operator, whose most important job is keeping the
X-15 lox tank topped off as the B-52 moves into position for launch.
Right now it isn't so vital that the evaporation of the volatile lox
oxidizer be completely replaced, and the tank kept brimful up to the
moment of launch. But·later, the record flights will depend on having
an absolutely maximum supply of oxidizer, to get the last ounce of
power from the rocket engines.

The launch operator has a station in the B-52 just above the level
of the X-15 mounting, and one of his jobs is to watch it like a hawk
on a small television screen inside the bomber cabin.

While I talked to Berkowitz, a group of about ten men in coveralls descended on the B-52—the Air Force crew of fliers, ground
men, mechanics, maintenance men. They wore a special kind of team
identification—long-billed Kelly-green baseball caps.

There seemed to be a spurt of activity everywhere in the mating
area now. Cooper Lindley was talking in animated tones with a tubby,
squat man whom I knew as the boss of the X-15 power-plant section, Bob Field. And the head of North American flight-test operations at Edwards, sharp-faced Ed Cokeley, had appeared at the
mobile-control van.

Cooper Lindley finished talking with Field, and I asked Lindley
what was happening.

"They just retopped the nitrogen system—they're now pressurizing the helium," he told me.

I asked him what were the unexpected problems this morning, and he said, "None" as he hurried toward the mobile-control van.

At seven o'clock Crossfield appeared. He was alone—had apparently just driven over from the North American hangar. He was wearing a short flight jacket and tan pants and carrying a canvas flight bag. He headed for the big yellow "suit-up" trailer, the air-conditioned Air Force van where experts dress him in his silver suit. The van was parked just off the hard stand.

Cooper Lindley pointed out to me the B-52 commander, Captain Charlie Bock, as he appeared next to the bomber. He is a big man with the deliberate, steady, capable look of a Strategic Air Command unit leader. He moved directly under the belly door of the B-52 and looked in, then hauled himself aboard with the experienced grace of a cowboy rushing off thataway.

At eight o'clock a silver-clad, waddling figure, evidently bound up from within by several layers of cloth, harnesses, bladders, came from the suit-up trailer—Crossfield. He was not wearing his helmet.

He padded inside the cordon of police guards and reached the cockpit. A couple of checked shirts stood by to help him up the work ladder.

"Okay," Q. C. Harvey's voice crackled on the public-address speaker atop the mobile-control van. "Board the aircraft now." He was speaking to Crossfield, to Charlie Bock and his copilot and crewman, and big Bill Berkowitz, the launch-panel operator; also to the scores of engineers and technicians who had to have official notification that the mission had reached this point in the check list.

At eight-ten Crossfield was in the X-15 cockpit and two technicians were working over him, screwing the white helmet into the neckpiece of his silver suit. I watched the heavy cockpit lid settle around the large, fragile shape of the helmet with its glinting plexiglas visor. With the canopy cranked down, through the narrow prison windows the helmet looked like a fragile half eggshell.

At this point there was a starting of automobile engines, and a group of vehicles started to move from the mating area. Some of the cars headed for the North American hangar, where Master Control of today's mission would be located. Other vehicles, blue Air Force sedans and trucks, North American pickups and station wagons, turned the other way, toward the vast dry ocean of the lake beds, where soon Q. C. Harvey would take his Mobile-Control van to direct field operations. We of the press—today only Cornell Capa, the photographer from Magnum, and I—were advised to go to Master

Control, where we non-productive types would be less in the way than amid the hurly-burly of Harvey's Mobile Control.

The Master Control station was set up in the tower of the North American hangar, a clean, bare, hospital-like room with huge panoramic windows that reached well up into the sky. At one corner of the room a couple of radio controls had been set up. A technician sat next to it with earphones clamped on his head, and the room filled with scholarly engineer types assembled to listen to the flight of their bird. I spotted the two youngish men who are the coassistant chiefs of the X-15 engineering project: Raun Robinson and Roland "Bud" Benner. Both are blond, alert, sensitive men. Today, considering this was the second flight of their baby and that the first one hadn't gone too well, they seemed calm. But I would estimate that this was only an appearance: both are well-disciplined individuals, with the faculty of keeping their emotions well below the surface.

From the tower window we watched the tall orange tail of the B-52 start to move, stop, move, stop—it was beginning to taxi out of the mating area. We heard the squawk and blurt of the radio calls, smothered occasionally by a band of annoying loud buzzing.

Robinson answered my question about it. "They got the noise out from last time. It was a middle A. But it was better last time, with the noise in it—mostly loud and clear."

"Better put the noise back," Bud Benner commented.

We saw the bomber, now tiny with distance, as it swept into the air at the north end of the runway, gaining altitude. As it spiraled into the sky, we heard Q. C. Harvey on the radio, taking the difficult communications problem in hand.

"Two flicks will be yes, one flick will be no," he was informing Crossfield, instituting a primitive semaphore kind of system to overcome the annoying abundance of static in Scott's voice transmissions.

"Is everything okay?" Harvey asked. His voice was coming through clearly. The radio problem was in the transmitter aboard the X-15.

"Dit-dit," came the answer.

So, on a communications level more like the hand-waving, flare-shooting level of World War I aviation than the latest in space travel, the second test flight of the X-15 was beginning.

We watched the curving of contrails now in the high sky. A fat white trail was leading—that would be the B-52 with the X-15 attached—and three smaller sprays of white vapor following it where the chase planes kept surveillance over their charge.

For a brief while Crossfield's radio seemed to be functioning again. We heard Scott say:

"Do you read me?"

And the firm bomber pilot's voice (Bock) answering: "Roger, Scotty."

But in a few seconds, as Crossfield was reporting something about the APU, it was lost in static—the grunts, thuds, and squeaks making it unintelligible to a layman's ear.

Bud Benner, his intelligence better trained to catch the garble, could make out some of it: "He's explaining about his power system being different from the B-52."

Today's flight, according to the blue-covered mission profile I had read, was concerned with checking out the controls of the X-15 (flaps, landing gear, etc.) while it was still attached to the B-52; also with such miscellany as a practice jettison of fuel by releasing the colored water from the tanks, calibrating the air-speed instruments, and simulating the drop procedure of the X-15 which will be followed on the occasion of the first glide flight in the near future —or before that if there should be an emergency.

The radio, in its fragmentary, staticky condition which allowed only a few of the communications to come from Scott, lasted long enough for the simulated-drop and the fuel-jettison test. The dit-dit, yes-no system was held in reserve in case the voice transmissions grew too fractious.

"Scott, this is Q. C. Let's go over this jettison when you're ready."

"Okay." Crossfield's voice was very faint. A minute later we heard something about "2–4 on page 39."

"Okay on phase 40." It was Charlie Bock's voice: "Five, four, three, two, one—*jettison!*"

Bock reported to Mobile Control: "There is a jettison."

We looked up toward the contrails curving in the high sky above us, but there was no visible sign from here of the releasing of the colored dye.

Q. C. Harvey's voice said: "We do have a jettison pattern?"

The firm answer from Captain Bock: "Affirmative. The jettison has stopped."

A new tracing of white arced up toward the B-52. "Charlie, this is Q. C. Chase Five is on its way up."

Bock's voice: "Chase Five is here."

As the airspeed calibration section came up on the check list, Scott

Crossfield's low voice disappeared completely from the communications channels, blotted out by radio static and malfunction. Q. C. Harvey went back to his blip-blip signal system:

"Everything okay, Scott?"

"Tick-tick."

"Thank you."

And the communications, instead of improving, got worse. As the bomber was lining up for some air-speed calibrations, Q. C. said: "Okay, page forty-two, give us a signal to go ahead."

There was no audible answer. After a few minutes Bock's voice reported:

"We just got an okay from Scott. You can go ahead."

Q. C. said: "How? Can you hear him?"

"No. I can see him."

By this time even Harvey's primitive blip system seemed to have failed. And the B-52 crew were communicating with him by means of hand waves and head nodding. Our most sophisticated and most advanced scientific effort, our first moves into the vast frightening frontier of space travel, to which our greatest mathematical brains had been bending their utmost efforts and techniques, had devolved, as most things do, down to simple mechanics and human error. The checkout of Einstein's theory of curved space and time compressibility, the determination of the origins of the universe, will probably be held up by humble, simple mechanical items such as radio transmitters and failures of mechanical preparation—in the future as right now. No matter how sophisticated our technology may become, simple mechanical and human failures will probably determine the success or defeat of our future battles, as they have so often in the past.

But men will fight through the maze of their errors then as now. Now we heard by the radio that even the visual method of communication between Crossfield and the mother ship was in difficulty. Some of the windows had frosted over in the high-altitude cold. But the fliers were determined to bull their way through the tests at hand —right now the air-speed calibrations and control checks.

Berkowitz, the launch operator, was reporting: "No horizontal stabilizer movement."

"Thank you, Bill," Q. C. Harvey told him. "Can you see through the windshield okay?"

"Yeah, no sweat," said Berkowitz nonchalantly.

The calibrations somehow were finished, and then Bock was saying: "Scotty is apparently signaling he wants to come home. He says, 'Let's go home,' and he nods his head to acknowledge my transmission." Bock meant that Scott had been able to hear Bock's report that the X-15 pilot wanted to go home, and had nodded his head in approval.

Q. C. Harvey gave the order, but wanted one more thing checked along the way—he being, I guess, the kind of fighting test conductor who knows you have to keep on trying, trying to wring the last drop of results out of every test, even those beset by hordes of difficulties.

"I would like the gear down if possible," Q. C. was saying, meaning he wanted to check out the mechanism for lowering the landing struts of the X-15.

Bock said efficiently: "The speed point will be 160."

Q. C. said: "I would prefer a countdown if he can hear me."

Bock reported: "He nodded his head and acknowledges."

Then the big B-52 commander's steady voice was heard: "Okay —counting down from five, four, three, two, one—*drop gear!*"

A few seconds later: "Looks good from the B-52. Timed at three and one half seconds."

In a few minutes we saw the curved white plumes of the B-52 and the chase planes arcing down toward the field from the west. The flight was ending with no major catastrophes as yet.

We drove over to the mating area and watched the big orange-tailed bomber taxiing across the plain of Edwards. And we watched with field glasses from behind the police lines while the canopy of the black dart went up and we saw that Scott had taken off his helmet. His dark hair was tousled. When the plane stopped, we watched him sitting motionless there while the inevitable swarm of checkered shirts, the technicians, pushed a work ladder up beside him and talked to him. He seemed to dally in the cockpit like a king deliberating on his throne. The crew didn't come out of the mother ship, I guessed out of politeness toward the king, the star of the show. They would let him descend first.

I watched Scott through the glasses and he appeared to be sweaty, disheveled, and uncomfortable as he talked to the technicians. At last he pushed himself out of the cockpit, put his booted feet on the platform of the work stand, then hung his head low as if he were about to keel over. But he didn't. He was apparently only thoroughly worn out by the rigors of the flight and—I found out later in the day —because the nitrogen supply which air-conditions his suit had run out just as the plane touched ground.

Crossfield climbed down, waddling with the bulk of his suit and its built-in harnesses. He strode toward the Mobile-Control van, with the small knot of engineers around it, and stopped to talk with the company brass there: Cokeley, Q. C. Harvey, and Harrison Storms. The company cops kept the rest of us away from him, so that he could make his way in peace to the yellow air-conditioned suit-up trailer.

I managed to catch Chief Engineer Storms for a moment, and asked for a comment on today's flight. He was miffed about the trouble with the radio.

"The things cost so much money, you'd think they'd do better. If you had the thing in your home, and it performed like that, you'd throw it out the window."

He explained what the trouble had been: the electrical circuits for the X-15's own radio system are far from perfect. "It'll take a lot of work," he said. But, he added, the test was good. "We were able to do the things we expected."

After the interview with Storms, I tried to arrange to see Crossfield. But he scooted off to a secret debriefing with the engineers, then shoved off for his home in Los Angeles.

This afternoon, though, I did succeed in penetrating the security-guarded confines of the test-pilot facility in Edwards, and talk to Captain Bob Rushworth, the No. 2 Air Force flier lined up as a back-up pilot on X-15 for Captain Bob White. White or Rushworth —or possibly one of the NASA pilots—depending on the breaks— will probably fly the most spectacular record missions, climbing up to 50 miles, then as high as 150 miles' altitude, well into the fringes of space.

With Air Force Sergeant Ivy Edmunds for an escort, I managed to get into the long, bare, barracks-type building where the fourteen Air Force experimental test pilots have cramped cubbyholes of offices, a day room, and a locker room. Next to the office building is a big, high-domed hangar where the latest military aircraft (some of them top secret) are kept between flights. Out on the hardstand on the field side of the office (the other side is fenced in with barbed wire) sat an array of special planes being tested this day. Most were jet fighters—none with rocket power. All wore the bright orange nose and tail paint of the Air Force Air Research and Development Command.

I saw Bob Rushworth in one of the little rabbit-warren offices. He is leathery-looking, tow-headed, with light blue eyes, and he's thirty-five years old. He had flown a 104 chase plane this morning and was still wearing a flying suit.

Rushworth, like White, is a combat flier of two wars, World War II and Korea. He is the kind of phlegmatic, cool, deliberative fellow you would trust with your life in an emergency.

I asked him what are the big problems in the X-15 program, and he said with scientific conciseness:

"Cn Beta—negative stability—that's one of the things we'll be looking for in the program."

Cn Alpha and Beta are scientific shorthand for roll and yaw, which can be compounded into inertia coupling, or tumbling, the dread phenomenon which killed Captain Mil Apt when he established the present world's speed record in X-2; and nearly killed Kincheloe, Walker, Murray, Yeager, and many other of the rocket pilots as they braved the frontiers of space travel in their experimental ships—the dangerous frontiers of thin air and bullet-like speeds.

I asked Rushworth what is the toughest nut to crack at this present stage of X-15 testing. The light eyes considered the question, then he said deliberately:

"It's going to be a pretty good thrill when they drop off for the first time." That was all he said. His calm understatement about the danger of that first flight set my scalp tingling. His easy-going language seemed to throw into sharp focus the perilous, white-hot and ice-cold, grim and breathless realm the space pioneers such as Rushworth, White, Walker, and Crossfield are braving.

FRIDAY, APRIL 3. Today I went down to the North American plant to look at one of the great training devices for X-15 flight—the static simulator. Dick Barton took me past the high, barrel-shaped wind-tunnel building to the simulator section where we looked at the gadget —a cockpit mockup of X-15. It's a duplicate of the black nose of the ship, with the same instruments and controls as the flyable birds, connected to a workable tail section. But that isn't all there is to the simulator. It also involves a huge roomful of calculating machines.

Norm Cooper, the head simulator man, was on hand to demonstrate. His correct title is more complicated than that: it's properly "engineering supervisor, flight-control analysis, systems and tactics, X-15," but the effect is the same.

Cooper showed us how the tail-control surfaces on the simulator, the rudder, and elevons respond just like the control system of the

X-15 in flight. These control surfaces are rigged on a boom, a kind of skeletal steel arrangement, behind the cockpit. Like the surfaces on the flyable X-15s, they are activated by a hydraulic system. The size and weight of the control surfaces and the hydraulic forces involved are exact duplicates of those on the X-15. But the mockup itself doesn't move during a mission. The instruments react as they would in flight, and graphs record the whole course of the mission.

Next to the simulator mockup is a big glassed-in room that holds the array of computing machines needed to record the flight and activate the instruments. The enclosure, about as large as a ten-room apartment or a small hangar, is filled with banks upon banks of gray calculating machines that look like rows of tall lockers until you inspect them carefully. Then you see that their fronts are filled with voltmeters, dials, and light signals.

Cooper, a small, youthful man who is very deliberate in his speech, explained how the simulator works:

"These electronic analogue computers enable you to fly the airplane on an actual mission," he said. "You can command the airplane any way you like, and the computers will estimate the response exactly."

Next to the cockpit mockup was a kind of bulletin board where a stylus was rigged to make marks on a big sheet of paper. On the paper a curved meandering red line traced some recent "flight" in the simulator.

"The plotter shows you exactly your course," Cooper said. "Another graph records speed and altitude."

Cooper pointed out another cockpit mockup near the X-15 simulator. It was the static simulator for a North American experimental fighter plane, the F-107. "The F-107 simulator had what we call five degrees of freedom. It could compute for movement on five axes— every kind of movement except fore-and-aft speed and drag.

"The X-15 simulator has six degrees of freedom. It's the first simulator allowing for change of altitude and velocity."

I looked into the cockpit, then climbed in to see how the chair felt. The cockpit was tight. Even without the bulk of a parachute, and without a helmet, the cockpit canopy touched my head when it was closed. If I had been dressed in a silver suit and helmet I would have had to hunch way down in the cockpit. The X-15 pilot's office is built for a small man.

The instrument panel doesn't seem more complex than that in any good-sized aircraft, but there is a dazzling array of switches and toggles. The plumbing, the power sources, the duplicate systems necessitate plenty of activators, and there are several batteries of switches on each side of the cockpit.

The throttle is not a conventional lever as in most aircraft, but a panel at the left hand with two lines of switches—eight altogether. Each switch activates a barrel in the array of rocket tubes in the tail. There are two engines, one ranged above the other, in the tail, and each engine is composed of four rocket tubes.

I checked over the three control sticks. There is a long rubber-handled stick between the pilot's knees that duplicates the old-fashioned joy stick in a conventional airplane. There are also conventional rudder pedals.

But there are also two side sticks, pistol grips mounted on the rim of the cockpit to the left and right of the pilot's seat. They can be moved up, down, or on sidewise arcs, and they cause movements of the body and wings of the ship with the same efficiency as the conventional stick and rudder pedals.

The pistol grip controls or side sticks are designed to effect the movements of the ship with very slight movements of the wrist. Instead of moving his whole arm, as with the conventional long joy stick, the pilot flies the plane with hand and wrist. The idea is that when he is under the strain of heavy g-forces—as when, for instance, he is pulling out after a steep arc into space—he can handle the ship by tiny movements around the pivot of his wrist.

The right-hand wrist stick activates the same control surfaces as the big center joy stick. The one on the left works the rocket or reaction controls—the rocket-jet tubes in the nose and wings of the X-15 which can change its attitude up above the atmosphere, where there is no air for the conventional control surfaces to push against. The reaction controls work on the principle that even in the vacuum of space a rocket push in one direction results in a movement in the opposite direction. It's all according to Newton's third law, that every action produces an equal and opposite reaction.

But whether the side stick activates the reaction controls or the conventional control surfaces that work in the air, the small, pistol-grip side sticks probably foreshadow the control knobs space ships will use, as they fly both in atmosphere and in space. The side sticks can be moved easily even when the pilot is undergoing great forces of acceleration or deceleration. If the pilot tried a pull-out with an old-fashioned big stick, his muscles might not be strong enough to move it. For instance, if the weight of his arm were normally 25 pounds and he were pulling six g's, the weight of the arm would become 150 pounds, or the weight of the upper half of his body would be increased from 100 to 600 pounds. With that much weight pushing forward he might not be able to haul the stick back. But with a side stick he could effect the pull-out with a very small force.

So I was looking at space controls—the stick at the right designed for high-strain flight in atmosphere, the one at the left built for flight in space. Both with their free-pivoting pistol grips, the controls of the future which will supersede the clumsy stick and rudder pedals of old-style aircraft. The inclusion of the old-fashioned center stick and rudder in the X-15, said Barton, is a gesture toward the conventional in aircraft manufacture. But the side sticks are the important ones for the future.

I asked Cooper and Barton if I could sometime soon have a chance to fly a mission in the simulator and try the side sticks. Barton said yes, I could be started at 100 miles up and see if I could successfully fly the bird back to earth. That will be something difficult to look forward to. Barton said he had tried it several times and several times crashed, such a crash being quite harmless in the simulator. If you auger in with the simulator, he said, you just crank it up and start all over again.

Barton told me the most experienced man in flying simulator missions is Cooper himself. He has made more than 1,000 simulated X-15 flights of different shapes and patterns.

I looked at the map on the chart board. Someone had been flying landing approaches over the Edwards Air Base lake beds, the red curving lines showing how the plane circled and landed.

"Who's been flying this thing recently?" I asked Cooper.

"Crossfield was in today," he answered. "We were plotting his landing pattern for the first glide flight." Cooper pointed to a sweeping large curve which made almost a complete circle over the center of the chart.

"He favors this pattern," Cooper said, "because he can break off anywhere along the curve according to how much altitude he has. If he's high, he can fill out the curve. If he's low, he can break off early." He put a stubby finger on the red tracing. "He could break off here—or here."

I asked Cooper if Crossfield considered a flight in the simulator an exact duplicate of an actual flight. It seemed to me that a practical test pilot would have some reservations about this.

"He says it's a simulator, not the real thing," Cooper said. "Scott says you can be lulled into a false sense of security by getting used to the simulator—and then the real flight might turn up something new and unexpected. But I would say he's a good simulator pilot. He follows instructions."

Cooper went into a rather lengthy and technical explanation of the simulator and the way it works.

"It involves 240 amplifiers and 27 servos," he said. "The amplifiers do the linear computing, which means the constant factors—like steady speed, fixed altitude. The servos do the non-linear or variable computing."

This was fairly clear to me, but I still had no idea what servos and amplifiers looked like, or how they worked. I wasn't so presumptuous that I thought I could pick up the knowledge in ten minutes when it takes the engineers years to learn, but I resolved that when I came back to "fly" the simulator I would make more inquiries.

For the present, I appreciated the simulator and its related calculating machines more when Cooper said these computers could solve equations instantaneously which it would take a man years to compute—years, that is, to measure the control movements and translate them to readings on the instrument panel and graphs and charts of the "flight."

Cooper was saying that the mass of calculating machinery gets greater as the simulators grow more sensitive and realistic. The F-107 simulator has only half as many servos and amplifiers as the X-15 mockup. I said I presumed that future simulators, duplicating spaceship travel, would be even more complicated and bulky, that huge hangars full of computers would be necessary for each one, and he agreed.

I turned back to the chart of Crossfield's practice landings on the simulator. Cooper said one of the great values of the simulator is that it can be used to sample the pilot's reactions to an emergency anywhere in a mission. He can set up almost any emergency—like, say, loss of APU power—and see how it could be solved.

"Speaking generally," Cooper said, "from the start of a High Range [maximum performance] mission over Utah to the landing at Edwards we have to have every emergency figured out. There wouldn't be time to figure it out on the spot."

SUNDAY, APRIL 5. Convinced that I need all the background I can get in the field of space and rockets, I've been spending my spare time reading a slew of books on the subject.

The literature of the space or rocket age is relatively meager. I have combed through all the bibliographies I could find, and discovered few good recent texts. There are two space encyclopedias: *The Space Encyclopaedia: A Guide to Astronomy and Space Research,* edited by M. T. Bizony and R. Griffin [New York: E. P. Dutton & Co., Inc., 1958; New Revised Edition, 1960] and the *Dictionary of Guided Missiles and Space Flight,* edited by Grayson Merrill [New York: D. Van Nostrand Company, 1959]. There is a text, *Space Weapons: A Handbook of Military Astronautics,* published by *Air Force* magazine in 1959, and up to date enough to include NASA, the civilian space agency established in August of 1958 at President Eisenhower's direction. But these reference books, being encyclopedic in nature, do not discuss in detail the careers of the space and rocket pioneers such as Wernher von Braun, Lieutenant Colonel Chuck Yeager, Scott Crossfield, Joe Walker, or Captain Bob White. The whole field is too new. And of course it is hopeless to look for any mention of the younger space-age figures in the standard biographical texts (even the latest editions) like *Who's Who in America* and *Webster's Biographical Dictionary.*

The whole nuclear, rocket, space age is far too new for historical scholars to have established and published the facts fully, but a general shape of rocket history does emerge.

There seems to be general agreement that the first recorded military use of rockets was in 1232 by the militia of a Chinese city variously called Kai-fung-fu or Pien-king. It seems to be the same as the present city of Kaifeng, an old, populous trading capital of central China.

There's also some uncertainty about the name of the Mongol conqueror, Ogadai or Ogdai, against whom the rocket weapons were used. There is agreement, anyhow, that he was the son of Genghis Khan, the great Mongol emperor, and that the inhabitants of the Chinese city used a battery of rocket tubes against him—"arrows of flying fire," as the French missionary chronicler St. Julien calls them. The skyrocket (and the necessary gunpowder) had existed as far back as the year 1000 in China, and the episode at Kaifeng is the first known occasion when fireworks were used as weapons. We infer from St. Julien's account that they were used without success at Kaifeng. Ogadai took the city, and there is no indication that he attempted to make any use of the novel weapons used against him.

There is some disagreement, too, about the authenticity of the first recorded attempt at rocket flight—which many writers credit to a Chinese nobleman named Wan Hu in the sixteenth century. Several authorities cite the Chinese legend that Wan Hu rigged a sedan chair with 47 rockets, sent up a huge kite to serve as a sky anchor, commanded 47 servants to light the 47 rockets—and succeeded in generating some rocket thrust, which, being misaligned, resulted in not flight, but the rapid disintegration of the intended aircraft. It's not clear just what happened to Wan Hu, but the rocket-propelled chair fell apart in a heinous burst of fireworks. John L. Russell, Jr., in *Destination: Space,* Beryl Williams and Samuel Epstein in *The Rocket Pioneers,* and Willy Ley (the most authoritative) in *Rockets, Missiles and Space Travel* include accounts of the Wan Hu adventure.

There is general agreement, anyway, that the Chinese were the first to develop and experiment with rockets, and that the Chinese rocket knowledge was carried to the Mediterranean area by Arab traders during the Middle Ages.

Through the Arabs, rockets reached India, and several of the Indian potentates formed rocket corps, as the Chinese of Kaifeng had done when attacked by Ogadai.

So it happened that a force of British troops, bent on imperial conquest in the principality of Mysore, received a rude shock one day in 1791 when a barrage of flying fire met them as they attacked the forces of Prince Hyder Ali. As the British cavalry charged, a barrage of long-shafted, flaming arrows sped into their ranks. More than 1,000 Indian troops, a rocket brigade under Tippo Sahib, Ali's son, were firing the missiles—iron tubes, about eight inches long and two inches in diameter, with a bamboo stick about ten feet long attached to each so it would fly straighter. The propulsive power was the same as the Chinese had employed: the mixture of charcoal, sulphur, and saltpeter the Western world now called gunpowder.

The British fell back in confusion. Casualties were not great but the effect on the morale of the close-packed British horsemen and foot troops was considerable.

A British artillery officer named William Congreve, a major in far-off London, read reports of the Mysore engagement and devoted some of his own funds to researching the new weapon.

Soon Congreve had developed a new rocket that could fly farther faster, and straighter than the Indian model. It was a bigger metal tube than the Indian weapon, had a 16-foot shaft, and a range of more than a mile.

Congreve won permission of the War Office to try out his rocket in combat, of which a plenitude was available with the cycle of Napoleonic wars. In 1805 a British ship equipped with rockets was used against the French port of Boulogne, but the effort fizzled out, largely because of the overcast weather. One year later, however, British rocket-firing ships came back and set the city on fire, burning out a large portion of it.

During the British siege of Copenhagen in 1807 Congreve led a fleet of rocket-firing ships into a night attack. More than 25,000 rockets were poured into the city, and they burned out about half the buildings in it.

This kind of success encouraged the British, and when they tangled with the United States in the War of 1812, they scored some spectacular successes against our forts with barrages from rocket-firing ships. At Bladensburg, Maryland, an American garrison supposed to be guarding an approach to Washington, D.C., was routed when the British rocket batteries fired. The American force of raw recruits fell back, the British forces marched into Washington and burned the White House and the Capitol.

The British rocket weapons reached their apex of fame when in 1814, still during the War of 1812, rocket-firing barges attacked Fort McHenry. Francis Scott Key, writing about the engagement in a song that became our national anthem, memorialized the weapon Congreve had developed with the phrase, "mid the rockets' red glare." Everyone knows Key's stanza telling how the flag was still there despite the fiery assault.

During the long stretches of peace that arrived with the nineteenth century, rocket progress, as usual in times of international tranquillity, came slowly. By the late 1800s artillery had improved greatly in accuracy because of the rifling of cannon barrels—and the rocket brigades of the European nations fell into discard. One of the last to go was the Austro-Hungarian rocket corps, disbanded in 1866.

It was only the use of rockets for maritime distress signaling that kept the science alive toward the end of the century—that and the theorizing of a few scientists and fiction writers.

The famed French science-fiction author Jules Verne speculated on space travel in *From the Earth to the Moon* (1865), but his imaginary aerial projectile, while driven by the mechanism of reaction, was pushed into flight by a gigantic cannon with a 900-foot barrel, not by rockets.

It remained for a Russian scientist, Konstantin Eduardovitch Ziolkovsky, just before the end of the nineteenth century, to write an article that accurately prophesied the big rockets of our century of war—and more than that, the way in which liquid-fueled rockets could be used for the motive power of space ships. Being a chemist and physicist, Ziolkovsky calculated weights and measures for a rocket ship, modern style, and envisioned accurately some of the fundamental requirements of space travel—such as the carrying of oxygen to sustain the travelers in space, and to make possible the burning of the rocket fuel out there beyond the atmosphere.

For fuel, he advocated a light oil much like the kerosene we burn in our present-day missiles, and he even foresaw the use of green plants to absorb the carbon dioxide breathed out by the crew and to provide oxygen for them. We are just now getting to experiments along this line in aeromedical labs of the Air Force.

One of Ziolkovsky's papers on space flight, written in 1898, was not published until five years later. It took that long to convince the *Nautschnoje Obosrenije* (*Science Survey*) to commit his ideas to print.

Late contemporaries of Ziolkovsky in the space-travel field were a Frenchman, Robert Esnault-Pelterie, and a German, Hermann Ganswindt. But neither predicted space-age rocketry with the accuracy of Ziolkovsky. Our American rocket pioneer, the secretive Robert H. Goddard, began his rocket experiments considerably later. His most important work didn't emerge until after World War I.

Strangely enough, the science of rocketry was not spurred by that war, even though the conflict gave a fantastic boost to other sciences such as aeronautics. Rockets were used in World War I mainly for signaling purposes—and rocket research dropped out of sight. It remained for World War II and the military-minded Germans to bring rockets almost to their present stage of development. In a space of nine years the German master minds pushed the rocket from a primitive signaling device and the cranky little sideshow item of Goddard and the amateur rocket societies to a proved, practical V-2 projectile that weighed fourteen tons, could climb to 100 miles and reach 3,600 miles an hour; in short, in size, weight, contour, and performance almost exactly the same as the X-15, but fifteen years earlier.

It was when I raised this point that such emphatic disagreement had come from Scott Crossfield. I know his contention was basically that the two could not be compared, because the X-15 has to be brought to a landing after its flight, and its rocket power has to be throttlable by the pilot. However, the parallel exists, and in fact the

German A-4b, a stub-winged version of the V-2, could be taken for a sister ship of the X-15 in looks as well as performance.

I made a mental note to comb through the copious library of the Institute of Aeronautical Sciences in Los Angeles, and dig into the history of the German pioneers who shaped our present-day space and rocket progress—on both sides of the Iron Curtain, for the Russians were quicker and more decisive than we in following the German lead.

So the research should be interesting, and meanwhile I'm looking forward to a flight in the X-15 simulator. It's set up for next Wednesday.

WEDNESDAY, APRIL 8. Down at the simulator with Dick Barton, I found that Norm Cooper had prepared for my X-15 mockup flight.

Another engineer, Arden Boyd of the flight-control analysis department, was on hand to indoctrinate me before the simulated flight.

I climbed into the cockpit, and Boyd and Cooper introduced me to the prelaunch procedures.

"First," Cooper was saying, "you've got to check your prime conditions—see if your lox tanks are topped—two minutes before launch."

"You have to make sure your APUs are on—over there on the right—those two toggles on the dashboard. In other words, you check your generator power and your hydraulic pressure—and your APU temperature, those two gauges. And you check your source for liquid helium: to push along the cockpit coolant."

It was partly Greek to me. But the prelaunch procedure was what anyone who had been following the bird might have expected: checking a lot of gauges and switches to make sure that the various gases and liquids were available in the right quantity, a kind of check list of plumbing connections.

It seemed like a lot of checking to keep in mind; but fortunately it's impossible to hurt yourself by forgetting something in the simulator. In the real thing any goof could cost you your life, but quickly.

Cooper and Boyd launched me without further ado. In the simulator you can do that—put a man up in the sky without any training or conditioning and see if he would make it or crash.

One change in the cockpit I'd had time to notice, since my last visit, was a new knob at the left. Where the eight switches for the Small Engine had been installed last time there was now a single throttle knob. That meant the Big Engine (the one that hasn't arrived yet) was being simulated.

"You'll need the XLR-99 engine to get up to 250,000 feet where you're going," Boyd said. I realized with a jolt of disappointment that the XLR-11 engine, the one that's in the bird at Edwards now, wouldn't be able to go very far out into space. I made a mental note to ask one of the senior project engineers later just how far up the X-15 will be able to go with the Small Engine.

My black-knobbed throttle was pushed forward to full throttle now for this flight, but the engine was of course 100 per cent simulated: no rocket noise, in fact no noise of any kind. Boyd and Cooper could talk to me in whispers as they stood beside the cockpit mockup. They could advise me on any problems on the spot.

And there were plenty, especially with the controls. The simulator you have to fly completely on instruments: nothing moves except your instruments and your controls. This means that you must "fly" by your instrument panel—meaning particularly the small airplane silhouette on the artificial horizon display right before you. The rear view of an airplane represented there has to be kept trimmed against the line of the artificial horizon. You must keep the wings level and the nose of the plane above the horizon during the climb, and later, during the glide back to earth, the nose must be kept below the horizon. This, of course, is just the way the X-15 itself will be flown, by instruments—instruments that will give an instantaneous reading on the position and attitude of the plane anywhere in space. They are the stable platform instruments, developed in missiles. They are geared to a spinning gyro behind the cockpit. That gyro instantly projects a flat position in space and tells you how much you deviate from it. In missiles, an automatic mechanism corrects the attitude of the bird to what it should be. In the X-15 that correction is up to the pilot.

The disconcerting thing with the X-15 control system, I rapidly discovered, is that you correct the attitude of the bird on your instrument panel by moving the stick just the opposite of the way you want the bird to move. In other words, to raise the right wing of the little plane on the dashboard, you don't move the stick to the left; you move it to the right. You fly that little bird on your instrument panel just the opposite of the way you would fly visually. To a pilot who had been given some training on instruments, it would be standard.

My experience in flying has been limited, although I once soloed, and this new task of handling controls, just the opposite of what I'd been taught, was disconcerting to put it mildly. Also, I was flying now for the first time with a side stick: the pistol-grip control at my left geared to the reaction controls.

Some of the new Space-Age instruments were unfamiliar, too: for instance, there were two mach meters or air-speed instruments, one geared in the traditional way to a pressure tube, measuring speed by checking the pressure of air against the wing; the other, a true space-age instrument designed to measure movement on a gyroscope principle where there is no atmosphere, i.e., in space. There is also an accelerometer, geared to a Space-Age gyro, that gives an accurate record of the speed with which the X-15 is accelerating, and an angle of attack indicator that tells exactly how steeply you are climbing or descending. These instruments have to be watched carefully to see that at the great speeds involved the pilot doesn't destroy himself by pulling too many g's. At the higher altitudes, to which I was climbing, the matter of g forces was not so critical, my mentors said; but in re-entry into the atmosphere they would have to be watched very carefully.

What with the new space instruments and the peculiar reversal of controls in handling the artificial horizon, I soon got myself hopelessly uncaged. The small silhouette of the plane on the dark board separated itself too far from its artificial horizon. When it dragged one wing and my instinctive efforts to correct only made the trouble worse, the small shape of the plane seemed to come unglued from the panel and was soon spinning hopelessly.

It would have been fatal in a real flight. But now Cooper only stuck his head solemnly into the cockpit and told me:

"You pranged it."

I looked at my altimeter and saw that it was reading something below sea level—well below the fatal level at Edwards Air Force Base, which is more than 2,000 feet altitude.

Boyd and Cooper set me up immediately, since I should by now be beginning to grasp the control situation—in another "flight" toward 250,000 feet, just about twice the present world's altitude record.

Now that I had already tried one flight, Cooper pointed out a couple of items I would certainly have to know about before I could tackle an actual mission. One was the ejection system: there's a yellow knob to the right of the pilot's chair that fires the canopy clear in an emergency. Then to fire the chair clear of the aircraft the pilot folds his arms behind braces so they won't get broken by the slip stream and pulls a trigger underneath him.

Another hitherto unnoticed item was the display of instruments for the stability augmentation system in front of the pilot's knees. It's possible to fly the bird, as I had, without paying attention to these instruments. But it's better, of course, to know about them.

The SAS, as it's called in pilot shorthand, is basically a system of dampers that prevents the pilot from overcontrolling. I found now that the practical matter to watch for with the SAS instruments is to see that there's no blinking of lights among the dials for yaw, pitch, and yar (combination of yaw and roll). Learning to fly this bird on the run as I was doing today had one great advantage: it taught you the bare fundamentals that you had to know to make the bird go. I might not know how the SAS controlled yaw and roll, but I learned rapidly that if the warning light doesn't blink, the system is working all right.

My first simulator flight hadn't been recorded, Cooper told me, but this second one would. The tape would be switched on so I'd get a graph of the mission. I was glad my first attempt, with its ignominious crack-up, hadn't been memorialized on a graph.

"They say you can get a graph that shows Marilyn Monroe if you have the right input," Cooper joked. But I was too concentrated this time on making a respectable flight to appreciate the gag.

Cooper saw it and told me to be sure to jettison the lower ventral at 17,000 feet, and I promised I would. I know landing is impossible with X-15 as long as that control surface is attached.

And the flight went all right. This time I didn't get confused about the reversal of the controls. I flew the small bird on the instrument panel without a hitch, moving the two side sticks and the big stick just the opposite to the way I'd learned in flying—and came in for a landing without uncaging my instruments.

But there was one thing that slipped my mind in the maze of remembering all the items to check and recheck: the altitude at Edwards. That desert lake bed is really a plateau 2,305 feet above sea level. The altimeter, which works conventionally on air pressure, would read 2,305 feet when you came into contact with the ground. So, since I was flying totally by instruments, I went on through that level and came to a perfect landing at zero feet, actually 2,305 feet below sea level.

My two mentors immediately prepared another mission, to see if I couldn't make one good flight without destroying myself.

They set me up again in the sky, and I ran through the check list: source pressure, APU switches on, lox tank pressure okay. And off we went into the Wild Black Yonder, flying the silhouette bird against the white of the artificial horizon, the black knob of the throttle full ahead; choosing the angle of attack for the climb by watching for a sign of approval from Cooper as he watched me manipulate the stick.

Then we were reaching the apex of the flight, the Space-Age altimeter indicating 220,000, and in seconds the course of the flight would level and start curving over for the down grade. My power had burned out at about 150,000 but the ship was still rising. Before we started today I had asked Cooper why the X-15 follows a ballistic curve, and he had answered:

"It's like when you throw a stone—gravity overcomes the inertia and it falls. The X-15 is falling as soon as the power is off, although the course is rising for a while. That curve follows the inevitable pattern depending on the angle and the force.

"With the reaction controls you can alter your course only to a slight degree during the ballistic part of the flight. Mainly the reaction controls are to alter your trim. They aren't powerful enough to do more than that."

I was doing just that—trimming the plane in the ballistic portion of the flight—and at a nod from my two coaches pushing the nose over slightly below the line of the artificial horizon as the simulator reached the top of its arc at 250,000 feet and hovered there before beginning to slope down toward home base again.

Now the simulator was coming back toward atmosphere, the speed picking up on the down slope. At the apex of the curve we had been down to between Mach 2 and 3 (between 1,300 and 1,980 miles an hour at that altitude). Now we were picking up to 4.5 as it slid down through space toward atmosphere; that would be 2,730 miles an hour.

Cooper was nodding to me to pull up a little to slow the speed. I knew the course of re-entry now through my brief acid experience with the simulator: speed must not go too high or the re-entry heat will grow dangerous. If you hit atmosphere at too great a speed, I knew, the nose and underside of the wings would glow red with the heat of friction.

I pulled up the nose a little (with, I must admit, a helping hand from Cooper), and the accelerometer reading tapered off a bit. The altimeter showed that we must be beginning to hit the edge of atmosphere—the needle indicated slightly above 100,000 feet. The Mach meter read less than 4—something about 2,470 miles an hour. A slight nod of Cooper's head indicated that I was doing all right.

Then I had to begin flying with the big stick and the right-hand stick, the controls for atmosphere. I flew the artificial horizon silhouette into the air, keeping the bird trim and level. And then came the problem of conventional flight, airplane style, in atmosphere. I brought the simulator into the curving S-shape pattern over Edwards, making a long approach in the approved pattern, ready to cut off the curve as the altitude checked out okay for the landing.

Soon I was at 20,000 feet with time for just a 180-degree turn, and in seconds it was time to hit the handle which would drop the lower ventral—a nod of the head by Cooper reminding me of this. I was only a performing horse, an educated Clever Hans waiting for a nod of approval from his master as he performed what was expected at the right time. I dropped the ventral at 18,000 feet, bearing in mind that the landing was to be at 2,305 feet on my altimeter.

I flew in on my big stick and my right-hand side stick. It was easy in the motionless, mechanical simulator, now that I had the hang of it, and with Norm Cooper leaning over to see that I was flying the pattern correctly. But I would be kidding myself if I thought this was more than very partial qualification for flying X-15.

The flying of the simulator got more complicated as one came closer to the ground, Cooper told me. He leaned over to correct my stick movement as the seconds grew fewer. Then I was in the curve of my final approach and landing, quickly, at 2,305 feet, and 180 knots (207 mph) indicated. The flight was over.

"You did okay," Cooper said, with a restrained note of praise. "Come on—let's see how you did with the graph."

I climbed out and the engineers shut off the machinery with a clicking and whirring of switches. Cooper pulled the wide band of paper from the computing machine. It showed more than half-a-dozen squiggly lines ranged one after the other, each different from the one before. Cooper explained they showed velocity, altitude, dynamic pressure, side slip, angle of attack, normal acceleration, side acceleration, roll angle. My squiggly lines varied between positive and negative, sometimes bouncing up or down to peaks and valleys, but the marks were within the desired limits, Cooper said.

I was proud of the lines marked on the paper, maybe more proud than Crossfield, White, Cooper, Boyd, and the others who had flown the simulator must have been their first time because they were really accomplished pilots, not amateurs, and because White and Crossfield had already come a lot closer to actual X-15 flight in the F-104 in the "dirty" configuration.

I carried off my diploma of simulator flight, kindly given me by Cooper—the wiggly red tracings showing that one flight anyway had been within accepted patterns of normality, the patterns which all of the X-15 pilots must go through scores and perhaps hundreds of times on the simulator before they can get a crack at the actual X-15.

Barton and I walked on past the West High Bay where the No. 2 and No. 3 birds are being worked over. There we met Al White, Crossfield's back-up pilot for North American.

I asked Al about his impressions of the simulator. Like Crossfield, he has had many workouts on this mockup. I was curious about the lack of any movement or g-forces in flying the simulator. He said yes, it's true this is a *static* simulator, but that the X-15 pilots have had plenty of experience with g-forces in other phases of the training program, such as workouts with the Navy centrifuge at Johnsville, Pennsylvania.

This centrifuge, supposed to be the world's largest, has a 50-foot steel arm that whirls around exactly like a cream separator on a farm. At the outside end of the arm is a gondola or mockup cockpit where the pilot sits. A gimbal or three-axis joint makes it possible to set him at any angle so that he can be exposed to different kinds and intensities of g-forces as the arm whips around.

All of the X-15 pilots went to Johnsville, White said, and had a fling at the centrifuge. "Everyone got nauseous," he told me. "We went backward. It was something, with the lights flashing by. We got urping feelings. They put a light on, you were supposed to put it off in the middle of g-forces."

The pilots got used to the centrifuge, White said, just the way one gets used to anything.

"At first I could only take three missions a day. Later on I could take ten."

Gradually, White said, four of the X-15 pilots were worked up to nine g's in their silver suits at Johnsville: Kincheloe, then scheduled to be the No. 1 Air Force pilot, White, Crossfield, and Jack McKay, the NASA pilot. "With all the g's we got petechiae [broken capillaries] in the feet and elsewhere. But jet and rocket pilots are used to them, and they disappear with time."

White said besides the centrifuge work the X-15 pilots were exposed to heat and cold and pressure chambers in their silver or MC-2 space suits. Also, they were each given a thorough physical checkup at Wright-Patterson Air Force Base and at the Air Force's Lovelace Clinic at Albuquerque, New Mexico. These physical tests, he said, were much the same as given the Mercury astronauts later on. In fact, these tests of the X-15 fliers set up a kind of pattern for the testing of future spacemen.

"We got the real works at Lovelace," he told me. "Day and night vision—night vision [the test] was a kind of luminescent circle with part cut out—hearing, physical capacity—we had to walk on a treadmill—blood pressure and oxygen consumption were measured. We also had a bicycle, to check respiration and heartbeat; they made an electrocardiograph. We had to keep time with a metronome—had to keep constant pressure on the pedals."

I asked Al how he and Scott Crossfield competed to prove their physical worth.

"That Crossfield," he said. "He's always thinkin'. I wore out on the bicycle, I pumped too hard. But Crossfield—he'd eat sugar cubes before he'd start. Then he'd pump away on the bike. He never stopped."

White went on to discuss a couple of the ever-present problems of the space pilot: the discomfort of the space suit and the perennial concern of the pioneer in these days when men are first climbing out of air into space: inertia coupling or Cn Alpha and Beta, the aerodynamic killer which has done away with or threatened so many of the rocket pilots.

On pressure suits, those portable torture chambers space pilots must adjust to:

"They're better than they used to be. The old partial-pressure suits of the first days—like Yeager and Everest and Murray used to wear— were rough. They worked on the capstan principle—just mechanical tightening, like string.

"It's like the old Chinese finger puzzle. The suit binds you, it just presses you in. You can't take it for more than a few minutes. . . .

"But the MC-2 suit, the silver suit, is a lot more comfortable. I can't say exactly how it's put together—that's still classified. Even how many layers in it. But it has layers and bladders so you can resist g's."

Al said by making a bodily effort you can resist g's somewhat even without a suit.

"You hold your breath and strain. In other words, you do just what the g suit does for you."

On the problem of inertia coupling, the great hazard of high-speed flight where the air grows thin on the way to space, White grew eloquent. He spoke at some length about this subject that must cross the

minds of all of the X-15 pilots many times. About one instance of
Cn Beta, the death of Captain Mil Apt in the X-2 the day he made
the world's speed record, White had a definite explanation.

"It looks as if he turned too sharply," Al said. "When he turned
at that speed he increased his angle of attack and got negative stability. And there were other factors involved. With the vertical stabilizer on top only (as on the X-2) you get negative stability as the
angle of attack increases, so instability increases. But we're lucky
with the X-15. With that lower ventral we shouldn't have the problem."

He led the way to an office where he borrowed a plane model to
illustrate how inertia coupling overcomes a fast modern jet or rocket
plane in thin air. It was a complicated explanation of the physical and
aerodynamic forces involved. He spoke clearly, though an aeronautical engineering degree on my part would have helped to make it
more apparent to me. The significant thing was how important the
whole question is to a man in White's position; it's literally a question
of life and death.

I told him I hoped he never had to face the problem at the controls of the X-15 or the B-70, the flight-test program scheduled to
follow for him. He agreed heartily.

Before I left North American I asked Barton when the next X-15
flight will be. He said soon—in a couple of days. It'll be only a captive
flight, with the bird attached to the B-52. The first free or glide flight
is still weeks off.

FRIDAY, APRIL 10. I was up at four-thirty this morning, with the
plan of bumming a ride to Edwards on the North American DC-3,
scheduled to haul some engineers from Los Angeles in time for
today's scheduled X-15 flight.

In the bare North American dispatcher's office at the edge of the
Los Angeles airport I found a crowd of engineers waiting for a ride
to Edwards. The building was a hangar where North American keeps
the company transport planes: Piper Apaches, Aero Commanders,
helicopters, and others. The DC-3 that would take us up to Edwards
stood out on the flight line.

Among the crowd of engineers I met Dr. Toby Freedman, the
head flight surgeon for North American. He has the job of caring for
the health of all the company test pilots, so I asked him about Crossfield as we took our seats in the cabin of the DC-3.

"Crossfield has a tremendous competitive drive," the chunky, convivial doctor said. "He's learned that with a little extra push you can make a win out of a marginal situation."

I agreed that the little extra push at the most difficult and agonizing moment of a contest was the mark of a champion. Freedman went on to talk about Crossfield's World War II days, when he was a fighter pilot on a Navy carrier. The carrier never got into any action, nor did Scott see any combat during his war experience, but he used to set up arbitrary contests for himself on routine missions.

"When he'd go out on a mission, he'd take pride in having used less oxygen and less fuel than the others," Freedman said. "He always seemed to feel the urge to be the best."

The physician told me that Crossfield idolized his father and felt an urge to live up to the paternal example. The elder Crossfield, now dead, had been a California rancher during his later days, following retirement as an oil company engineer.

We took off, headed over the Pacific for a few moments, then were climbing over the cloud-draped black bulk of the San Gabriel Mountains north of Los Angeles. Soon we would be over the brown desert plateau where Edwards lies between the San Gabriels and the Sierras. It's the kind of country Crossfield knew as a boy, when his father used to take him on camping trips.

"His father was the kind of man who used to go on long trips in the wilds with light rations, and make the rations last a long time," Freedman said. "He was practically indestructible. He was like Stapp [John Paul Stapp, the Air Force space pioneer who did aeromedical research on a 600-mile-an-hour rocket sled]. If he broke his arm, he'd just bind it up with a handkerchief. Crossfield feels he never measured up to his father. He used to say if he could be as good a man as his father, he'd be satisfied."

We were flying over the tan-colored lake bed which a million years ago, geologists say, was the bottom of an inland sea. Here, today, the sky was clear and as we swept over the nine-mile stretch of pancake flat the desert heat began to seep into the cabin.

The pilots set our DC-3 down near the silver North American hangar on the edge of the lake bed and we taxied onto the concrete plain of the taxi strip.

Toby Freedman hurried off to get into flight clothes. He would be flying as usual on X-15 missions, in an Air Force helicopter that would hover in the Edwards vicinity in case the B-52 or X-15, or both, should crash and medical attention should be needed.

I followed the engineers up the back stairs of the North American hangar into the sunny tower room where they would be watching the flight.

At one corner of the room, beneath one edge of the panoramic window, the Master-Control desk had been set up. Behind it, with radio mikes, speakers, and switches ranged before him, sat Q. C. Harvey, the test director. He was as tidy as usual, wearing black sunglasses, white shirt, and tie; and, as usual, he was flipping the pages of a check list. He grinned a greeting as we came in, then went back to his work. Take-off was scheduled right about now and the spools of two tape recorders were turning on a shelf behind him, noting the preflight events of this, the third captive flight of X-15.

We saw the tall orange mast of the B-52 tail moving across the airfield as it taxied toward the south end of the main runway. Take-off, as usual, would be to the northeast along the runway, into the prevailing wind.

It was 0820—the take-off had been held up twenty minutes by miscellaneous delays—when we saw the F-100 chase plane barreling up into the sky above the runway and Q. C. told the B-52 crew via one of his mikes:

"Okay, chase off. Oh-eight-two-zero."

In a few seconds we heard the B-52 pilot, Charlie Bock, counting down for the release of his brakes, which would mark the beginning of his take-off: "Five, four, three, two, one—*release!*"

"Brake release at oh-eight-twenty-three," Q. C. commented for the official record.

We watched the B-52 emerge at the east end of the mass of hangars, off the ground and climbing, but with landing gear still down. And the usual plague of niggling mechanical troubles began to harry the flight: first, the minor difficulty in retracting the landing gear, then more fundamental trouble with the radio.

While the B-52 crew were still wrestling with the landing-gear problem, Q. C. Harvey suggested into the radio: "We can knock off the low-altitude speed runs and check the X-15 systems."

Scott Crossfield's low-pitched voice added distantly: "We want to make this complete—as much as possible."

Then the louder, crisp voice of Charlie Bock, the B-52 pilot "Sergeant Brantley got the gear up. Don't know whether he fell out or what, but he got the gear up."

The B-52 continued with tests, making speed runs so that Scott could see if his instruments were reading correctly. Charlie Bock said: "Now indicating 272."

Stormy Storms, the North American chief engineer and X-15 master mind, had come into the tower to join the engineers and now he asked Q. C.:

"Still got the gear down?"

Q. C. shook his head to indicate the negative: "It's clean."

But by now the radio in the X-15 was giving trouble again. Q. C. was saying to Scott: "Can hear you. But weak. Speak clearly and louder."

Scott (faintly): "Okay."

Charlie Bock was reporting, with refreshing volume: "Thirty-five thousand. Indicating two-four-six."

The speed runs were finishing, the B-52/X-15 combination moving on to the jettison tests. Again—they had tried on the last mission—they were going to try out the system that dumps the fuel. Colored water was being used, as last time, for the test, so that it would be visible.

"Five, four, three, two, one—*jettison!*" Charlie Bock ordered.

The launch-panel operator, who was Bill Berkowitz as on the previous two missions, sounded dejected as he reported: "It just petered out."

We in the tower had moved so that we could see the contrails of the B-52 and the chase planes as they moved around the southern sky toward the east. But from our distance we could see no sign of the jettison of the dye water.

Now the B-52/X-15 crew were progressing to their simulated launch. In this, as on previous missions, they would go through all the moves preceding launch of the X-15, would go through everything except the actual drop of the rocket ship.

Charlie Bock was saying: "Thirteen minutes to simulated launch." By now the contrails, the fat, multipronged cloud trail of the B-52 and the white-pencil stripes of the chase planes, had progressed to the eastern sky, and Berkowitz told Q. C. Harvey by radio:

"This is the launch-panel operator. I read Scott but I cannot understand him at all."

A few seconds later we heard the same voice saying rather plaintively to Crossfield: "I cannot read you, Scott."

Crossfield's radio calls were nothing but faint blobs of static, with a few syllables of words projecting unintelligibly. It was five minutes before the simulated drop that Q. C. said: "About fifteen seconds before the drop, if Scott does not come back on, we can have a hold."

Scott was supposed to turn on his APUs, the generator power units he would need for any launch, but there was no audible transmission about this from his radio.

Q. C. Harvey told Stormy, who was now leaning over the Master-Control desk in an attempt to hear the radio: "He can hear, he just can't transmit."

On this day the telemetering units of the National Aeronautics and Space Administration tower near us were supposed to be recording information sent by the 1,300 pounds of instrumentation installed in the X-15 behind Crossfield's cockpit. Stormy, irked by the fractiousness of the X-15 radio system, asked if the telemetering was working. He said to Q. C.:

"Ask 'em for a reading on anything. I don't give a damn what it is."

Q. C. called NASA:

"This is Coconut One. What are you getting on telemetering?"

NASA answered: "The hydraulic pressures are fluctuating. We're unable to give you a reading here."

Stormy asked: "What are they fluctuating between?"

But in the excitement of the simulated drop, which was coming up right now, the question was lost.

"Thirty seconds," the L. O. was reporting. Then "fifteen," and "five, four, three, two, one. No drop."

Then NASA reported something about not being able to make any reports, but most of the message was lost in static on the radio.

"Saved by the radio," cracked one wag among the engineers. But the temperamental radio system hadn't finished raising Cain for today.

The B-52 was supposed to make some more speed runs to check the X-15 instruments. Q. C. said on radio: "We'd like to have acceleration up to the limit."

Charlie Bock heard the call and answered: "Okay, we'll use full power."

But the fainter voice of Crossfield's radio was blanketed in a buzzing sound.

Q. C. said: "I can't read you, Scott."

During the set of speed runs Scott's voice could be heard faintly. Then, as a series of tests were run on the APUs, the pilot's transmissions came through better. But the reports were disappointing: he was having trouble with his No. 2 APU.

"The No. 2 APU will not start," Scott was saying clearly, and then something about "vibration and external hammering."

Then Q. C. asked for an external check on the aircraft. One of the chase pilots reported: "There's a little bleeding under the right wing." And now again Scott's transmission was clear:

"Probably the drainage from turning off the APU." Charlie Feltz, the head X-15 project engineer, was beefing about the APU to Roy Ferren, the assistant chief of the engineering flight-test section: "The goddamn system . . . and it's not our fault."

The pulses and data bursts of the last runs were finished now and the B-52, low enough so there were no contrails, was sweeping in for a landing. We heard Charlie Bock saying, "The gear is down and locked," and the big plane was coming in from the west. At nine forty-four we saw it trundling along the runway to the east of hangars, its big drag chute popped behind the tail to slow its landing run.

Q. C. was saying on the radio: "When you get to the mating area I want you to put power on the thing but don't de-mate it. We can kick it around a little." He meant the engineers and crewmen could go over today's difficulties a little better if the X-15 were kept attached to the B-52.

He said to Roy Ferren, one of the crowd of engineers who now huddled around his desk: "If we can find out why it shut down on him, it's worth its weight in gold."

He was evidently talking about the APU system, which had shut off automatically. The engineers, five of them grouped around Q. C., now, were riled about it. The Auxiliary Power Units had given plenty of trouble before, especially in the first mission, when there had been the big fire scare. Q. C. was saying:

"He said the noise was associated with the shutoff."

Roy Ferren said: "He tried to restart it twice."

An intense dispute ensued about whether Scott had shut down the APU or it shut itself off automatically. Q. C. got onto the radio and told the flight-line crew at the mating area:

"Get a man into the cockpit as soon as Scott is out and kick it and have a look at the hydrogen peroxide [the fuel of the APU system]."

The engineers trooped out of the room, some of them heading for the mating area to have a look at the bird and make their own observations about what had caused the difficulty with the APU system.

And there would be plenty of work to be done on the radio system, too—and the telemetering. This program was working as I had seen military campaigns work many, many times before, by guess and by God. It didn't matter how good any plan or bit of equipment looked on paper, there was always the agonizing process of trial and error by which simple mechanical details and elementary things such as communication systems had to be perfected. That meant that mistakes had to be made, and men if they were lucky and tried very hard could learn from the mistakes.

About a half-hour later, near the tower, I looked out the window to where a huge flat-bed truck had pulled up next to the hangar, with the second X-15, Bird No. 2, tied on its wooden deck. Two company cops were on hand to guard it, and a big yellow crane truck was inching out of the hangar toward it. Canvas slings held the nose in place, steadied the fuselage so that it would not be damaged in the long truck ride up from Los Angeles. Sheets of protective paper shielded the stub wings and the tail. This, the day of the third mission of Bird No. 1, was epochal in another way: it was also the delivery day of the second X-15, the one I had seen being finished at the North American plant.

I asked the dynamic chief engineer, Harrison "Stormy" Storms, about it. He smiled confidently. "We'll crack Kincheloe's and Apt's records with the second airplane, if we can ever get the damn radio fixed."

After the debriefing, the session of Scott, the crewmen, and the engineers in a back room which is still set aside from members of the press as secret, I saw Crossfield for a moment, now in white shirt and slacks. I had heard snatches of their talk—much of it about the radio. The session went on for an hour. I asked Crossfield how the flight had gone.

"Other than this communications business, things went pretty normally," he said, brief and to the point. Then he shoved off, as usual not inclined to discuss the details of his job with the press. But at least he was doing the job well, like the other devoted men I have seen since the start of this X-15 project. One thing you can say categorically about them is that they are trying very hard.

2   Space Pioneers in Action

WEDNESDAY, APRIL 22. There has been a veritable blank spot in the chronicle of the X-15 for the last ten days. The first three captive flights were duly noted in the newspapers and newscasts (with very little about what actually happened). There was editorial comment, briefly, about the significance of the X-15, its destiny to be the first man-carrying craft into space. *Aviation Week,* the enterprising trade journal of the aerospace industries, scored a scoop by getting hold of the tape recording of part of the first mission—the one on which there had been smoke in the cockpit and a fire scare.

But after these bits of public notice, the black rocket disappeared from the public prints and the TV and radio newscasts. This was understandable, because while the engineers and technicians have been frenetically busy with engineering improvements at the Edwards and Los Angeles installations of North American Aircraft, no new flights have been scheduled. This has been—and is and will be for a few weeks—a period of what the engineers call the E.O., the engineering order. More than 250 E.O.s have been drawn and blueprinted and the appropriate parts worked from one end to the other of Bird No. 1. Right now the engineers, draftsmen, and technicians are working over Bird No. 2, incorporating the same changes into this second ship at Edwards.

This is what my friends at the North American engineering drafting rooms at the factory tell me. I make a note now to find out what most of the changes are—at least in what part of the X-15 most of them have been concentrated. I gather from what I have heard so far that most of the E.O.s have been in the radio system and in the auxiliary-power units, both of which have been principal causes of trouble in the missions so far.

I have been anxious to find out when the first glide flight is to be attempted. The best information from the North American plant now is that there will have to be at least one more captive flight before the craft can be cut loose from the mother ship and the first landing attempted. The original plan was to have only two captive flights to work out the rough edges of the different systems within the ship, but as usual there turned out to be more rough edges than expected, and some which hadn't been anticipated at all.

I've taken advantage of the slight slowup to catch up with my reading on the fascinating subject of space. I've also been trying to arrange to see Chuck Yeager, the first man to break through the sound barrier, and really the dean of the rocket test pilots. Yeager, now a lieutenant colonel, is stationed at George Air Force Base, near Edwards. He's no longer a test pilot; he got his wish and became a squadron commander. His squadron is composed of F-100s, hot jet fighter planes.

I've been trying to reach Yeager by phone but arrangements are nip and tuck. He hops all over the country in his jet, and is now planning a squadron trip to Japan to be followed by a personal flight to Russia for the Moscow fair. I've finally succeeded in making arrangements to see him at his home in Victorville (near George Air Force Base). I'm planning to drive up there tomorrow.

This morning and afternoon I kept on with the process of cramming on the subject of space. My space library now is a five-foot shelf of 35 or 36 volumes.

Most of the reading I've done has immensely increased my respect for the Germans as fathers and developers of rocketry, especially for that member of the Prussian aristocracy named Wernher von Braun.

In 1931 Von Braun was one of the small group of rocket enthusiasts working at a kind of clubhouse, a former ammunition storage building in a marshy suburb to the north of Berlin.

At the time Von Braun was nineteen, and, like many of the *Verein für Raumschiffahrt* (Society for Space Travel), he was a student. He had been an inferior student, much to his wealthy father's dismay, until he became a rocket enthusiast—and suddenly, where he had been flunking in mathematics, he could see the importance of math to rockets and space travel, and he became first in his math class and a teaching assistant in the subject at the university.

Thanks largely to the genius of Von Braun, the Germans were able to develop the V-2, and successfully fire 3,340 of these 46-foot, 14-ton, 3,600-mile-an-hour missiles in the winter of 1944–45. It's too bad more than 3,000 men, women, and children had to be killed and 6,500 seriously injured as a result of these flying bomb firings into London and Antwerp, but on the other hand the conquest of space would probably be lagging fifteen years behind the present level if the United States and Russian governments hadn't inherited the know-how Von Braun and his force of engineers developed in the V-2 program.

Before the German war-rocket program got under way in 1933, with considerable money from Hitler's rearmament funds, rocket research had been on a piddling scale.

In the United States the frail physics instructor Robert H. Goddard, at Clark University, Worcester, Massachusetts, had been pursuing a lonely course of research in rocket flight, until the early thirties when a group of amateurs and science-fiction writers formed the American Rocket Society and began their experiments. Goddard was a member of the ARS, but being a secretive type who felt the world was bent on stealing his inventions, he refused to tell the ARS people what he had learned about rocket construction.

Beginning in 1914 after a bout with tuberculosis, Goddard experimented with signal rockets, the kind used at sea for distress signals. His basic idea was to use a rocket to push meteorological instruments higher into the sky than they could be lifted by balloons.

He soon found that the black powder used in signal rockets didn't burn evenly and didn't yield enough thrust to push a load up high. So he began experimenting with smokeless powder, which he estimated would give him five to six times the thrust or exhaust velocity.

The state of international communications being primitive at that time, Goddard didn't know about the Russian Ziolkovsky's previously published rocket calculations, nor about Ziolovsky's conclusion that liquid fuels, and oxygen to burn them, would be the solution for the problem of powering a rocket or space ship.

And Goddard couldn't know, nor would the world know for some time, about the space-travel calculations even then being made by a medical corpsman named Hermann Oberth who was serving in the army of Austria-Hungary. In a relatively inactive sector of the European battle front Oberth was using his spare time to work out the mathematical problems of rocket travel. Later on, in Germany, Oberth was to become the designer of successful liquid-fueled rockets.

Meanwhile, Goddard was working with smokeless powder, and he spent months fencing with the difficult problem of feeding the dry stuff into a combustion chamber in uniform quantities that would burn evenly. He designed and patented a combustion chamber that burned the powder efficiently and yielded a thrust potential of 6,000 feet per second. He checked this out in a laboratory test bed. The rocket wasn't flying—it was a heavy steel bench-type arrangement— but the findings encouraged him.

He was continually running out of money, his assistant professor's salary being a poor source of support. He sent a paper on his rocket experiments to one research foundation after another, in the hopes of getting a grant, but with no success.

At last he received a favorable reply from the Smithsonian Institution in Washington, and some time after that a subsidy of $5,000. He went ahead with his research into ways of feeding powder charges into a combustion chamber.

America's entry into World War I detoured him for a while: he and two assistants, working in a shed at Mount Wilson, California, invented a short-range rocket weapon quite similar to the anti-tank bazooka of World War II. But the end of the war canceled out the work on the project, and Goddard could go back to his first love, the space rocket. He prepared a paper entitled *A Method of Reaching Extreme Altitudes,* in which he included tables on rockets that might go to 400 miles altitude, driven by smokeless powder, and he also dared to suggest that an 8-to-10 ton rocket of similar construction might reach the moon. With a payload of explosive magnesium powder, it would make enough of a flash when it hit, so that the impact could be seen from earth with a high-powered telescope.

Goddard's paper was published by the Smithsonian in late 1919, and it occasioned the New York *Times* story of January 12, 1920, headlined:

BELIEVES ROCKET CAN REACH MOON

The story pointed out that Goddard proposed to power his hypothetical moon rocket by a multiple-charge system in which packets of powder in metal containers would be fed into a combustion chamber. This time, as often before and subsequently in rocket history, something conceived as a military invention had been applied to peacetime use. Goddard had proposed such a multiple-charge system during his World War I research, as a means for powering long-range rocket artillery

The story about Goddard's moon-rocket proposal permeated the public prints, and one of the readers who saw a rehash in a German newspaper was Hermann Oberth, the former medical corpsman in the Austro-Hungarian army who was then a mathematics student in Munich. Oberth had been working on his own treatise on space travel. He envisioned a liquid-propelled space ship, because even gasoline would produce more thrust than a powder rocket and could be more easily stored and handled. He didn't know that Ziolkovsky had come to the same conclusion about liquid fuels twenty years earlier. The Russian's writing had not been translated from *Nautschnoje Obosrenije* (of which, Oberth, incidentally, had never heard), but the New York *Times* made a bigger mark in German journalism. Oberth wrote to Goddard in May 1922 asking for a copy of his pamphlet, *A Method of Reaching Extreme Altitudes*. Goddard sent a copy to the German —but of course in his pamphlet Goddard wrote about solid, not liquid, fuels. Oberth took exception to this—also to Goddard's idea that the explosion of a rocket-borne charge of flash powder at impact with the moon could be visible from earth.

In 1923 Oberth's booklet, called *Die Rakete zu den Planetenraumen* (*The Rocket into Interplanetary Space*) was published in Munich. Oberth had to pay part of the printing costs from his own pocket. But the booklet helped to stimulate European interest in rockets, and, some say, contributed to the founding of the German Society for Space Travel (*Verein für Raumschiffahrt*). Two men who would be among the VFR's founding fathers, Max Valier and Willy Ley, wrote popularized versions of Oberth's book. Within three years interest sparked in amateur rocket clubs in Germany, Russia, and France. The foremost was the VFR, founded in the back room of a restaurant in Breslau, Germany, June 5, 1927. The first president was Johannes Winkler, elected after Max Valier, the popularizer of Oberth, turned down the honor because of the press of lecturing engagements.

In the United States the first rocket society was not to be formed until 1930. Meanwhile, working in lonely obscurity and keeping his findings to himself, Goddard had shifted from powder to liquid fuel and had fired the world's first liquid-powered rocket. The date was March 16, 1926. The rocket was a two-foot-high metal tube mounted at the top of a ten-foot-high frame of steel tubing, with two tanks for gasoline and liquid oxygen at the bottom. The ungainly, spindly device, started with the flame of a blowtorch, lifted from the ground, traveled a distance of 184 feet along a curved path, and hit the ground just short of three seconds after take-off.

However, Goddard made no public announcement about the flight. He reported it to the Smithsonian seven weeks later; and his account was not made public until four years later, when the Smithsonian finally printed an account of his early liquid rocket work. Goddard by now decided to be very secretive about his work. He refused to answer questions mailed him by the members of the German VFR—just as later on he refused to give information to the American Rocket Society.

Because of Goddard's penchant for secrecy, the history of the American Rocket Society (first called the American Interplanetary Society) took a strange turn. When the members set about building their first rocket in 1931, they modeled it not on Goddard's work but on a small liquid rocket built by the German VFR—a rocket which Willy Ley and other VFR members had openhandedly shown to the president of the American society, G. Edward Pendray, and his wife when they visited Berlin in 1931.

But the German VFR rockets and the rockets built by Goddard were of tiny thrust, less than 300 pounds, and the altitudes and speeds, and the weights carried, were small. The Goddard shot of 1929—which broke through his wall of secrecy because it aroused the Auburn, Massachusetts, fire department and thus brought newspaper publicity—went up 90 feet and traveled 171 feet horizontally. It was a spindly rocket frame like the earlier ones, although it did carry a barometer, a camera, and a thermometer, in line with the professor's avowed intention of using rocket thrust to push meteorological instruments to high altitudes.

The best the Germans of the VFR could brag about by 1930, aside from reams of books and pamphlets, was an engine of 15 pounds thrust, Oberth's *Kegelduse*. The rocket designs persisted in a mistake in design which Goddard had abandoned in 1926: they placed the engine at the head of the rocket, the tanks behind. In May 1926 Goddard had flown a liquid rocket with the modern configuration—the engine at the bottom end. But the Germans in the VFR didn't know that. They didn't even know that Goddard was by then using liquid fuel, as they did in their first flyable rockets.

Other German efforts had centered in a field of endeavor that most VFR members thought was a detour, even an aberration. This was a series of attempts to apply rocket power to automobiles, railroad cars, and gliders. This seemed a heresy to the space-minded VFR enthusiasts, who insisted rocket engines were for powering vehicles beyond the atmosphere: furthermore, heresy of heresies, the source of thrust was the antiquated dry powder rocket.

Nevertheless, Max Valier, a natural-born promoter, managed to raise funds for a rocket automobile driven by banks of signal rockets, the whole sponsored by the German Henry Ford, Fritz von Opel.

In 1928, after a few trials with conventional cars that had batteries of rockets attached to the back, and a racing driver named Kurt

TOP: Major (now Lieutenant Colonel) Charles "Chuck" Yeager, U.S.A.F., who in October 1947 was the first to fly faster than the speed of sound, climbs from his supersonic aircraft, the Bell X-1A, *(Official U.S. Air Force Photo)*. CENTER: Captain Milburn G. Apt, U.S.A.F., flew the X-2 rocket plane to the former world's speed record of 2,094 mph in September 1956 but lost his life in the same flight. *(Official U.S. Air Force Photo)*. FOOT: Captain Iven C. Kincheloe, Jr., U.S.A.F., set the former altitude record of 126,200 feet in the X-2 in September 1956. Captain Kincheloe, who was to have been top Air Force pilot for the X-15, died in the crash of an F-104 fighter. *(Bell Aircraft Corporation Photo)*

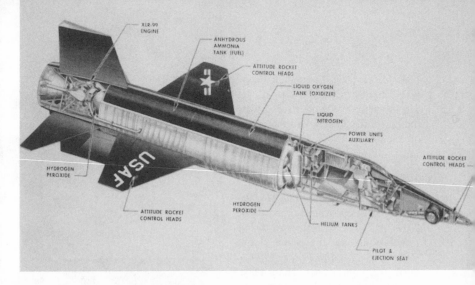

The X-15: a diagrammatic sketch *(Courtesy U.S. Air Force)*

The ultimate X-15 mission *(Courtesy U.S. Air Force)*

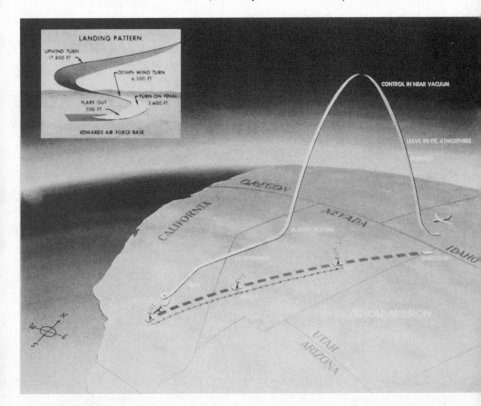

ABOVE: Overhead view of X-15 Bird No. 1, October 1958, at roll-out (*Official U.S. Air Force Photo*). BELOW: Supersonic ejection of X-15 pilot's seat, containing a dummy, from high-speed sled run at Edwards Air Force Base (*Official U.S. Air Force Photo*)

Four of the X-15 pilots. *Left to right,* Captain Robert A. Rushworth, U.S.A.F; Captain Robert M. White, U.S.A.F.; Scott Crossfield, North American Aviation, Inc.; Joseph A. Walker, NASA. *(Official U.S. Air Force Photo)*

Dawn: the X-15 *(center)* hangs beneath the wing of the B-52 bomber. The exacting preparations for the coming flight have continued during the night. *(Official U.S. Air Force Photo)*

ABOVE: X-15 being raised by hydraulic jacks to the pylon of the B-52 mother ship *(NASA Photo)*. BELOW: Scott Crossfield about to board the X-15 *(Official U.S. Air Force Photo)*

ABOVE: Lifting after take-off *(Official U.S. Air Force Photo)*. BELOW: Carrying the X-15, the Air Force B-52 bomber sweeps majestically toward the drop position. *(Official U.S. Air Force Photo)*

Looking down at the X-15 from the B-52. Chase plane in background
(Official U.S. Air Force Photo)

Volckhart at the controls, Opel built a specially-designed streamlined rocket car, Rak 11, which he drove at the startling speed of 120 miles an hour.

One year later, on September 30, 1929, Opel became the first man to take off and fly under rocket power (dry fuel). Before this flight, in fact more than a year before, Opel had sponsored a glider flight in which the plane was launched by a rubber towrope, and rockets attached to the wings had caused it to fly from there on, for a maximum distance of one mile. Valier, with customary enthusiasm, had convinced Opel that rocket airplanes could be easily made: it was simply a matter of substituting rockets for the usual internal-combustion engine and propeller.

However, Opel wanted to make a flight wholly under rocket power. On September 30, 1929, a glider pushed by six powder rockets, with Opel at the controls, took off from a wooden track at Frankfort airport.

The aircraft climbed, reached a speed of about 100 miles an hour as the rockets were fired, and then the rocket blast set the wings on fire and Opel brought the ship to a crash landing. The improvised rocket plane was a wreck but Opel crawled uninjured from the debris.

For his part in these powder-rocket ventures Valier was nearly expelled from the VFR by purist, space-minded members. However, Oberth interceded in his behalf and he transposed his efforts at automobile propulsion to liquid rockets, which were acceptable to the VFR. He built a car driven by a rocket engine using liquid oxygen and gasoline. One day in May 1930, alone in a Berlin factory building, he was working late, idling the engine, when it exploded. A steel splinter struck Valier in the region of the heart, and he bled to death, another of the long train of pioneers who have risked their necks and given their blood for rocket progress.

The VFR, taking the same chances and plagued by a chronic shortage of funds, and numerous unexpected explosions, forged ahead with their liquid rocket experiments. Hermann Oberth's eyes were injured in one early VFR rocket explosion, but he recovered.

By 1932 the VFR had fired 87 rockets into flight and made 270 test runs of rocket motors. The best they had been able to do in terms of thrust was 110 pounds, and the altitude record was 3,300 feet.

On the other side of the Atlantic, Goddard, supported by a Guggenheim grant, had been working with methods of control for his rockets. From his experimental station near Roswell, New Mexico, in 1932, he launched the world's first gyroscopically guided rocket. The gyroscope, set spinning before the take-off, was supposed to react whenever the projectile deviated from the vertical, and set it back to a vertical course through a series of vanes. The device didn't work, and at the same time Goddard's Guggenheim funds ran out. He had to struggle along with small funds from the Smithsonian Institution and a pro-tem grant from the Guggenheims. He had to close up his New Mexico shop and go back to Clark University, and it wasn't until 1934 that he could get together enough support to reopen the New Mexico station and start flight-testing gyro controls again.

Meanwhile, a big powerhouse of monetary support, in the form of Adolf Hitler's desire for conquest, had moved into the sphere of the VFR.

In 1932 Colonel Walter Dornberger, an artillery officer entrusted with the job of researching rockets for war use, hired the twenty-year-old Werner von Braun of the VFR as his first assistant. He also took in Walter Riedel, an engineer for the Berlin firm which had financed Valier's liquid rocket car. Dornberger also acquired the services of several mechanics who had worked with the VFR. The VFR was beginning to disintegrate, partly because some of the leaders fled from Hitler while others went to work for his war machine.

Dornberger's new group moved to a rocket-testing base at Kummersdorf, south of Berlin. They tested their first rocket engine in December 1932. It exploded, wrecked the concrete chamber and testing rack—no casualties.

They rebuilt the rack and chamber and engine and tried again in three weeks, and the tremendous heat of the large aluminum combustion chamber rapidly melted it to slag.

But the scientists bulled ahead. They were on the trail of something never realized before—a liquid rocket of 660 pounds thrust. The biggest engine the VFR had tried before, Willy Ley's Aepyornis Egg, had been designed for 140 pounds, and produced 110. Goddard had excelled him in 1930 by launching a rocket of 300 pounds thrust, which was to be his thrust record for life. He died in 1945.

The Dornberger group had their 660-pound engine working consistently in 1933, and they had raised their sights toward an engine of an unheard-of 2,000 pounds thrust.

And while Goddard was still fiddling with gyro and pendulum devices for rocket guidance, Dornberger had engaged a gyroscope manufacturer to build a system, with a relatively advanced servomechanism or automatic control, designed especially for a rocket. In 1934 the Dornberger group had completed their 660-pound thrust rocket, called the A-1. Research with a high-speed wind tunnel and an improved test stand, however, led to a host of quick revisions, and that same year they had built an improved, 660-pound-thrust A-2 (the letter A stood for Aggregate). They had two prototypes, which they slangily dubbed Max and Moritz, after the original Katzenjammer Kids.

Max and Moritz were fired just before Christmas, 1934, from Borkum on the North Sea. They reached altitudes of more than 6,000 feet. The best Goddard had been able to do by this time was 2,000 feet altitude, with a considerably smaller rocket. But he knew nothing of the German experiments, which by now were covered by a veil of secrecy even deeper than his own—in the name of military security.

And by this time the hottest secret of all was that the Dornberger group had built their duraluminum rocket engine of 2,000 pounds thrust, and were working on the design of an even larger one that would yield 3,000 pounds. The new big engine was to be incorporated into the A-3, a beast of 1,650 pounds gross weight, 21 feet in length and two feet in diameter.

By 1937 the Dornberger group was given sharply augmented funds and installed in a new, more spacious base near a Baltic fishing village called Peenemunde, an area that had once been a favorite duck-hunting ground of Von Braun's Prussian father.

The official move into the new base was to be celebrated by the launching of the first two A-3s. The 3,300-pound-thrust rockets fired and were airborne, but the flights were failures because the new gyroscope guidance system didn't work. The German scientists grimly flung themselves into their plans for bigger and better rockets, the A-4 and A-5.

In 1939, before the outbreak of World War II, they flew the A-5, a one-ton rocket, to an altitude of more than seven miles. It was returned to earth by parachute. The Germans were jubilant, and Dornberger wrote later: "The liquid-propellant rocket was equal to the tasks set for it. Seven years after starting work, we had created the A-5, a unit which, since it could be recovered, enabled us to test the many interior mechanisms required for the large-scale rocket in actual flight. We could now develop these mechanisms for incorporation in the A-4 [which was later renamed the V-2]."

By 1939 very little, comparatively, had happened in the United States. The American Rocket Society, following the lead of the old

German VFR, had designed and built half-a-dozen small thrust
motors. Like the VFR, they had relocated their rocket engines at the
bottom end of the rocket, they had come to using water alcohol as
fuel, and had begun to employ the cold fuel or cold liquid oxygen, the
oxidizer, to cool the combustion chamber. But in 1939 100 pounds
of thrust was a lot to them (compared to the 3,000-pound-thrust
engine the Germans were flying in routine trials), and the American
rockets were flyweight affairs; the rocket which the American Rocket
Society hailed as a major advance in 1938 was designed around a new
engine, of 90 pounds thrust, built by James H. Wyld, a new member
who had recently graduated from Princeton. The rocket which the
Society proposed to build around this engine was to weigh 35 pounds,
including fuel. It was to have a gyro mechanism and a parachute so
that it could be recovered after flights, and it was supposed to be the
supreme achievement of the American Rocket Society.

However, the ARS rocket was never built, partly because of the
Society's lack of funds, partly because the men who backed Wyld's
engine (they later called themselves Reaction Motors, Incorporated)
had financial trouble, and partly because the nation, somewhat alerted
by the outbreak of international conflict in Europe, was beginning to
mobilize man power in war jobs.

The three men who had been most active in building the 90-pound-
thrust Wyld engine were finally—in late 1941—encouraged by a
United States Navy contract (for $5,000) to build more of their
rocket power plants. They formed Reaction Motors, Incorporated,
one week after Pearl Harbor Day, and set up shop in a storeroom in
Pompton Lakes, New Jersey.

The creative genius of James Wyld, John Shesta, and Hugh Frank-
lin Pierce (and a relative newcomer, Lovell Lawrence, Jr.), founders
of Reaction Motors, was handled with a stupidity that I hope is not
typical of our present government. The Navy contract called for
several of the engines, to be used not for rockets, but as a power
assist for Navy flying boats when in an overloaded condition.

After a few successful trials of this rocket assist for take-off of
Catalina flying boats, the Navy discarded the Wyld engine even for
take-off assistance of conventional planes; they transferred their interest to solid-fuel rocket motors for this purpose—the famous JATO
or jet-assisted (actually rocket-assisted) take-off.

The Wyld engine didn't come into its own until after World War II
(our leadership was blind to the possibilities of the liquid rocket all
through the war), but after the war in 1946, Reaction Motors ex-

panded Wyld's basic design into the power plant of our first series
of rocket planes, the X-1. Four-rocket barrels much like Wyld's original engine, but with thrust increased to 1,500 pounds each, were
combined in the engine of the X-1 series; and two of those X-1 engines
were eventually combined to form the power plants for the first two
X-15s, while Reaction Motors, by now absorbed in a larger corporation called Thiokol, works to perfect the larger XLR-99 engine
for the X-15.

But that story we will get to later. For now, to return to the year
1939, our military and other leaders were displaying a singular short-
sightedness about rockets, while the Germans made mammoth strides
under Dornberger and Von Braun.

Goddard had been making piddling small progress by comparison
with the Germans. Still handicapped by a shortage of funds, and his
own peculiar penchant for isolation, he had scored his best rocket
flight in 1935, when a 300-pound-thrust vehicle had climbed to 7,500
feet. He had achieved a few satisfactory performances of his gyroscope control mechanism—but the Germans had done far better
even with guidance: they had evolved the gyro guidance system they
were later to use for 4,300 successful V-2 firings before the end of
World War II.

Of course Goddard didn't know what remarkable progress the
Germans had made. If he had known, he might have been more
openhanded with American rocketeers, even about his own small
progress. He was falling into the trap that seems to afflict us characteristically when it comes to rocket and space matters: the automatic, self-important assumption that we are ahead of anybody else
so therefore we must keep our progress a secret. The fact that we
frequently find we have been surpassed by vast margins doesn't blunt
our egoism or prevent us from being caught in the same trap all over
again, time after time.

Anyhow, in 1939, the Germans were accelerating far out of the
ken of the rest of the world. And in October 1942, when the intrepid
partners of Reaction Motors were being threatened by a citizens'
committee with a suit for disturbing the peace of Pompton Lakes with
100-pound rocket blasts, the Germans were launching their first successful A-4, the 14-ton, 3,600-mile-an-hour, 50,000-pound-thrust
rocket that was later renamed V-2.

That day, October 3, 1942, a group of Dornberger's engineers sat
at a safe distance from a test stand at Peenemunde and watched the
take-off of the fifth A-4 the Germans had built. Two had cracked up

in tests earlier that summer. The first had been built in 1940, ground-tested, and modified with changes built into later models.

The launching of October 3 went beautifully. The great engines burned for fifty-eight seconds, the big turbopumps (improvised from fire pumps) cranking nearly ten tons of water alcohol and liquid oxygen into the engine. The guidance system, a gyro coupled with carbon steering vanes set in the rocket blast, held the bird on a straight course. It went serenely to nearly 60 miles altitude, as planned, came back into the thicker air without overheating, and hit the water 118 miles from launching point.

We in the United States and Britain, of course, knew nothing of this startling success at the time. But tremendous progress had been marked that day. For the first time man had put a rocket through the speed of sound (760 miles an hour at sea level, 660 mph at 50,000 feet) and gone to four or five times that speed. As Dornberger told his engineers at a celebration that night (the quote is from his book, *V-2*):

"We have invaded space with our rocket and for the first time—mark this well—have used space as a bridge between two points on the earth; we have proved rocket propulsion practicable for space travel. . . . This third day of October, 1942, is the first of a new era, that of space travel. . .

"So long as the war lasts, our most urgent task can only be the rapid perfecting of the rocket as a weapon. The development of possibilities we cannot yet envisage will be a peacetime task. Then the first thing will be to find a safe means of landing after the journey through space. . . ."

Nowadays, nearly eighteen years later, with X-15, a very similar space vehicle about the same weight, size, and performance as V-2, we are still trying to implement Dornberger's prophecy.

The safe landing of the manned rocket craft has yet to be achieved. So, in the X-15, do the speed and altitude the V-2 achieved that day in 1942. This performance in the X-15 depends on the engine we haven't yet seen, the 50,000-pound-thrust XLR-99 engine which has been built, and now is being tested, by Reaction Motors.

With the small XLR-11 engine now in birds No. 1 and No. 2, the X-15 can climb out of atmosphere, break the world's altitude record of 126,200 feet set by Kincheloe, September 7, 1956, and break the world speed record of 2,094 mph set by Captain Mil Apt on the day

of his death, September 27, 1956. But to equal the performance of
V-2 in 1942, we must wait for the Big Engine that will give the X-15
the same thrust as the V-2. I make a mental note now to go back
East to the Reaction Motors plant, which is still near Pompton Lakes,
and get a look at that engine, and maybe catch a firsthand idea of how
it is progressing.

To finish the story of the V-2: after being slowed up by Hitler's
initial slowness to "buy" it, the weapon was thrown into a schedule
in August 1943. Then Hitler, beginning to taste his forthcoming defeat, jumped with frantic energy into a rocket program, a series of
"vengeance weapons" (*Vergeltungswaffen*) which he thought might
turn the tide of battle in his favor. The A-4 became *Vergeltungswaffe
Zwei* or V-2.

From intelligence reports that came out of Sweden, the British
became aware of the V-2 in 1943 and actually got hold of parts of
one, which the Swedes fished out of the Baltic.

And British intelligence agents sent information about Peenemunde,
although they were not clear just what kind of work the 4,000 employees were doing there. On August 17, 1943, some 300 British
bombers came over, each carrying 10,000 pounds of bombs. They
reached the target, dropped their explosives on the test stands, the
liquid-oxygen plant, the electric power plant, and the settlement
where engineers and workers lived. The count of the dead was 735,
including one engineer, Dr. Walter Thiel, on whom Dornberger had
depended heavily. Thiel had been largely responsible for developing
the V-2 engine. He and all his family were killed.

The bombing wasn't the end of the killing that night. Several German night-fighter squadrons caught the bombers on their way home
and shot down 47 of them, with more than 250 casualties.

But the damage to Peenemunde's heavily reinforced bunkers
wasn't crippling. The engineering test stands, built for both the V-2
and the smaller, slower V-1 or buzz bomb, were soon working again.
And the new underground V-2 production line, at a place called
Niedersachswerfen in the Harz Mountains, was untouched by the raid.
In the next year and a half this and other assembly plants produced
12,000 V-2s.

To train guided-missile crews, a rocket range was set up at a
former Polish artillery ground at Mielec in southern Silesia. The target
area was in the Pripet marshes, about 200 miles to the north.

Owing to an underestimation of the accuracy of the V-2, the
search group assigned to inspect the impact sites was located right

in the target area. One V-2 landed less than 100 yards from Von Braun on one occasion, but didn't injure him.

Another time, later in the V-2 program, Von Braun's life was endangered when a Gestapo agent reported having heard him say that he was more interested in space exploration than in the destructive potential of the V-2. Heinrich Himmler decided Von Braun should be executed, and Dornberger (by this time a general) had to plead with Himmler that his chief of engineering was irreplaceable.

The first assault of Hitler's new terror weapons was the discharge of 8,070 V-1s, or pilotless buzz bombs, toward London. Since the bombs were relatively slow (360 mph), more than half were shot down. But they did knock out more than 75,000 dwellings, kill 5,864 people, and seriously injure 17,197 more.

In September 1944 the V-2s were ready to fire. In a warm-up run two V-2s were fired at Paris on September 6. One hit the city and one fell short.

On September 8 the V-2 attack on London began. Two V-2s were fired at London from a mobile launch battery near the Hague, on the Dutch North Sea coast. London was nearly 200 miles away, but both missiles landed and exploded in the city. The first one killed three people and seriously injured 10 more. The second knocked down some sheds but hurt no one.

In the next ten days 26 V-2s landed in England or just off the English shore. Half of these 26 hit within the London boundaries.

For the next seven months a thousand V-2s landed in England, killing some 2,000 people, seriously injuring 6,000 more. In the closing months of the war the Germans fired 2,100 more V-2s at Antwerp Harbor, trying to interdict the use of that Belgian port that was so important a supply source for our armies pushing eastward across Europe. I haven't yet run across any statistics about the dead and injured in Antwerp, but it's safe to assume that if, as Dornberger writes, 1,500 V-2s were launched at England (and 1,015 landed, killing 2,727 people and seriously injuring 6,467 more) then probably those casualties were exceeded when 2,100 V-2s were fired at crowded Antwerp. It's probably valid to assume that the 4,300 V-2s which were fired operationally killed more than 5,000 people and seriously wounded at least 12,000 more.

Fortunately, the Allied armies overran Europe (and Peenemunde and Niedersachswerfen and four other V-2 manufacturing and research centers). Fortunately for us, the big German rocket effort came too late. General Eisenhower wrote in *Crusade in Europe:* "It seemed likely that, if the German had succeeded in perfecting and using these new weapons earlier than he did, our invasion of Europe would have proved exceedingly difficult, perhaps impossible."

Having been based in London as a correspondent during the onset of both the V-1 and V-2 weapons, I can testify that the morale effect of both kinds of guided missiles was considerable. To be surprised at any time of night or day by a missile carrying a ton of high explosive (both types had 2,000-pound warheads) at hypersonic speeds and fired at you from 200 miles away, had a harrowing effect on the nervous structure.

It was surely the weapon of the future. And if the Germans hadn't been overrun by our armies, we in the United States would have felt the might of the new weapon. Dornberger's scientists had been working on an enlarged V-2, called the A-9/A-10, an 85-ton rocket which would have reached a speed of 6,300 mph so that it could glide in space to New York and crash its load of explosive there.

The Dornberger group had been testing a developmental version of this rocket, which they called the A-4b. It was a V-2 with stub wings, and it looked very much like our X-15. The wings were to give the super weapon longer range: having arced through space it would re-enter atmosphere where the wings would enable it to glide to its target.

The long-range missile would be guided by a gyro mechanism, like the V-2s, so that it would be kept vertical for a time, then tilted as the gyro was angled by a preset electric clock. It would probably also ride a radar beam to the target, as about one third of the V-2s had done.

Dornberger, dreaming of the future, of international and space-rocket travel, envisioned controllable rocket ships that would come to a safe landing after space travel:

"It was possible to cause rocket aircraft to fly at many times the speed of sound, and they could certainly be landed by means of braking and landing flaps. We were well on the way to solving a problem which, together with high-altitude research, was the first I had set myself to tackle after the war: the landing after a flight in airless space. We had taken a long stride forward in developing the first intermediate stage preceding the space ship.

"Basically the problem had already ceased to be a problem. It was only a question of working out the technical details and devoting enough time to development. But the evacuation of Peenemunde put a stop to this experimentation, too."

The troops who took Peenemunde were Russians—and they succeeded in taking away with them many of the German engineers and technicians.

But the top engineers, entrusted with long-range planning, fortunately for us had fled with Dornberger and Von Braun into the Harz Mountains. At first they had a Gestapo guard, then Von Braun's younger brother Magnus went out to find the advancing American tanks and the Dornberger group surrendered to the United States forces.

The Russians later boasted they had taken over four or five times as many of the German rocket experts as the Americans, but the highest-grade leaders, the planners, did go over to us.

The Russians, however, seem to have made more immediate, intelligent use of the talent and matériel they inherited. They operated in many of the existing V-2 bases, most of which were in East Germany, and they went ahead with many of the 140 German rocket projects, especially with the long-range A-10. Apparently it was an improved and augmented A-10 combination that enabled them to get the world's first satellite into orbit, and open the Space Age, on October 4, 1957.

As everyone knows, we were much slower to take advantage of the German know-how. Fortunately, our troops were the first to reach the underground V-2 factory at Niedersachswerfen, and a bright colonel managed to pinch 300 boxcar loads of V-2 components before the Russians arrived. For six years these parts, enough for 100 V-2s, were our basic hardware for our rocket experiments at White Sands, New Mexico, and in the first stages of rocket flights at Florida's Cape Canaveral.

And it was a V-2, fired by our engineers and technicians, which held our (and, we thought, the world's) altitude record for rockets, for five years, 1946–51.

During the World War II years our record in rockets had been shameful. In 1941, twelve years after the Germans did it we finally got around to sending up a piloted aircraft with rocket power. It was a tiny Ercoupe light plane with 12 powder rockets attached. A group of California Tech scientists who favored solid-fuel rockets had arranged the flight.

In this case, the experimenting group didn't go as far as Von Opel had twelve years before. Von Opel had insisted on take-off under rocket power alone; but this group at March Field, California, used a truck and a towrope to get the plane up to 20 miles an hour before the pilot, Captain Homer Boushey, fired his rockets. (Boushey is now a general in the Pentagon.)

Anyway the rockets fired correctly, burned for eighteen seconds while the Ercoupe climbed steeply, leveled, and glided in for a landing.

This flight helped to determine the direction which our rocket-propulsion efforts were to follow during World War II: take-off assistance for conventional propeller-driven planes. And for these JATO rocket-assist engines, solid-powder fuel, held together with a kind of asphalt, was the only acceptable power source.

The director of the Boushey flight, Professor Theodore von Karman of the Guggenheim Aeronautical Laboratory, California Institute of Technology (GALCIT), was asked by the Air Corps to go into mass production of the rocket-assist boosters for take-off. The request led to the formation of Aerojet Engineering, which produced the JATO units. The United States Navy became the principal customer.

On an experimental basis, solid-propellent rockets were built and tried out as airplane-carried weapons during the final year of the war. Most were ordinary glide bombs with solid-rocket power assist and radio controls to get them to their target.

But there was not a single operational liquid rocket in our arsenal at the end of the war. The only ray of hope was that in November of 1944 Bell Aircraft had begun work on a supersonic experimental plane for the Air Corps, and in 1945 they were looking for an engine that could power it. A Bell engineer named Robert J. Woods was exploring the possibility of having Reaction Motors build a beefed-up version of the liquid-rocket engine that James Wyld, one of Reaction Motors' founding fathers, had built in 1937.

The results of the Bell effort, eventually, were the X-1 and its 6,000-pound-thrust rocket engine which flew in 1946, and in October of 1947 it became the first man-carrying aircraft to crack the so-called sonic wall and fly faster than sound. Chuck Yeager, then an Air Force captain, was at the controls.

In jet planes we had trailed far behind the Germans—just as sadly as we did in the field of rocket-propelled missiles.

The Germans had flown the world's first jet aircraft, the Heinkel 178, in 1939. The British weren't able to follow until May of 1941, with the Gloster E-28-39. The British sent us a Whittle engine of the type which had powered the Gloster E-28-39, in 1941. We used it in the Bell XP-59A, our first jet, in late 1942.

Neither we nor the British were able to put a jet fighter into action during World War II, but the Germans did. The German craft was the Messerschmitt 262, of which 1,433 were produced before the war ended.

In rocket-powered aircraft the Germans also led us by a disgracefully large margin. The Bell X-1 rocket plane first flew under power in December 1946. But the first German rocket plane designed and built as such, the Heinkel 112, had been taken off and flown under rocket power in 1937. And a production-line rocket-powered fighter, the Messerschmitt 163, had seen action in World War II. This Me-163 Komet had a 4,000-pound-thrust rocket engine and a maximum speed of 590 mph. The Germans built 360 of these, and they saw action against our B-17s at Leipzig, and at Stettin, where they were guarding synthetic fuel plants. They were proving very dangerous to our bombing raids when the war ended. One German ace, Kapitan Olejnik, gained fame during an American raid at Altenburg, in Thuringia, when he shot down three B-17s in one dogfight.

But while we had a very slow start with both rocket ships and guided missiles, we managed to accelerate somewhat in the years after World War II. A principal source of assistance was the advice of the German engineers from Peenemunde, and another was the hardware we took from the underground V-2 factory at Niedersachswerfen. General Dornberger eventually got a job with Bell Aircraft, which had the job of building the X-1. Dornberger took with him to Bell one of his able engineering assistants, Krafft A. Ehricke. Wernher von Braun eventually was sent to the United States Army ballistics-missile center at Huntsville, Alabama. There he headed up the work of building large missiles. A number of his staff from Peenemunde assisted him, and they were largely responsible for the Redstone missile and its later development, the Jupiter and Jupiter-C. When the Russians embarrassed us by shooting Sputnik I into orbit, October 4, 1957, and our much-touted Vanguard missile proved itself a flopnik, it was Von Braun's Jupiter-C that finally got our first satellite, Explorer I, into orbit, January 31, 1958.

Vanguard finally got a 3.25-pound sphere, six inches in diameter, into orbit on March 17, 1958. But our next two satellites, Explorer III and Explorer IV, were also shot into orbit by Von Braun's rocket. Like Explorer I, which had saved our international face after Sputnik I and Sputnik II (Muttnik), these satellites were of respectable size compared to the tiny Vanguard. Like Explorer I, they weighed more than 30 pounds and were 80 inches long. They were nowhere near the size of the two Russian Sputniks which were respectively 184 pounds and 1,120 pounds. But they were much more impressive than the grapefruit-sized Vanguard which provoked the jeers of Premier Khrushchev. (But, NASA says, Vanguard provided a very large amount of data.)

It had been President Eisenhower's policy, up to Sputnik I, to be very secretive about our military missiles, and to forbid the use of these military missiles for the launching of satellites. The idea was that the Vanguard missile, a puny "civilian" rocket cleared for scientific investigation, would supply the necessary power. The Russians had no such limitation on rocket power. They used the combinations of their military rockets, devolved from the root of the A-9/A-10 which they had picked up from the Germans and from the expert advice of the captured German engineers and technicians, to yield the 350,000 to 500,000 pounds of thrust needed to put their Sputniks into orbit.

Incidentally, when we finally got our Atlas intercontinental missile into action in 1958, it too had 350,000 pounds of thrust. Curiously enough, several of the German Peenemunde alumni contributed greatly to the Atlas program. One was Krafft Ehricke, who had moved to Convair from Bell, and became assistant chief engineer for the Atlas program. Others were Hans Friedrich and Walter H. Schwidetzky.

All in all, the German genius continued to supply the root of rocket progress on both sides of the Iron Curtain.

In our immediate postwar years, the years in which we lapsed into a general state of unpreparedness for war, the captured V-2s gave us most of our hardware for rocket-missile research. Out at White Sands Proving Ground (New Mexico), Army Ordnance, with very limited funds, undertook a program of V-2 firings in 1946. It was called Project Hermes, with General Electric engineers in charge of readying the rockets.

V-2 Rocket No. 17, on December 17, 1946, went up to an altitude record of 116 miles, which continued to be the record until February 1949 when another V-2 with an American-made WAC-Corporal on the nose as a second stage set up a new record of 250 miles. The WAC-Corporal, a liquid-fueled, 16-foot rocket of 1,500 pounds thrust, was separated from the V-2 at 100 miles altitude and went on with its own increment of power to a speed of 5,150 mph, carrying it to the record.

The V-2 continued to hold our altitude record for single-stage rockets until our first considerable rocket, the Viking, climbed to 136 miles in August 1951.

The V-2-WAC-Corporal two-stage combination held our absolute altitude record until 1956, when in a secret military test one of Von Braun's Jupiter-Cs, fired in a ballistic curve, arched up to 600 miles.

But this test had been to check it out as an intermediate-range ballistic missile, for purely military purposes. When President Eisenhower allowed the Von Braun missile to be used for the "civilian" purpose of launching a satellite, it did well, climbing up to 1,600 miles—well beyond the Sputnik I missile, which had reached 560 miles (with a satellite that weighed six times as much).

The Air Force's Thor, the intermediate-range missile which was close to a copy of the Jupiter-C, eventually did as well at the job of putting satellites into space. And the Atlas-Score project, of December 1958, put a 5,800-pound rocket hull into orbit for a time; in terms of sheer weight projection, that was a record.

In general, our career in space exploration with rocket missiles has been spotty, and a good deal of it has been based on the German contribution.

In the field of experimental manned rocket ships, though, we have been able to make significant progress on our own, through the X series.

The Bell Aircraft Corporation built six X-1s, one of which enabled a man (Yeager), on October 14, 1947, for the first time to fly faster than sound—and survive. A German pilot had never done that, even in the Me-163. And one of the two Bell X-2s, as noted earlier, carried one man (Kincheloe) to the present world's altitude record of 126,200 feet (23.9 miles); and another man (Apt) to the present world's record, 2,094 mph. Both records were set in 1956.

The other Xs were not so spectacularly successful. Their achievements were important to the engineers working on rocket flight, and their limited missions added to the know-how we see today in the X-15.

One of the X type, which did not have an X designation because it was built under United States Navy auspices, was the first plane to carry a man at twice the speed of sound, on November 20, 1953. The ship was the Douglas D-558-11, and the pilot, Scott Crossfield.

The Douglas X-3, which looked a good deal like the X-15, was about the same size and had similar stub wings. It never attained record speed or altitude because it was underpowered; and sufficient power was not available in its time, 1952. With a decent rocket engine (it never had anything but jets) it might have supplied answers to many of the questions now to be tackled by X-15. But even with limited power, it helped with the design of X-15 and the fast 104 jet fighter.

The Northrop X-4, also jet powered, was used for research in the problems of tailless aircraft.

The Bell X-5, first flown in 1951, had wings built so that the amount of sweepback could be varied. It was useful in determining the degree of sweepback to be used at various speeds. But it, too, had a jet, not a rocket engine, so its speeds were limited.

The XF-92, built by Convair, was also jet powered, and slow by comparison with the rockets, but it supplied much valuable knowledge about delta-wing aircraft—the delta being the wing shape of the future for fast airplanes.

The other Xs, X-7, X-10, and X-17, were all pilotless aircraft designed to aid in missile research. Since they carried no pilots, their flights were not so dramatic as the missions of the other Xs.

The hazards—inertia coupling and instability, explosion and fire —stalked the series of brave men who piloted and tended the X-1s and X-2s. Three men were killed testing X-2. A dozen other times pilots and crewmen narrowly escaped death in accidents involving the X-1 and X-2. A civilian technician, Herbert Lilly, was killed when a turbine wheel exploded in the first D-558. An Air Force pilot was killed in the crash of the X-5.

Besides Captain Milburn Apt, who died in the crash just after his world-record speed run, a Bell Aircraft Company test pilot, Skip Ziegler, was killed early in the X-2 program when his rocket ship exploded over Lake Erie. Dead in the same accident was Frank Woklo, a crewman in the B-29 mother ship.

Two of the X-1s exploded in midair, and the pilots narrowly escaped with their lives, in both cases managing to scramble into the mother plane and dump the flaming rocket ship. The pilots were Joe Walker, now first NASA pilot on the X-15, then flying the X-1A; and Colonel Frank K. ("Pete") Everest, Jr., who later for some time held the world's speed record, 1,900 miles an hour, in the X-2. The plane that exploded under him was the X-1D, in 1951.

Another pilot, Joe Cannon of Bell Aircraft, was badly burned when the third of the X-1s exploded on the ground. He was burned, curiously enough, by 300-degrees-below-zero liquid oxygen when it was spilled onto the hard stand by the explosion. He slipped and fell into the fierce coldness of the lox as he exited from the plane.

And almost all of the pilots had their bouts with inertia coupling, the instability that afflicts fast rocket planes in thin air. Right now I am looking forward to asking one of the famous and brave X men, Chuck Yeager, about this and other hazards of rocket testing. I'm planning to see him tomorrow.

THURSDAY, APRIL 23. On the way up to Victorville, while my wife Walton did the driving, I finished reading William R. Lundgren's book about Chuck Yeager's life and his feat of breaking the sound barrier. It's called *Across the High Frontier,* and I was anxious to read it because I felt I should have all possible preparation for the meeting with Yeager, one of the most famous personalities of our Space Age.

Yeager showed great courage when he flew beyond the speed of sound, because many of the authorities, including plenty of well-qualified engineers, had predicted grievous trouble for anyone who essayed the job.

Many pilots had found out that when airplanes approach sonic speed, frightening things are apt to happen. Unless they are designed to resist the special strains of transonic air waves, the wings of the planes are apt to start buffeting.

In this speed range many pilots had discovered that conventional airplanes also lost stability, and even suffered control reversal, so that, for example, when you pulled back on the stick, instead of climbing, as it was supposed to, the plane went into a dive.

Many pilots had lost their lives exploring the transonic range, including Geoffrey De Havilland, the test-pilot son of the famed British plane maker. De Havilland was killed when his experimental jet plane, the DH-108, fell apart as he approached the Mach, the speed of sound, on September 27, 1946. About a year after that Yeager managed to fly through the Mach in the X-1, October 14, 1947. Apparently, when an aircraft was designed, as the X-1 had been, with the specific idea of going supersonic, the progress through the so-called sonic wall was very smooth.

But Yeager had no way of knowing that before it happened. Even an eminent aerodynamic authority, Professor Theodore von Karman of the California Institute of Technology, had voiced the fear that flying through the Mach might be like hitting "a brick wall in the sky." And the civilian test pilot who made some of the early tests of the X-1 for Bell Aircraft, Chalmers ("Slick") Goodlin, had quit his job when he asked for a fat bonus if he risked flying through the sonic wall and his request was turned down.

It remained for Yeager, an Air Force pilot on captain's pay, about $150 a week including the extra stipend for hazardous duty, to do the job. Lundgren quotes Yeager as saying he was honored to have the chance to risk his neck in the assignment, and after seeing and talking to him today, I can believe him completely. He's the kind of man who would like to handle a difficult assignment with honor—and he loves to fly.

Victorville, where Yeager lives with his wife and four children, is an agglomeration of bare houses strewn around the crossing of two large highways gouged across the desert.

The desert is the same Mojave dry lake-bed area where the buildings of Edwards Air Force have been put down, and George Air Force Base, where Yeager works, is only about 40 miles away from Edwards across a wilderness of sage, tumbleweed, and joshua trees.

Yeager's house is an example of contemporary housing-tract architecture, one of many ranged along one of many streets in a suburban grid. Being a desert settlement, this one has characteristically few trees and the houses have a bare look, as if they had just been painted but the desert wind and dust had already begun to work on them.

I was lucky to catch Yeager in the United States—let alone here at home in Victorville. I've been trying to arrange to meet him for several weeks, but he's been on the run—or rather on the wing—as you might expect of an F-100 squadron commander. Today he was making preparations for a trip to Japan.

He'll come back from that operational trip and go immediately on his personal semi-official trip to the forthcoming Moscow fair, with Jackie Cochran Odlum, the famous aviatrix who married an industrial tycoon (head man of the General Dynamics Corporation). Jackie and Chuck, both being international notables in the aviation field, will be, in effect, good-will ambassadors to the Moscow conclave.

During the last few weeks, while I was trying to locate Yeager, I found that he spent a good deal of time with the Odlums at their ranch in Indio, California, on the Arizona border. He had visited there between trips to the Air Space show being put on by Air Force and various Space Age contractors at Las Vegas and his usual rapid hops to Air Force bases all over the country. Yeager has become, besides being a working squadron commander, a sort of ambassador for the Air Force. But he does the good-will work as a kind of collateral duty, and gets only a straight lieutenant colonel's pay, which with flying pay and quarters allowance runs out to about $200 a week for an officer with twenty years' service, which Yeager has.

Yeager's present life could be viewed as a prediction of the future that lies in store for the Air Force test pilots who are lined up to fly the X-15, Captains Bob White and Bob Rushworth—provided they don't get killed in the program. If they survive, and if they have achieved feats in the X-15 program comparable to what Yeager did with the X-1, they, too, could be fighter-squadron commanders and collateral-duty good-will ambassadors for the Air Force. And their families and houses might well be mirrors of the kind of establishment Yeager calls home.

Both White and Rushworth are started in this direction, and are about at the point Yeager had reached before he cracked the sonic barrier—as to rank, number of children, experience, etc. There is one big difference in education: both White and Rushworth are graduate engineers, whereas Yeager never took a college degree. But it's the trend of aviation progress that the typical test pilot grows more highly educated as time goes on. In the old days he was a daredevil willing to take chances, a pilot with well-developed reflexes, a superb flier with a seat-of-the-pants type of swift reaction and skill. Then as aerodynamic knowledge increased, the test pilot was called on to make more penetrating analyses of the plane's behavior, and a higher degree of education, especially in scientific subjects, began to be an advantage. Nowadays, in a program such as that of testing the X-15, the man at the controls must be as much engineer as pilot. And if the trend continues, the test pilots of future space ships will probably be more engineers than drivers.

Lundgren makes this point of the increasing emphasis on engineering knowledge in the book *Across the High Frontier.* He tells about a conversation with Jack Ridley, an engineer and chase pilot on the X-1B. He quotes Ridley: "The pilot is surrounded by instruments that tell him what to do. On radio alone he's got half-a-dozen channels he ought to monitor. He may have four or five different radar systems. He's almost got to be an engineer. The plane has a complex electrical system, an intricate hydraulic system, and on top of that, servo-mechanisms that work faster than any pilot can."

Those words, from one of the last chapters of the book, were fresh in my mind as we pulled up in front of Yeager's house—which was

distinguished, as he had told us by phone, by the presence of a re-
cent-vintage Mercury sedan in the front driveway.

Yeager was doing some gardening work on the front lawn. He
wore slacks and a sports shirt. Seen closer to, he was a sturdy, taut-
faced man of about forty, with curly hair well back on his forehead
and a peaked forelock. He has a battered nose and bright, sharp Irish
eyes.

I had read that Yeager came from a little farming town in West
Virginia, that he was, as he said, a country boy, although his father
worked as a technician in a power plant in the town of Hamlin. He
and his brother Roy had "fished the Mud River and caught mostly
bass with grasshoppers and worms or little frogs for bait. Hunting,
there were rabbits, squirrels, deer, quail or grouse, pheasant and bear,
'most anything a boy would want to hunt."

The inside of Yeager's house showed he still likes to hunt. There
were white, dry-looking roebuck horns, impersonal because they were
only horns with no stuffed animal head attached, at several places in
the living room, and Yeager showed me his favorite hunting weapon,
an ornately worked bolt-action rifle he keeps in a gun cabinet. It
has a slick, rubbed and grained stock, checkered pistol grip, etc.—
all that a rifle should have to appeal to a gun nut. He told me he had
done all the finishing, custom graining, etc., himself. His sharp eyes
took on a nostalgic glow momentarily when he told me that the roebuck horns had come from a tour of duty in Germany with his Air
Force fighter outfit.

It was a rare privilege to ask Yeager, the best known of all the
test pilots, about the trade that had made him famous—a trade that
he had forsaken since 1953.

From reading the book and from talking to some of the other
pilots, I knew a little about what had happened to Yeager when he
gave up the test-pilot job. At that time he had just flown the X-1A,
and in it broken the world's speed record by flying 1,650 miles per
hour; and on the same flight, after the speed run, had fallen into one
of the worst recorded encounters with the deadly inertia coupling.

I knew—because I had read a transcript of the radio tape made
that day—that Yeager had taken a frightful beating then.

He was semi-conscious after the uncontrolled, end-for-end tumble
down seven miles of sky.

Yeager reported on the radio: "I'm . . . I'm down . . . I'm
down . . . to 25,000 feet . . . over Tehachapi . . . don't know
. . . whether I can get back . . . to base or not."

Kit Murray and Major Jack Ridley, who were flying chase for
Yeager, both asked him for a position report, and Yeager answered,
his voice still thick with confusion and the beating he had taken:

"I'm . . . I'm . . . Can't say more. Christ!"

"What say, Chuck?"

"I say . . . don't know . . . if I tore up anything or not, but
. . . Christ!"

Murray was asking: "Tell us where you are, Chuck, if you can.
Give us a heading if you can, please."

"I think . . ." Yeager's voice was still unsure, "I can get back
to the base . . . okay, Jack [Ridley]."

There was another pause, and then Yeager said: "Boy! I'm not
going to do that any more!"

And shortly after that Yeager did give up test piloting. But it was
not fear that led him to seek a transfer to a fighter outfit. He was
beginning to realize, as the book reported, that high-speed aircraft
were growing more complex by leaps and bounds, and that the test-
pilot trade was changing, too, growing more sophisticated and intellectual.

Besides being dismayed by the increasing complexity and intel-
lectuality of being a test pilot, Yeager, who liked the companionship
and good fellowship of his World War II fighter outfit, was weary
of being a star performer and prima donna. He yearned for the feeling of the team. "I missed being in an outfit," he said, "working with
an outfit."

Yeager had won his share of glory and proved his courage working with an outfit in the war, a P-51 fighter squadron with the Eighth
Air Force in England. He had shot down two enemy fighters before
he himself was shot down and escaped from France to England; and
later, still in there fighting, he had once shot down five enemy planes
in one afternoon, and another day, four in one fight. His total kills
were 11.

He missed the camaraderie, the joking, and the pranks, the horsing around. Being an experimental test pilot was in many ways a
lonely job, one that sometimes incurred enmity and jealousy.

"It's too individualistic," Yeager said. "There's no teamwork, like
in a squadron. It's a job for one man. You end up at each other's
throats."

And he added: "Besides, there's too much politics. A guy gets
caught in it."

I've already observed the importance of political elements in the

X-15 program, as in the earlier Xs. The man who has to sit at the controls is only, in effect, the visible spray on top of the wave, the culmination of various forces rising from below, some of them conflicting. The pilot must do his job and we all see him, but we don't know about the many forces pushing him. Each of the forces quite naturally has its own special interests.

For instance, three separate government agencies are involved in the X-15 project, all working together, but each with different responsibilities and financial obligations. The budget is about $123 million so far, and about 95 per cent of that is Air Force money.

The Navy has about $7.4 million in the program, so they are entitled to some voice in what shall be done. And NASA, the civilian space agency, is probably going to be in over-all command, even though the NASA budget obligation is mainly in terms of supplying engineers, technicians, testing facilities—and technical direction—and the largest percentage of the test pilots.

Without hesitation Yeager said in his opinion Joe Walker, the first NASA pilot, was the best of all the fliers lined up to pilot the X-15.

"Walt Williams [the director of the NASA facility at Edwards] would probably boost his own boy, Walker. But Walker's still probably the best."

I've been aware that in every step of the building, testing, and flying a ship such as X-15, there are bound to be rivalries. As long as people are involved in anything of the magnitude and complexity of the X-15, there will be cliques and conflicts—as in any large enterprise. Still, I wouldn't want to be the one man, the pilot, whose life is at stake in such conflicts.

I asked Yeager about his celebrated bout with inertia coupling: how it came about.

"I had a yaw, then dihedral effect," he said. "It started with a yaw, then there was a breakdown of stability on three axes." Yeager might be a seat-of-the-pants pilot in the opinion of the more highly trained types, but to me he sounded impressively like an engineer on this subject.

"Directional stability is the first thing to go in a high-speed airplane," he went on. "And if you get into instability, the maneuverability of the airplane is increased a thousand per cent. You get extreme reaction to control movement." He specified the way in which a fast rocket ship might start rolling violently if you tried to bank.

"It might be 550 or 570 degrees per second. That's two complete rolls per second." That kind of loss of control, I knew, could lead to the loss of control in all directions—to the head-on tumbling that is called inertial coupling.

"That's what happened to the first F-100," Yeager said. "It killed old 'Wheaties' Welch. Afterward they put 27 per cent more stability in the F-100."

With the same objective, the North American engineers had put the large lower ventral stabilizer into the X-15, and also the system of electronic dampers designed to make the control system less sensitive when the ship hits high speed. Yet the X-15 is designed to go far faster than men have ever flown before, and the unknown quantities have to be tested out the hard way in flight.

I knew the story of "Wheaties" Welch that Yeager referred to. George Welch was the chief test pilot for North American when the F-100 was first being flown. He put the plane into a high-speed dive and pulled up sharply. He lost control, the tail broke off, and he paid with his life. That was in 1953. After that bitter lesson, North American added a larger vertical tail to make the airplane more stable at high speeds. While Yeager was being so frank, I asked him his opinion of some of the other test pilots who had flown the fast rockets in their shakedowns.

Of one he said: "He had a personality problem. He couldn't fit in with the boys. He'd try hard. He didn't drink. He'd be having a ginger ale. And I'd tell him: 'Have a drink, even if you don't drink it.' But he couldn't get with it."

Of another he commented: "He had a Napoleonic complex." Of another: "He's too much of an engineer, it interferes with his flying."

Yeager introduced us to his wife, Glennis, whom I felt I already knew slightly because I had read about her in the book. It told what a strain she had been under during the X-1 program, how her temper sometimes grew fragile under the tension.

As reported in the book, Yeager had frequent nightmares toward the climax of the X-1 program, and these occasioned some nervous outbreaks on the part of Glennis. The nightmares circled around the fact that Yeager had no provision for bailing out of the X-1 if serious trouble occurred. There was no ejection system and the cockpit canopy was so set up that if he tried to climb out, the slip stream would whack him back into the sharp-edged wing. He used to dream of getting a fire-warning light, then trying vainly to pry his way out of the cockpit. He would wake beating frantically with his hands against the wall or the window latch beside the bed.

To quote the book:

" 'Chuck,' Glennis finally says, after the third nightmare, 'I want to ask you something.'

"It's six in the morning. The boys are asleep. Glennis is in the kitchen scrambling eggs. But even when you come into the room to ask her sleepily what she wants, she doesn't look up from the bowl held in her hands.

" 'How dangerous is this plane you're flying?'

" 'Well, honey, it's built—'

" 'Please,' she says sternly, not looking up. 'Never mind the specifications. I've never asked you before about anything you've had to do. But these nightmares—I'm scared, Chuck.' She looks up now and the tears are running down her face.

"Then Glennis, who has never questioned your right to fly, buries her head in your shoulder and sobs out the whole of her complaint. 'All day long,' she begins, 'I sit here waiting. I don't even like to think what I sit waiting for.'

" 'Easy, honey. Take it easy.'

" 'It's bad enough when you're on an ordinary flight—'

" 'Don't cry that way, Glennis.'

" 'But this—this *thing*. I hate that damn airplane!' . . .

"You raise her chin so she has to look at you. 'It's just that I get too tired. I'm not really worried because I'm scared. Hell, I'm always scared in the air. Everyone is. It's natural. What makes me dream that way is there's so much at stake in the project.'

" 'There sure is,' Glennis says. But she's not crying any more. 'There's you, and me, and Mickey and Don. In the beginning, before the children were born, I was perfectly willing to accept whatever risk there was. You were flying then and I knew you were going to fly. But it's different now, Chuck. It isn't just you and me. There are the children and they sense these things. I don't think we have any right to take any more chances than we have to take with the rest of their lives. I feel so terribly guilty when I see them alone, asleep at night, or when Don wanders through the house at three o'clock because he knows it's time to go after you and he senses, without knowing it, that you might not come home. I don't know.' Glennis dries her eyes and stares at the floor. 'I hate to talk this way. I feel as if I were letting you down somehow. But aren't we letting them down in a way?' She looks at you. . . .

" 'Well, what do you want me to do?'

" 'Nothing.' She tries to grin. 'I guess I'm just tired. You and
your damn nightmares—' " [1]

Yeager had named his X-1 *Glamorous Glennis,* and Glennis looks
the part nowadays, too. She's trim, slim, and athletic-looking, very
glamorous, though there is a sort of steel temper about her, as if she
had been tested and heat-treated in the many fires of being wife to
a fighter pilot (she was affianced to Yeager even during the days
when he was listed as missing in action in World War II) and an experimental test pilot braving the supersonic unknown.

When my own wife Walton set up her cameras and lights to make
photographs of Yeager, Glennis seemed jumpy and didn't want to
be photographed. I agreed that was her privilege. Anyone who has
been through the feminine side of harrowing scientific research, such
as breaking the Mach, is certainly entitled to an occasional moment
of nervousness and tension. I will try to remember that when I talk
to the wives of the X-15 pilots, who are facing an even greater and
more terrifying unknown.

TUESDAY, APRIL 28. This morning I went down to the North American engineering department to seek out the two assistant heads of
the X-15 project—Roland "Bud" Benner and Raun Robinson.

I saw these two youthful, vigorous, sharp, slide-rule types in the
brightly lit big room where drawing boards are ranged in endless row
on row and hundreds of men work in white shirts under swivel-
mounted mercury-vapor lamps.

The highest echelon in the department, the section where I saw
Benner and Robinson, is dignified and distinguished by partitions
that separate the desks of the head men from the rest.

Robinson and Benner came in from the row of drafting boards,
where a wag had hung a sign saying APU DEVELOPMENT GROUP—
an ironic reference to the amount of trouble the engineers have been
encountering with the Auxiliary Power Units of X-15.

It was in the tiny, semi-separated office of Charlie Feltz, the head
of X-15 engineering, that I interviewed his two principal assistants.
I was anxious to find out the status of the two flyable birds, to find
out what changes are being made on them, and when the first glide
and first powered flights would be.

[1] From *Across the High Frontier: The Story of a Test Pilot—Major Charles
E. Yeager, USAF,* by William R. Lundgren. Copyright, ©, 1955, by William R.
Lundgren. By permission of William Morrow and Company, Inc.

The blond, crew-cut Benner (the same description also fits Robinson) told me: "There have been 280 EOs (engineering orders for changes) submitted for No. 2 and those changes have been made in No. 1."

To think of 280 engineering changes having been made in the bird during the short time it has been tested is staggering; but development proceeds fast in this kind of experimental ship.

I asked what most of the engineering changes had been so far, and Benner answered: "Most in the radio system." I asked about the gag sign, APU DEVELOPMENT GROUP, and he nodded. "The APU changes were next to the radio changes in numbers."

I asked about the first flight when the generator had blown up and the cockpit filled with smoke. He detailed the effects of this accident that could have been so costly to the X-15 program.

"We got the plane off the B-52 by four o'clock [after the flight] and took it over," he said. "We saw that the generator case was cracked and the shaft was sheared. We saw the turbine buckets broken off—20 of 'em missing."

The engineers found the root of the trouble inside the generator —a burned-out bearing in the armature. The bearing had burned because "the bearing was too light and the tolerance between the inner and the outer race wasn't enough."

He went on with the long chain of cause and effect: "The bearing froze—friction crushed it. In the system the way it was set up then, the cooling system circulated around the generator, then was ducted to the windshield to defog it, like a defroster in your car. So when the generator burned up, the smoke was fed with the nitrogen into the cockpit."

The engineers quickly set about remedying the defect. They had to get a new generator from General Electric, the subcontractor. And to prevent a recurrence of the nearly-disastrous fire alarm, they rerouted the nitrogen cooling pipes. "We tapped the nitrogen for defogging the windshield from another source, and dumped the generator exhaust overboard."

I asked about the changes made in the radio systems of the X-15/ B-52 combination, since they were the most numerous engineering modifications.

"We found out the radio wires will have to be shielded from the power wires," Robinson said, "to cut the noise."

I could see again what an infinity of detail has to be threaded before the ship can be considered ready for delivery to the customer

—and what a nerve-rasping and frequently dangerous process it is. I asked Robinson and Benner a question that has been much on my mind of late: until the Big Engine comes, what will be the maximum performance that can be achieved with the Small Engine now installed in Birds No. 1 and No. 2?

I told them I understood that Crossfield, as the North American chief company X-15 pilot, was instructed to prove only that the ship is flyable and all its various systems workable—not to break any records. Crossfield is not supposed to fly faster than Mach 2 or higher than 100,000 feet altitude. But when the NASA and Air Force (and maybe Navy) pilots start flying the space ship, they will be breaking records for speed and altitude. By how large a margin, I asked, could the X-15 with the present Small Engine break the world's altitude and speed records?

Robinson said: "It could be 150—160,000 feet—and for speed, over Mach 3." (Mach 3 is about 1,980 mph at the altitude where rockets fly, 50,000 feet and up.)

Benner amended Robinson's estimate: "I'd say 140,000 at Mach 1: you trade speed off for altitude, so you'd have to slow down to get up that high. And as far as straight speed is concerned: I'd say the Small Engine could hit Mach 4 [approximately 2,640 miles per hour]."

There was this much difference in the estimates of these two top engineers on X-15. They were just talking off the tops of their heads, it was not intended to be an official statement. But they agreed on one essential—that even with the Small Engine, the X-15 has the power and speed to fly beyond the existing altitude record and probe into space, beyond the earth's envelope of atmosphere.

I asked about the space instruments of X-15, which, like the space controls, will be used for the first time on a man-carrying vehicle.

Robinson said the so-called stable-platform instruments, which are geared to a gyro to give a true reading on speed and altitude in the vacuum of space, haven't arrived yet. Bird No. 1 has been flying so far with conventional instruments, which take speed and altitude readings by measuring air pressure. But, he said, the stable-table gyro and instruments are expected soon. The X-15 simulator, as I had found out the hard way, is already equipped with the space instruments, but not the bird itself.

Robinson, Barton, and I went down to the West Bay factory wing where engineers and technicians still are working over the plumbing and wiring of Bird No. 3, which still has an open tail: no engine yet.

This will be the first of the three birds to be equipped with the Big Engine.

I asked when the Big Engine will at last be arriving, and Barton said: "It's been supposed to be arriving every month now for four months. God knows when it will be." He said the original plan, last year, had been to put the large engines in all three birds. But the engine was delayed and delayed, and finally the X-15 engineers decided to change the mount in the first two birds and use the small type XLR-11 engines which had been the power plants of the X-1 series.

We walked by the mockup version of the XLR-99 engine which the Reaction Motors people had sent so the engineers could make measurements and simple tests. It was a dummy engine, but it was the same size and shape as the real item which we all hope will be coming soon. According to the cover story on X-15 which *Newsweek* magazine ran in their February 2 issue three months ago, the expectation was that the Big Engine would be flying in X-15 this summer —at least, *Newsweek's* projection of a flight pattern assumed the Big Engine. But it didn't come.

Looking at the dummy Big Engine, I was struck by the fact that it looks very different from the small one. The Small Engine has eight rocket tubes, one set of four ranged above the other (actually two engines, one set above the other), so the effect is jagged, like the exhaust tubes of some racing cars.

The Big Engine, about the same size over all as the double-mounted small power plant, has a very different shape. Instead of eight small pipes, it has one huge trumpet-shaped horn that makes it look like the business end of an Atlas or Jupiter C missile. One is struck with the feeling that this engine will blast out plenty of power. But perhaps that is a purely subjective judgment, influenced by what I have been told about the Big Engine: I know that it is supposed to put on twice the horsepower of the world's largest ship, the *Queen Elizabeth,* and four times the power of the Small Engine.

Robinson, Barton, and I moved to the cockpit area, where the usual group of men in checkered shirts, technicians, had converged around the compartment behind the cockpit, the instrument bay, where 1,100 pounds of electronic black boxes, wiring, oscillographs, and telemetering equipment are being installed in Bird No. 3—as has already been done with No. 1 and No. 2.

I asked Robinson how the research information will be recorded here in the instrument bay, and what most of it will be.

"Pressure, strain, thermocouples [for heat measurement], telemetering, oscillographs that make ink lines like the charts they make of your heart in the hospital."

Robinson pointed out the location in the belly of the plane where two automatic cameras will make movie film of the flights, aimed to cover structural deformations in the stress of flight, or accidents like fire or explosion.

The space researchers of Air Force and NASA are relying on the pilot's judgment, on that brain so far superior to a whole shipload of thought machines when it comes to making on-the-spot decisions; but there is plenty of reliance, too, on automation to record vast amounts of data with accuracy and great speed.

MONDAY, MAY 4. The need for engineering modifications—for incorporating some of the object lessons learned in the first three flights of the X-15—has slowed the program of flights for the time being.

So I've been making arrangements to fly East during this slack time to have a look at some of the East Coast facilities involved in the X-15 program, such as the Reaction Motors plant in New Jersey where both the Big and Little Engines are built. And also, I want to see the Johnsville centrifuge (at Johnsville, Pennsylvania), where the X-15 pilots had an important part of their training and physical testing. I'd like to stop at Washington, where the nerve center of X-15 and other space programs is located, even though the muscles doing the work are far flung, as at Edwards and Cape Canaveral. I also hope to visit the Air Force research and development center at Wright-Patterson field in Ohio, where many of the problems of the X-15 program were solved—and more are still being solved.

While I'm waiting to bum a ride with the Air Force, I went up to Edwards again today to have a look at Birds No. 1 and 2, and ask the engineers there how the program is faring. I was glad I did, because I met several engineers who have been with the various Xs since the beginning, and was able to pick up some of their stories of the dramatic, dangerous early days of American rocket-ship progress.

I flew up to Edwards with Dick Barton, and we wended our way up to the engineering department offices on the second story of their hangar building on contractors' row. Through a window near the rows of metal desks we could look down at the No. 1 and No. 2 birds on the hangar floor. The birds are now partly torn apart, pieces of their black skins pulled off, and groups of engineers and technicians hovering around like worker ants, making the engineering modifications.

We checked in with the North American head of X-15 flight-test operations, the neat, crewcut Q. C. Harvey, and he introduced us to two of his men who had worked for Bell Aircraft in the early rocket days. They were Ollie Kramer, once crew chief on the third X-1 and the last X-2, now a project engineer on X-15; and Blake Staub, who also worked on the X-1s and X-2, and now is a senior engineer in charge of the stability augmentation system (the system of control dampers) in the X-15 project.

Kramer is tall and lean, Staub is compact, suave, and has an olive complexion; both wear the deliberative manner most engineers I have met manage to achieve. I asked them how they feel about the X-15, in some ways a stupid kind of question, but one I've found effective: it's such an outrageous question that it sometimes brings a frank, basic answer from the shocked interviewee.

"I feel about the way we felt about the X-2 over the X-1," Kramer answered. "But the changes are a lot more—especially the safety capabilities for the pilot.

"They've gotten more safety-minded. You were supposed to blast off the nose in the X-2 if you wanted to escape. It was an explosive escape capsule, the nose."

He was talking about an emergency escape system which has been abandoned in X-15. In the X-2 design, dropped since the crash that killed Captain Mil Apt on his record-breaking day in 1956, the pilot pressed a button that blew the nose of the ship clear, and the nose was supposed to protect him from the murderous 2,000-mile-an-hour slip stream. When the capsule slowed down, the pilot was supposed to loosen his safety belt, pull himself out of the capsule, and take to his parachute. A new design was evolved for X-15, the theory that the pilot would do better to stay with the aircraft, which, after all, is designed to withstand tremendous speeds until it slowed down; then he would trigger an explosive charge that would blast his 300-pound chair clear of the ship. An automatic device would free him from the chair. We've already noted the amount of research work devoted to making that chair stable, the stub wings that are supposed to fold out and prevent it from tumbling.

Now Kramer talked about the tests which he, as a Bell employee, had seen applied to the X-2 escape system to prove the contention that it would work.

"We put a mass on the firing mechanism to simulate separation, but we couldn't really test it. The mass—650 pounds—would go 93 feet when you fired the charges. It was held by four bolts and the blast agent was a telescoping 37-mm. cylinder a foot long. "We thought the pilot could get out as in a regular plane—release the canopy, and climb out. Apt got it [the canopy] off and his seat-restraint harness was unfastened. He was just getting out when it [the capsule] hit the ground."

Kramer said the X-15 ejection system seems to be an improvement in that there's less for the pilot to do. "He just moves his arms up, his arms are protected by armpieces automatically, his ankles are locked in by leg pieces—then he's automatically ejected."

Kramer summed it up with scientific objectivity: "Apt proved that what they needed was a completely automatic ejection system."

I said it was a hard way to prove a point, but Kramer was thinking ahead, thinking now as a pilot as well as an engineer; Kramer had been a Navy pilot in World War II. Now his mind was on the X-15, and he was thinking about a strange facet that had never crossed my thoughts.

"The interesting thing," he said, "is that he [the pilot] doesn't want to eject on the way up—if he did, he'd follow the path of the plane on its ballistic curve."

That was a bizarre thought; if the pilot, starting up on an altitude flight, should bail out at say 80,000 feet, he would go right on up to 250,000 feet, or however high the plane was going, because he'd be carried along with exactly the same momentum, just as when you throw a stone up, if it should split, the two parts will follow roughly the same trajectory.

I asked Kramer what he thought would be the most critical moments in the current stage of testing the X-15, right now when it is being run through its first captive flights.

"I think the most critical point is when he has a full load of fuel," Kramer answered.

And the dark, slender Blake Staub agreed about the danger of a full load of fuel—although he pointed out that some of the fuel hazards had been knocked back: engineering has found answers to problems such as the combustibility of liquid oxygen when it is struck: is "impact sensitive" in his wordage. All of the X ships which exploded, he said, exploded in the lox tanks. The worst explosion, the blow up of X-2 in flight near the Bell plant, where two men were killed, apparently was caused by an impact against a seal gasket of ulmer leather, a variety that absorbed enough of the lox so that it became very sensitive to any impact. Engineering changed the material used there and in many other spots where there was danger.

Staub told the story of that X-2 accident, an accident in which he lost one of his best friends, the X-2 company test pilot Skip Ziegler.

That May day in 1953, Staub was on the ground watching the flight over Lake Ontario. The crew of the B-50 mother plane were filling the lox tanks, and Ziegler, a tall Texan who was chief test pilot for Bell, was in the cockpit of the X-2.

They were at about 25,000 or 30,000 feet, and on the radio they were calling out "Forward lox pressure 27 psi," and so on.

"Then the explosion: there was an orange ball of flame," Staub related. "The B-50 was driven up 200 feet vertically. The chase pilot [who was following closely] was flipped. He recovered and said: 'We lost the beast.' [The X-2 was blown free and into pieces.] Then he reported a body coming out of the B-50.

"What happened was Bob Walters and Frank Walco were in the back, and Walco went out without a bail-out bottle, and in a hurry —and died, maybe of anoxia. But right after the explosion the pilot, Bill Leyshon—he was a veteran Pan American pilot and we used to call him the Silver Fox—refused to panic until he saw how much damage had been done.

"It looked as if the B-50 was wrecked, but Leyshon wouldn't give the order to bail until he found out about the damage. He found out it was still relatively in one piece, but by that time Walco was out and Ziegler was gone. . . .

"Leyshon brought the B-50 back—with Jimmy Dunne, the flight-test engineer, and Bob Walters [the remaining members of his crew]. It was a wreck, but Leyshon got it down and it was patched up." [And later scrapped.]

I could see that it saddened Staub to tell the story, and what he said indicated just how much: "Right then I swore I'd never get that much attached to a test pilot."

Staub's dark eyes mirrored a sudden depth of sorrow, and I changed the subject, told him I had just been over to see the premier X-1 test pilot, Chuck Yeager.

Staub brightened. "Yeah," he said. "Yeager was the last of the 'Show me the stick and rudder and I'll fly it' pilots. Nowadays, they go a little deeper in the engineering—a little heavier on the slip stick."

Later in the afternoon, as we took off for Los Angeles in a pretty little red-and-white Piper Apache, and looked down at the tan lake bed marked with the figures 1 through 9—1 through 9 miles, the

X-15 runway—I thought how the concept of a rocket pilot has changed in a very few years—twelve, to be exact, from 1947, when Yeager broke the sound barrier, to now, when eight graduate engineers, two with masters' degrees, line up to fly our first space ship.

The rapid increase of learning makes me aware of my own relative ignorance. Writers in the Space Age, too, should have familiarization courses lasting months and years.

When I got home, I checked with the Los Angeles Air Force office to see if there was any news on the flight back East, where I hope to add to my own knowledge of the field, get a look at the biggest brain center of the age of space: the Air Force and NASA offices in Washington.

I am glad to be living close to the heart (and brain) of the age of space discovery, I tell my wife—probably boring her because I have told her before quite often. But she understands that I am excited by watching the bright and brave men of this new age, as they work their hearts and minds out in the name of space exploration.

DALLAS, TEXAS, SUNDAY, MAY 10. This morning I succeeded in catching a ride with an Air Force plane heading for Washington. It's a C-131, military jargon for a Convair. It's a relic of the propeller age, but about the best the Air Force can muster now, because every time they ask for new transport equipment in Congress, the request is beaten back by the combined lobbies of the air lines, which maintain that new transport airplanes for the service would be unfair competition.

The Convair, although it's just about the best the Military Air Transport Service has, can't make the run across the country nonstop; it's too slow and can't hold enough gas for that. So we're stopping in Dallas. All of which seems a strange contrast to the Space-Age research Air Force is involved in: the world of 4,000-miles-an-hour rocket ships such as X-15, ballistic flights into the void, the maintaining of life in space, and surviving the furnace heat of reentry into our atmosphere.

Coming into Central Texas, we hit a thick, wild black overcast, which seemed to go on endlessly. The plane was whip-snapped, sashayed, racked up, and smashed down. Black clouds swallowed us and lightning flashed, and rain blasted against the windows. When we landed we discovered we had flown through the edge of a hurricane, which killed a score of people on the ground and wrecked several towns.

WASHINGTON, D.C., FRIDAY, MAY 15. I've been knocked out all week, since the flight here from Dallas, by some stomach bug picked up en route, possibly aided and abetted by the rough weather we hit in the lower altitudes of Central Texas.

I've been holed up in this Washington hotel trying to fight the bug into submission—and so far not doing so well. But I have arranged with Colonel Pug Evans of Air Force Air Research and Development HQ by phone to get clearance for a visit to the New Jersey factory where the rocket engines of X-15 have been made and are being made.

Things are set up now for me to go to Denville, in northern Jersey, next Wednesday or Thursday, to have a look at the rocket engine plant.

NEW YORK, THURSDAY, MAY 21. After two hours in the bus I came to the little town of Denville, in the Pompton Lakes area of New Jersey—which is to say 40 miles out of New York City to the west, the locale of Reaction Motors Incorporated.

Denville is like the small towns you sometimes see on *Saturday Evening Post* covers: a main street with shops and lots of cars, a bank building, and a couple of drugstores, and suburban women on foot doing their shopping at the supermarket while the husbands work; the whole effect bright, clean, and tidy.

I took a cab from the main intersection, and arrived at the city limits, where stood a severe modern building which could have been any kind of suburban manufacturing plant.

I reported to the cop at the reception desk just inside the front doors, and after about an hour of circling with sub-functionaries finally won my way to the head public-relations man, Dick Whitcomb. Up to that time it had seemed that Reaction Motors was dead set against any contact with the outside world.

But Whitcomb introduced me to several of the company officials, and later on I was assured that I might go out to the test-stand area, where from just outside the gate I might be able to see in the distance the stands where the Big Engine is being run up these days.

A couple of hours later I had made some progress in negotiation and it was mentioned that I might even get beyond the gate to look more closely at the test stand. Even though I had been introduced by the Air Force, and had presented proof positive of my intention to write an authorized book, the Reaction Motors people were guarding their military secrets jealously.

There were some aspects of this which I didn't fully understand, because *Aviation Week* magazine has just published a full description of the XLR-99 engine, complete with photographs, and the whole obviously approved by the Defense Department.

However, this is the empire of space; like any mammoth human endeavor, it is ridden with legalistic restriction, and like any area so dedicated, it can become sticky and frustrating with no effort at all. And maybe there's a need for extra caution in a factory area like this, which with all the high-explosive fuels needed for testing is a kind of bomb, ready to be set off by anyone carelessly admitted. Or maybe they just don't want me to see how much progress has been made, or not been made, with the Big Engine.

Anyhow, negotiation eventually cleared the decks somewhat. At last I was able to climb aboard an old sedan with one of the test-stand engineers, a good fellow named Harry Burton, and trundled over to the test area. It was carved into a sequestered green hillside.

Burton, after some considerable negotiation with the security cop at the barbed-wire gate, got me into the clearing which is the test area.

There were two metal shacks at the edge of a ravine that bordered one edge of the clearing. These were the test stands, so aimed that the blast of the rockets being fired would shoot harmlessly out into the air.

Away from the slope stood a concrete blockhouse, where Burton said the engineers watched the engines through television during tests. Scattered around the clearing were long silver tanks of fuel and the oxidizer, lox. From the top of one of the tanks a plume of white vapor trailed, marking the blue sky. And a hideous, nose-puckering scent of ammonia chopped through the air, so that one instinctively breathed absolutely as little as possible. The over-all sound was the waterfall noise of generators somewhere nearby building up electricity. Already in my space education the noise of generators makes me uneasy, since generators usually run hard before any scientific effort. Power is always needed.

No firing of the rockets in the test beds seemed to be immediately in the offing, though; in that case, the men clustered in the open-sided shacks would have been long since cleared away.

Harry Burton told me about the Big Engine tests which have been run here recently.

"We just ran the 101 engine—that's the ground model of the XLR-99—for thirty seconds at full thrust. The day before we had been trying one-minute runs." Burton explained that the 101, the so-called "ground" engine, would be the first of the Big Engines to be sent to Edwards Air Force Base. But as the name implies, it will not be installed in a plane. It will just be used for trial runs and familiarization of engineers and technicians at Edwards.

Harry said the engine we could see at the bigger of the two test stands—with a spotting of shirt-sleeved technicians around it—was a flying engine. Tests were just being started with it; it wouldn't be fired for a day or two.

I asked about the sound the engines make when fired, and he said:

"This engine is about the loudest so far—about 140 decibels. You can't stand it. You can feel it in your stomach and chest. Some guys can stand there and listen to it. I can't. It's like pain—some people can stand it, others can't. Some people have impaired hearing because of rocket blast—so they don't mind some of the frequencies so much. You get insensitive because your eardrums are beat in.

"I can hear 13,000 cycles in one ear, 16,000 in the other. That's from engine noise. I worked on engine testing at Wright Field in World War II. Propeller engines—but they can be pretty noisy, too.

"On rocket engines—generally the bigger ones are deeper toned. Very heavy. They're lower frequencies. That's why the 99 gets you in here." He motioned to his rib cage.

But, Harry went on, of course the noise isn't bad inside the blockhouse. He took me into that concrete structure, as thick walled as a Spanish fort.

"You can stand here with the door closed, during an engine firing, and it'll be little noisier than what you hear now," he said. The noise now was only a faint whirring of generators.

I looked around the blockhouse interior, where a few men in shirt sleeves were puttering over the television screens. There are two big-screen television viewers, and through one now we could see technicians working over the engine in the larger of the two test stands.

One wall of the blockhouse was faced with 26 barographs, charts about the size of a sheet of typewriter paper, with ink styluses to make graphs of pressures, temperatures, flow rates, and vibration.

Nearby was an array of recording spools, Ampex tape recorders set against a wall, maybe 35 of them.

"The procedure is," Harry said, "there are about 14 men in the room. The engineer calls for the recorders on first. The instrumentation group puts the run number onto the tape—like R3 P422, date

5/21/59—then they make a marker pip so they can start that part of the tape. The test engineer calls for what he wants—the idle switch or the fire switch."

Harry pointed out the round throttle handle and fire switches on a board near one of the television screens. I could see that the round-headed throttle knob—like the one I had used when I flew the simulator—started at half throttle, where it slipped into a notch, and from there on it moved smoothly. In other words, when you start your engine, you have half your maximum power. You have 25,000 pounds of thrust, as much horsepower as the *Queen Elizabeth.* You can't go lower than that if your engine is going, but from there on up you can throttle to any setting all the way up to 50,000 pounds, or twice the *Queen Elizabeth* power.

Harry Burton drove me back to the administrative offices for more conversations with company officials, who were loud in their praises of the new engine. They said it is the first truly throttlable rocket engine.

One of them said: "Throttlability is the biggest problem. And it gets nastier as the engine gets bigger—with the big flow rates and fluid dynamic problems, a lot more mass." He indicated that there are still plenty of problems to be licked.

But Art Sherman, the chief of test activity, bragged that the engine was a going concern. "No other engine gives that throttlability," he said. "People are amazed: you don't just turn a rocket engine on and off and on and off, especially a beast of this size. She'll play music for you."

I wish I could stick around a couple of days, and hear some of that basso-profundo music played, if it is played. But I have to be on my way to some of the other eastern points that figure in the X-15 story: Air Research and Development Headquarters; Langley Field, NASA center where some of the wind-tunnel research was done; the Navy centrifuge at Johnstown; and Wright Air Development Center, the Air Force research base where many of the systems of X-15 were developed. I'm hoping to see and hear one of the XLR-99 engines tested at Wright's power-plant section. There, I'm told, one of the flying engines is now being wrung out prior to shipment to California. From all I have heard today, I'd say this might take awhile. The problems of the Big Engine seem to be a long way from licked—despite all the enthusiastic talk of most of the RMI engineers. If they *were* all licked, it would have been flying on schedule, which is to say before now.

FRIDAY, MAY 22. Today, getting ready to shove off for Washington, I telephoned the West Coast and talked to Earl Blount, the public-relations chief at the Los Angeles plant of North American, to check on the X-15 flight schedule. And as a result of that call, I abruptly changed my plans. Earl said the first glide flight of the X-15 might be next week, and I'd better haul myself back pretty quickly if I wanted to see it.

I certainly do. The time when they cut the X-15 loose and Scott Crossfield has to bring it to its first landing is going to mark an epoch, whether he cracks up, as many people expect he will, or whether he makes a smooth landing. Several engineers and some of the qualified test pilots have said that this stub-winged missile can't be landed because of its high wing loading and expected instability.

So the space world will be watching as this step is passed or not passed. I called Washington and checked with Major Jim Sunderman, in the Office of Information, to see what pot luck I might have getting back to the West Coast in time for the flight. He says there might be an Air Force C-54, a Douglas DC-4—heading west on Sunday.

SATURDAY, MAY 23. Sunderman called me to say a seat has been set up for tomorrow from Washington on a C-131 (Convair). The plane will have to stop overnight in Denver, but I'll go right on to Los Angeles, which is fine; the X-15 flight will probably be toward the middle of next week.

3 ⎯⎯⎯⎯⎯⎯⎯⎯⎯⎯⎯⎯⎯ Flirting with Disaster

LOS ANGELES, MONDAY, MAY 25. Home again, I checked with North American about the flight. Dick Barton says it's scheduled for Thursday, but might well be off till next week.

TUESDAY, MAY 26. The flight is definitely postponed till next week. There's some trouble with the stability augmentation system, the complex of dampers and gyro controls which will help stabilize the ship.

TUESDAY, JUNE 2. The flight was scheduled for tomorrow, Earl Blount told me, so this morning I arranged to hitch a ride with him on the North American shuttle plane running up to Palmdale and Edwards.

We landed about three-thirty and headed for the engineering office on the second deck of the hangar. Before we could clear the security guard, though, Ed Cokeley, the taciturn chief of test operations at the North American installation, came by and told Blount: "It's off till Thursday."

Upstairs in the engineering rooms I had a clue as to what went wrong this time: it is still the SAS, the stability augmentation system, that is acting up.

Up there, engineers and secretaries were bustling around and talking on phones. I saw Scott Crossfield in a flying suit; he'd been out in a 104 practicing landings in the "dirty configuration" (that is, power off and full flaps, to simulate the landing characteristics of X-15).

I saw a familiar face on one of the phones. It was the lean, sardonic Cooper Lindley, a key flight-test engineer, and from him I learned of today's trouble.

Lindley was talking about the SAS system. When he finished with the phone, he answered my question precisely:

"The starboard potentiometer is producing only half of its output in the SAS system."

I remarked that the ship would fly cockeyed that way.

He shrugged and turned away. "It'd fly, but—"

Beside Lindley's desk lay the metal drum of a 300-foot steel measuring tape. I asked him about it, and he said: "When the flight comes off, I'll go out and measure the depth of the landing-skid penetration." He seemed to have no doubt that there would be a successful landing, and nice landing-gear marks for him to measure.

A small colloquy was going on between Earl Blount and engineer Cokeley. The subject was the expected presence of a large group of newsmen for the glide flight—probably 50 or 60. Cokeley was exploding: "We'll have newsmen lined up all along the runway."

Blount, ever tactful, answering: "Yes, it's a matter of compromise."

The usual battle was raging between the engineering type, who doesn't want to be bothered with explaining to the public what he is doing, and the public-relations man, who knows that it is good business to help the reporters to get information: good business because in a government project such as the X-15 the better known the project is, the more apt it is to get financial support in Congress.

I saw Bill Berkowitz, the bulky launch operator who had been in the crew of the B-52 in the first three captive missions, and asked him about the fourth captive mission, which had been flown while I was back East at Reaction Motors. I asked him about the radio and the APU system, which had given so much trouble in the first missions.

"The radio worked perfectly last time," he said. "Like you and me talking. And the APUs were fine—no problem."

Evidently the engineering modifications had done what they were supposed to do: the bird was working well, all the systems could be taken for granted on the critical glide test—that is, all except the SAS system, which is currently acting up.

LANCASTER, THURSDAY, JUNE 4. Here in the nearest oasis of civilization to Edwards Air Force Base, we of the press came in last night to be on hand, we thought, for the first X-15 free flight.

But the flight was destined for another postponement. A mechanical difficulty held up the works again: still the stability augmentation system acted up.

We stayed around the local mecca for newsmen, the Caravan Inn, after we had telephonic word from Edwards that the flight had been put off again. At 1 P.M. the dashing Colonel Charlie Brown of the Edwards PIO came in to brief us on the plan for tomorrow. Nothing new: the B-52 take-off scheduled for 0800, the drop to be between 0830 and 0900, as today

Tonight, at the dining room, Harrison ("Stormy") Storms showed up to talk to us.

He was carrying a handsome new model of the X-15, and he exhibited it proudly. On the base were cut these words:

> FIRST FLIGHT X-15
> JUNE 5, 1959
> PILOT: SCOTT CROSSFIELD

Evidently Storms has a conviction that tomorrow will be the day, after the numerous postponements. But he seemed drawn, and perhaps even a little more pale and intense than usual. I asked him how he felt about the flight, and he said, "Confident." But he added:

"This is the most critical flight of all—more critical than an orbiting flight would be, or a flight with the Big Engine. Because we're going to see if the aircraft will fly; because it's been designed, and checked out in the tunnels, but now it has to be really done. And in four minutes."

Four to five minutes will be the outside time dimension of the X-15 flight, from the time it is dropped from the B-52 at 38,000 feet, until it hits the ground.

I asked how Crossfield felt about the landing, and Storms said: "No problem. He's shot about 50 landings in the 104s in the dirty configuration, so he should have the feel—the equivalent. He's made 10 of these landings in the last ten days. Day before yesterday he made it in a crosswind. There haven't been any mishaps."

The chief engineer said Crossfield will bank, try his elevons, and increase speed by diving. He will have three alternate landing places on the lake beds, in case he has any trouble.

In the crowd near me in the dining room were two of the North American Company photographers, who had joined the group of newsmen. They were Bill Kettrick and Jack Murphy, young eager beavers I had seen on previous X-15 go-rounds. Jack was saying: "There's no sense in going to bed—I'm too excited." Kettrick said this was the most exciting thing in his life, and he'd be staying up, too. He'd have a date to keep him company—no hardship.

FRIDAY, JUNE 5. Up at 4 A.M. again for the flight. In front of the ARDC Headquarters building at Edwards, 50 or 60 correspondents, from newspapers, news services, radio, and TV milled around, waiting for the word to form up and drive out to the runway. There was a blue Air Force bus to carry most of us. Some newsmen had "official car" placards for their windshields so they could drive their own automobiles in the cavalcade. We all wore blue identifying ribbons on our coats. A coffee wagon did a good business while we waited.

At last the column, led by Charlie Brown in a blue Air Force sedan, shoved off, the bus waddling along at the tail end. Out on the edge of Runway Zero Four we waited in the accelerating heat of the desert sun, and Colonel Brown got up on top of the green NBC sound truck to announce that the take-off would be delayed forty minutes.

At the end of an hour, after some hurried phone conversations with the Edwards tower, Colonel Brown announced that the flight was again being aborted owing to mechanical difficulties. The event was following the pattern of space events, which usually seem to go according to the tradition of military operations: hurry up and wait. Probably the pattern is inevitable when so many thousands and millions of individual efforts—many of them highly skilled—have to be made to happen at the same time. One unexpected event can make the whole machine falter and stall.

At last the word passed on by Colonel Brown was that the flight would now be set up for Monday. I thought about Chief Engineer Storms waiting around somewhere in this vicinity with his presentation model dated June 5. He'll have to have some emergency engraving work done over the week end to be in shape for Monday's flight; if it happens Monday.

MONDAY, JUNE 8. During the night a high wind had been blowing—higher than the 15 knots allowable for the B-52/X-15 combination. But by three this morning the gusts had subsided; the rattling fronds of the fan palms around the hotel were quiet.

Our press calvalcade assembled again in front of the Headquarters building, and this time on schedule shoved off for Runway Zero Four to see the take-off. And strangely enough, this time everything happened on schedule.

At seven-fifty three blunt-nosed fire trucks with blinking red eyes, two ambulances bearing red crosses, and an AP prowl car ranged themselves near our vantage point at the 8,000-foot mark on this main runway. At seven fifty-eight the bright orange banana-shaped air-rescue helicopter (the one that would be carrying the flight surgeon, Toby Freedman, and his assistants) flew low down the length of the runway and hovered at the far end.

At seven fifty-nine the silver bullet of an F-100F with a scraggy, high orange tail screamed down the runway and blasted up into the clear blue, with the flame of an afterburner glowing bright in her tail—which is to say under crackling full power. That would be Chase No. 1 with Al White, the North American back-up pilot at the controls, and in the other seat a motion-picture photographer.

Half a minute later another orange-tailed Air Force F-100, Chase No. 2, belted into the air. We knew that one was being flown by Captain Jim Wood of the Edwards Flight Test Center.

At 0800 a missile-like Lockheed F-104 jammed itself into the sky, afterburner kicking it hard in the tail. In seconds it had disappeared into a dot, high up. That dot would be Captain Bob White, the third of the chase pilots, and the first Air Force pilot waiting in line to fly the X-15. While waiting, he could be this close to her.

At eight-one, the F-100s circled the field, and over the curve of the long runway, at the far end, we saw the towering orange mast of the B-52—and around it, now, eddying gray shreds of smoke, like thin liquid. We knew the B-52 engines were being gunned for take-off.

The big bomber came up, the wide wings spreading above the desert mirage reflected on the runway. The assemblage of wheels that were the landing gear floated eerily in that optical illusion. We heard the drumming of the big engines, and at the same time two chase planes came out of the sky, passed the lumbering bomber, and whipped over our heads.

At eight-three the B-52 with the tiny black dart under its wing was still rolling down the runway, almost on top of us; now the wheels were inches off the ground and the engines thundered like a trackful of race cars. The gear was folding fast into the fuselage and the plane was off at about the 7,000-foot mark.

There was a scramble then to the cars, and the press cavalcade took off on the heels of fire truck No. 3 and other emergency vehicles for a vantage point on the edge of the lake bed where we were scheduled to watch the landing, or at least the impact with the earth.

At eight-five we were heading across the hard, shiny surface of the lake bed, cheerfully eating the tan dust of the fire trucks and other emergency vehicles as they headed for the three-mile marker on the nine-mile bed, the point where Crossfield was supposed to land.

Colonel Brown's Air Force car led us to a dune area, a small knob of land with a sparse growth of desert grass. This was to be the press knoll. The Air Force public information people had strung telephone wires out here and rigged a public-address system so Brown could tell us what was happening.

The next knoll or dune to ours was rapidly marked by an agglomeration of trucks, cars, and emergency vehicles indicating it was the Mobile-Control center for the flight. I saw the North American Mobile-Control van at the center, and near it the long yellow trailer where Crossfield has been dressed in his silver suit before every flight, and undressed afterward. Near the suit-up van sat the gawky shape of the crane, on hand to clean up possible crack-ups; and an ambulance and a couple of fire trucks. I heard the radio of the nearest fire truck saying something about the B-52 being at 30,000 feet. We could see the spread of chalk marks upstairs where the contrails of the B-52 and the chase planes rolled their traceries against the blue.

At eight-eighteen Colonel Brown's voice on the public-address system told us: "Ladies and gentlemen, the mission is proceeding satisfactorily. . . . At this point it makes a wide sweep toward Mojave . . . after launch, the X-15 will be performing what we call a lazy S. It then comes in for a landing. As I noted before, it will be landing from your right."

The colonel's commentary made me feel that this lake bed is a kind of arena for one of the great shows of history, and in fact it was today. All the world was watching today through the press representatives; and the arena was fittingly large for the show to be presented.

At eight twenty-six we watched the white comb marks of the contrails curving around the high sky to the north. And Colonel Brown told us: "We have an estimate at this point, ladies and gentlemen, of fifteen minutes to drop." A minute later: "You'll see something drop as he comes in, ladies and gentlemen; it will be the lower vertical fin purposely dropped."

At eight thirty-five: "We are estimating five minutes till drop."

Eight thirty-seven: "The B-52 is making its turn toward Rosamond Dry Lake. Estimating three minutes till drop." And the colonel added, now that the event was imminent and even out in the wide space of the desert you could feel the tension among the newsmen: "No matter what happens, the condition is: we want you to stay here." He was obviously concerned that if the ship should prang, the newsmen might run out and impede the rescue operation.

Now, at eight thirty-eight, the chalk marks of the contrails were curving into the western sky, and Brown told us: "Two minutes to go. It's reported that Scotty said: 'Yes, sir, we're gonna go.'"

Eight thirty-nine: "One minute to go." The planes were west, over Rosamond.

We all watched the contrails with field glasses, and on a neighboring knoll I could see the long white barrels of the telephoto movie camera trained on the same target.

Suddenly a gusty wind seemed to have sprung up: the coarse grass waved in it. I worried for fear the drop would be canceled now: a strong wind could ruin the successful landing—or a wind at the higher levels could cancel the flight because it would make it hard for Crossfield to make a decent glide toward the lake bed.

"There he goes!" somebody shouted, and I saw a new white trail penciled against the sky below the shape of the bomber; that would be the X-15 cut loose at last on its maiden venture alone in the blue.

"Zero—he's on his way," said Colonel Brown on the public-address system. The time was eight-forty.

The clumsy, broken-backed orange shape of the rescue helicopter was trundling toward our press knoll, getting into position for the landing. It was hovering now, the big rotor beating the air noisily. Behind it I could make out a silver speck in the distant sky. That would be the black X-15, catching the light of the bright sun, and curving in its landing approach.

Brown was saying on the public-address system, his voice all but drowned by the heavy beating of the rescue chopper: ". . . making a right turn. . . . Lazy S."

I lost the dot of the ship in the immensity of the sky for a moment, frantically searched with the binoculars, and found it again, gliding with apparent smoothness in from the west. Now it was close enough to be recognized as the X-15, the long black cigar with no visible wings, holding steady and moving fast. It seemed strange that such an un-aerodynamic shape would be able to glide like an airplane. But it was also sinking toward the lake bed rapidly.

I lost the bird again for a moment, then caught it again just as it was coming in for the landing flare out—the overgrown dart shape only a few feet above the tan lake bed. The tail was holding way down, awkwardly, like a chicken squatting to alight.

The tail seemed much too low, ridiculously low, the nose was pointing steeply toward the sky so that the bird looked ungainly, hanging on its tail, scooting along, dragging its hindquarter. But Crossfield was holding it down, feeling for the ground with it. He went past us, past the spot where we expected him to land. The slick body shape now was encumbered with the projecting jagged struts of the nose wheel and the two wide-reaching skis of the main landing gear below the tail.

The ship rocked up and down, bounding like a porpoise, looking very insecure. The tail oscillated, returning to its ridiculously low position. Crossfield held it down, still feeling for the ground.

Then pale dust spewed up around him in a cloud, the X-15 was in contact with the ground. With a thud you could feel even from this distance, the up-angled nose slammed down hard. But it stayed in one piece, the plane held steady on the lake bed, a thick tan wedge of dust rising behind it, spewing up high. The cone of dust ran straight and in a few seconds it stopped. The black shape of the space ship was sitting still and level now, on its gear.

"A perfect landing—a perfect landing—a perfect landing," Colonel Brown said fervently on the public-address system. The time was eight forty-five and a half. The colonel added, "Quote from Crossfield: 'The APU is working real well. I wish I could do a barrel roll on the way in.' "

Now the helicopter thrummed the air over us as it streaked toward the immobilized X-15. Near us the trucks, fire engines, the crane, the ambulance, the Air Police, the Air Force cars, and the green North American sedans, the Mobile-Control van and the yellow suit-up trailer all were starting out on the lake bed with a roaring of engines. Shooting up dust, the cavalcade rushed toward the X-15. Behind me I heard a buzz of talk among the newsmen, and Clete Roberts, the TV commentator, saying excitedly to someone:

"Six minutes—I don't need any more than that." One of his cameramen was reporting to him:

"I got cutaways to Colonel Brown."

Now a crowd of vehicles had agglomerated magically where the X-15 sat and blocked it from our view. The dust of the caravan's passage was like a smoke cloud over the lake bed. Through it I saw the moving bright red blinker of a fire truck near the spot where the X-15 must be.

A puffy cloud of white smoke belched up from the X-15 vicinity. I saw another red glittering fire beacon in the dust, below the white cloud. Two fire trucks: I wondered if the X-15 could be on fire. But the white cloud was the wrong color for that. In a moment it lifted above the crowd of vehicles and began to dissipate, and I guessed what that meant: Crossfield had flushed out his hydrogen-peroxide tanks. He must be all right.

The chopper was down, now, beside the knot of vehicles, and

much of the dust had settled. We could see the assemblage of steel supported on a wide, wavy gray band of mirage on the face of the lake bed. It seemed as if the flight must be successfully over.

The time was eight fifty-seven and we were being held here at the will of the Air Force, while scores of little dots of men clustered around the now visible dark cigar shape of the X-15: the usual crowd of semi-official rubbernecks, technicians, and engineers without much to do at the moment except look: look, now at Crossfield. His cockpit canopy was up, he had probably long since been extracted, and must be amid the crowd beside the X-15, talking to the North American head men.

One engineer at least was working out there. I saw the figure of a man on the hard, reflecting surface of the lake bed bending over at about the spot where the skis of the main landing gear had first impacted the lake. That would be Cooper Lindley with his measuring tape, gauging the depth and length of the skid marks.

The flying banana helicopter was lifting from the lake bed with a great thrumming of its rotors. He hadn't tarried on the ground long— evidently long enough for Dr. Toby Freedman to make sure that Crossfield was okay.

"The chopper's going home," said Lieutenant John Kirkley, of the PIO office. He borrowed my binoculars and leveled them at an Air Force sedan that was streaking across the lake bed, tailing a cone of dust. The car was heading toward the huge yellow suit-up trailer.

"I see Scott in the car," Kirkley said, which would figure. Crossfield would be taken to the suit-up trailer to shed his cramping silver suit and take a shower before being exposed to questioning by the press— which, if I knew Crossfield, would be a kind of ordeal by fire to him. He seems to have little in common with the world of newsmen.

In a few minutes a green North American sedan left the suit-up trailer and zoomed across the lake bed to the press knoll. The assembled press surged around the car as it squealed to a halt. They surrounded Scott, who looked freshly showered and now wore slacks and a white shirt. In the background, from the car, came Storms, Earl Blount, and J. O. Roberts, a North American test pilot.

Several of the newsmen were shaking hands with Crossfield, and one said:

"Beautiful job, Scotty."

The newsmen crowded close around Crossfield, some of them extending microphones toward him. The cameramen backed around and popped bulbs at him.

"How did she handle, Scott?" was the first question.

"Just as good as we expected," Crossfield answered quickly.

Q. "How fast was the landing, Scott?—160 knots?"

A. "About 160 knots—plus or minus 20."

Q. "How'd she handle, Scott?—stiff or loose or just right?"

A. "Just right."

The photographers were climbing all around to get their shots. One cameraman, fortunately in stocking feet, was walking around on the hood of the sedan, leaving footprints in the dust there. Several photographers had climbed on the nearest Air Force station wagon to get high-angle shots.

Q. "Did you land where you expected?"

A. "I landed just a little longer than anticipated." It looked to me as if he had touched down about two miles farther down the runway than we'd expected.

Q. "What were your sentiments just before release?"

There was no need for an answer right then—though the question was repeated later on—because several of the photographers were yelling to Crossfield:

"Scotty—give us a wave!"

"Scotty—give us a wave up here!"

Somebody asked a question about Mrs. Crossfield, but that also was ignored. Crossfield has said several times that he wants to keep his family out of the X-15 program.

Clete Roberts, anchored next to Crossfield with mike in hand, was asking in authoritative tones:

"We noted some apparent oscillation as you were landing—a kind of porpoising."

"I was just feeling out the controls—trying to see how much [reaction] I could get." (Later on, I found out that Crossfield had been almost completely out of control of the airplane during the landing. The control linkage was very slow to respond to his stick movements, and his SAS wasn't working to damp out the pitching. It wasn't till nine months later that Crossfield told me his sensations at that moment. "It was like driving your car when one wheel hits a soft shoulder. You overcorrect with the wheel, trying to get it back on the road, then you steer too far, so you turn back again too far, so you weave back and forth." By the next flight the control linkage had been corrected so it would be more responsive.)

Then the newsmen were asking J. O. Roberts, the North American test pilot, about the landing. "The landing was at about the five- or six-mile mark," he said. "He slid a mile. He had three miles to go." Then Roberts was signaling the end of the interview: "Okay, let's go."

Blount told the newsmen that after the briefing Crossfield would be available for more questioning and television filming.

The second session was at an improvised pressroom set up at the Oasis, a military service club near Edwards Headquarters, after Scott's debriefing with the engineers. The questions were much the same as before, but there was more time; and this time Crossfield had to answer the question about his emotional reactions to the flight.

"I was so busy," he said finally. "I had so much to do. I had no sense of personal feeling or attitude. I've been doing this practically all my life, and I don't have any aesthetic reaction to it."

(But later, in a national magazine article, Crossfield said that he had been quietly praying to God to help him, so that he wouldn't let his team down. He also related he was terribly disappointed after the landing, and the discovery that the airplane, as the controls were then set up, was completely unstable.)

The newsmen were also anxious to get the emotional reactions of the B-52 crewmen who were present this time: Captains Charlie Bock and Bill Allavie, pilot and copilot, and Bill Berkowitz, the launch operator. Bock is an old hand at this kind of thing, since he dropped both Pete Everest and Iven Kincheloe on some of their X-1 and X-2 runs, and now, faced by questions about his emotions, he was playing it cool.

"Did you and your crew have any emotions before the launching?" someone wanted to know.

Bock hesitated. "I couldn't say that we didn't have any emotions." And he let the rest of the answer slide while someone else asked a question of George Mellinger, the North American head-of-flight test operations.

Crossfield, hard pressed with questions about the flying qualities of X-15, declared firmly:

"There has been some conjecture that the plane would be difficult. I have always denied it. I deny it now. It's a nice airplane to fly. Now we've established what we set out to establish: that the plane will fly and that the systems will work."

Someone asked about the schedule of flights, and when Scott would be flying into space in X-15.

"The airplane will be turned over to NASA and the Air Force," Crossfield said. "I won't be making the spectacular flights."

Later on I asked Blount about the schedule—and when the first powered flight will be, the first of the flights which will lead up to the turnover of the ships to NASA and the Air Force. He said the first powered flight won't be for perhaps two months. So this afternoon I explored the possibility of hitching another Air Force ride to the East where I could gather some information from the brain centers contributing to the development of X-15. I called Washington to find out, and was told I might get a ride with a general who was expected to be flying East in a few days.

Tonight the newspapers, radio, and TV stations gave today's X-15 flight a big play. Clete Roberts in his six-thirty TV show kept saying it was very exciting, and he seemed almost breathless as he told about the mission. The Los Angeles *Mirror-News* lead summed up the event concisely:

"Rocket ship X-15 streaked out of the stratosphere high above southern California today in history's first manned space-ship flight."

MONDAY, JUNE 15. Talking to Dick Barton today, I was reminded that there will be another important X-15 mission before the first powered flight. That will be the first "wet flight," in which for the first time the bird will be filled with its full load of highly explosive fuel. The firecracker, in effect, will be loaded for the first time and taken aloft. It won't be launched, but this captive flight will be a dangerous one since it will be the first time the bomb has been armed; hence an important "captive" mission. Barton says the wet captive flight will probably be in about six weeks, and the first powered flight two to three weeks after that. So I had better be on my way East to see some of the X-15 installations and people, and still get back here in time. But the Air Force has bad news about the general's expected flight back East—it has been canceled.

TUESDAY, JUNE 16. The Air Force PIO office at Los Angeles tells me a KC-135—which is a military version of the Boeing 707 specially built for aerial refueling—will be coming into Los Angeles on Thursday, and heading back East almost immediately. It will deliver the commander of Wright-Patterson Air Force Base, Major General Stanley Wray, to Los Angeles, then turn around and fly back to Wright-Patterson. A ride on this plane would be fine because Wright-Patterson has been, and is, very important in the X-15 program. The chief Air Force project officer for X-15, Major Kit Murray, has his headquarters at Wright-Patterson. So do the aeromedical experts who tested the X-15 pilots and helped to design the silver suit and helmet, and the aerodynamic experts who played a large role in designing the control system; and the power-plant specialists who are right now trying to iron out some of the bugs in the Big Engine.

Wright-Patterson was once the headquarters of the Air Force Air Research and Development Command, and now it is noted for continuing research work on various advanced Air Force projects such as X-15. These projects are called WISPOs, in Air Force slang: WISPO being short for Weapons System Project Office. Major Murray is the head man for the X-15 WISPO. (To be exact, WISPO should be spelled WSPO, but there would be difficulty pronouncing this, and the word is pronounced WISPO. I add this note to pacify NASA critics who say it should be spelled WSPO or WESPO.)

So it will be smart for me to promote the ride back to Wright-Patterson on the general's ship, if I can. The chances look pretty good, Captain Tom Moore of the Ballistics Missile Division office tells me.

THURSDAY, JUNE 18. General Wray, a short, compact dynamo type, got off the big KC-135 on schedule this morning on the south, or Air Force, side of the Los Angeles International Airport.

The general was cordial for a moment before he hurried off to conferences at the Ballistics Missile Division.

"The airplane will have to shoot a dozen landings at Edwards on the way back," he told me. "Touchdowns. This is a test run. They're checking out some equipment."

I said that was fine with me, as long as the ultimate destination was Ohio and Wright-Patterson. The general introduced me to the airplane commander, Major Louis Kesterson, and Kesterson, a deliberate, capable man with the cool manner of the test pilot, told me the equipment being tested was cabin air-conditioning. This is a research aircraft.

The plane is basically a tanker, with the long boom for aerial refueling underneath the tail, but it also has an array of regular air liner seats. Now, an assortment of servicemen, including a couple of sailors, were stowing their gear near the seats.

There was the usual wait in the military tradition. Then three hours later, at two-five, two crewmen pulled up the ladders, Kesterson said "Ready to taxi," and the big jet began to move.

The test landings at Edwards used up about four hours, so it was seven fifty-five in the evening when we finally took off for Wright-Patterson. But since this is a research airplane, it is fast, unlike the outdated equipment of the Military Air Transport Command. So our flight plan across the country to Ohio was three and a half hours.

Now it is deep night, and we are riding over Ohio at 35,000 feet. It's eleven-fifty by Pacific time, or 1:50 A.M. local time. Down below the lights of Dayton are like a spread of stars, diamond dust on night's dress. And we are nosing down, sinking toward Wright-Patterson at 6,000 feet a minute. Kesterson has had lots of flying time on this aircraft, but he still seems excited about piloting it—even now at the end of a flying day that started eighteen hours ago. He and the copilot, Lieutenant Joe Schiele, are practically singing out their check list as the plane whistles toward the earth. The check list on a jet has to move fast anyhow, but they are enthusiastic about the plane, too. As Schiele says: "It's a real goin' bird."

DAYTON, OHIO, FRIDAY, JUNE 19. This morning at the Wright Air Development Center (part of the Wright-Patterson Air Force complex) I talked to Murray's assistant on the X-15 project, Chester McCullough. Murray was not on the base today.

McCullough went over the history of the project, beginning in December 1954, when the Air Force sent out letters to twelve aircraft manufacturers, asking for bids on X-15. Much of this I had heard before, except for this item:

Up until late 1957 the Air Force involvement on X-15 was only as a research project. But after October 4, 1957, when the Soviets opened the Space Age by launching Sputnik 1, the X-15 program was boosted several steps and transposed into what the Air Force calls a weapons system; that meant that it immediately gained more attention in the Air Force, and a better budget. (NASA contends it is not a weapons system but a research vehicle.) And the X-15 staff at Wright Air Development Command—then only two officers—was increased to five. In the same way, more money was shoveled into the X-15 contracts with North American Aircraft and Reaction Motors. The rude shock of foreign competition made us jump, and had even effected a fast reaction in an organization as vast and cumbrous as the United States government.

This afternoon I went with a public information escort to the aeromedical section of Wright ADC, to seek out some of the experts who had worked with the X-15 pilots on their problems of survival in space.

We made a tour of the aeromedical lab, which was scattered

through several aging buildings—a potpourri of assorted schoolhouse architecture, 1920 style.

We went through the torture chambers where the scientists inflict simulated hazards of space upon themselves, and measure the results. First we saw the four altitude chambers, bare rooms not at the moment in use, where partial or complete hypoxia can be achieved in the interest of testing men or equipment for space flight. Here Scott Crossfield and Al White had been checked out in their silver suits at a simulated altitude of 100,000 feet and the suits adjusted to fit better. Here, before the X-15 advent, several brave flight surgeons had risked lives and health to evolve some of the principles of pressure suits.

One of these pioneers in a Wright pressure chamber was Dr. James P. Henry, who in 1944 tried out a system of bladders arranged in a space suit to maintain pressure on the trunk of the human body when in thin air, so that it would not blow up like a balloon. (In thin air, the blood begins to boil at body temperature.) On that occasion, Dr. Henry had been wearing no special protection over his hands—so at 55,000 feet altitude the hands began to blow up grotesquely. Dr. Henry didn't immediately give the signal to depressurize: he was too interested in studying the phenomenon. The people outside the chamber saw what had happened and rapidly brought the simulated altitude down to 40,000 feet. But that experience led to Dr. Henry's prescription that high-altitude pilots (it was too early for space pilots) should wear tight garments on their arms and hands, as well as over their torsos.

Later on, to measure the effects of altitude on man's blood, Dr. Henry and an assistant, Eli Movitt, took their own blood samples at the various chamber levels. They worked with a needle fixed in the arm during the whole session, with an inner plunger so they could take samples frequently. Their research work into the amounts of oxygen in the blood helped ultimately in the design of the MA-2 helmet, the one that goes with the silver suit. They found out that the blood's oxygen content had to be above the 80 per cent mark for safety; they discovered this at the cost of growing woozy at altitude, and taking blood samples while woozy, a rather scary process.

From the work done by Henry and Movitt and many others like them came the T-1 altitude suit, the one worn by Yeager, Murray, Everest, Kincheloe, Apt, and the other X-1 and X-2 pilots. It was called a "capstan suit" because when the suit was inflated the laces threaded down the arms and legs of the flier were tightened mechanically around small capstans like pulleys, and the bladders thus were pulled tight against the flier's body. Of this tight kind of suit Colonel Everest said: "The longest I could stand it was about an hour before the pressures created by the helmet [which had a tight seal against leakage] and the suit would overcome me."

The T-1 suit and helmet led eventually to the more comfortable silver suit (called MC-2 by the Air Force) and the MA-2 helmet, which had a tight seal but no oxygen mask to worry about. Oxygen is fed directly into the helmet.

I knew I would find out more about these Space-Age flying suits from the Wright ADC specialists. Meanwhile our guide, chunky Charley Lutz, an aeromedical specialist, told us that plenty of T-1 and MC-2 suits had been tested out in these chambers.

However, he said, most of the tests weren't so dangerous as people would have you think. "The biggest problem is boredom," he said. He pointed out the TV set in the largest of the altitude chambers.

"We've also got tape recordings of everything from classical to rock and roll," he said. "Sometimes the altitude tests last pretty long."

We progressed to the Wright centrifuge, a heavy girder mounted at the center of a large room, with a gondola at the outer end of the arm. Crossfield and Al White, the X-15 pilots, have both been checked out here in a mockup of the X-15 cockpit, to check their reactions to the g-forces they might have to face in pullouts, sharp turns, or in going over the top of an arching ballistic flight. Lutz said both had made their centrifuge checks in their silver suits, and without them, and it was found the suits gave about two and a half gs more resistance; or in other words, the suits enable them to withstand that much more accelerative force.

The X-15 cockpit was long since gone. Now the gondola is occupied by a reclining seat—like a pilot's chair pushed over on its back, the mockup for the Mercury capsule. The chair was filled by a light-colored dummy which, despite its plain, blank face, managed to look agonized. It was the position that produced the effect: the figure's back against the floor, his knees in the air, he looked helpless and sad.

We went on to a heat chamber, a bare room with a table and straight chairs, like the day room in an army camp.

"Scott [Crossfield] tested here for the X-15 re-entry temperature tests. But it wasn't glamorous enough for *Life;* they moved him where there were a lot of lamps."

We moved to a new heat chamber, an oversized oven of shiny metal, where, Lutz said, there is a 450-degree wall temperature and

400 in the seat. He flicked the switches to make batteries of quartz light bulbs flash into action. Their heat, he said, corresponds to the heat of re-entry which may flare up and die down as future space ships coming back into atmosphere go into the air, get heated from the friction, then pull up momentarily to cool off.

"The roast is basted here," Lutz said. "You want it well done or rare?"

Right now it was too late in the day, and the week, for any tests to be under way in the heat or altitude chambers, but I told Lutz I would like to come back on Monday and see some of the space research in process.

"The division heads always try the experiments on themselves first," he told me. I said that figured: all through the world of space the leaders I have met are long on courage and intellectual curiosity. You wouldn't expect less of the scientists here at Wright ADC.

MONDAY, JUNE 22. Lew Zarem, the public information director of Wright ADC, took me in to meet Major Arthur "Kit" Murray, the Air Force X-15 project officer. I knew a bit about Murray's background. He had been an X-1 rocket pilot, who had been flying altitude runs while Yeager made runs for pure speed in the rocket ships. In the X-1A in 1954 Murray had set up a world's altitude for a time: 94,000 feet. On that same flight Murray's ship fell into inertia coupling, tumbled down eight miles of sky before he could establish control. But nowadays, Zarem told me, Murray has said he'd give his eye teeth to fly the X-15. He hasn't lost his pioneering urge to reach out into the unknown; and probably it galls him to hold down a desk job as chief administrator for the Air Force X-15 program and be involved with every development and yet not be able to fly the bird.

Murray is blond, handsome, and well spoken, one of those lucky ones upon whom nature seems to have lavished many gifts. He seemed especially impressive in an Air Force uniform.

He said that his group at Wright ADC had the function of tying all the X-15 contractors together—the makers of the air frame, North American; the power-plant manufacturers, Reaction Motors; Sperry, who make the gyros and the stable platform (space) instruments; David Clark Company of Worcester, Massachusetts, brassière manufacturers who tailor the silver suit; and many miscellaneous contractors such as General Electric who make the APUs.

"One of our functions here is to pass on information to the various contractors. We're a clearing house of information on all the subjects concerned, and if we see that a contractor, say an engine or airframe contractor, is going off on a tangent, or trying something which somebody else has tried and found unworkable, we can supply the pertinent information and guidance."

That's the way it was, Murray said, with the power plant, the XLR-99 Big Engine.

"These people had standard development troubles with a new power plant," he went on. "The subtle establishment of flow rates, control rates, sensing rates, the development of ignition and combustion, a whole group of hardware difficulties.

"And we could help because we were in touch with all the other power-plant manufacturers, and could supply information on the state of the art among all the manufacturers, and save some time that way."

I asked Murray what has been the most important contribution of Wright Air Development Center, and he said without hesitation:

"The most important input was the aeromedical work with the suit." He meant the research with the silver suit and helmet and the suits that led up to it.

A lot of the other development work on X-15, he said, had to be done in the West, where there were certain facilities you couldn't duplicate in the more congested sections of the country—such as the Edwards lake beds or the rocket-sled tracks for high-speed testing at Edwards or Holloman Air Force Base, in New Mexico.

Only rocket-sled tests, he said, had told the true story about the X-15 pilot's chair: the way it would behave aerodynamically at high speed if the pilot had to use it to escape. In tests made in the wind tunnels, the chair checked out as stable enough when it was hurled through supersonic winds on simulated emergency launch. But in tests at Edwards, where it was driven by a rocket sled at 780 miles an hour, its design seemed to set it to tumbling violently.

"It was a shock that the wind tunnels didn't correlate accurately," Murray said. "We had to run actual rocket-track runs to determine the stability. We instructed North American to try something different. They used two telescoping booms, which came out like wings, to stabilize the chair. Then they had an open-escape system that would work at those altitudes and speeds."

Incidentally, while he was speaking of rocket sleds and their value to research, Murray said I should see Colonel John Paul Stapp, one of our most famous space pioneers, who is now head of the aeromedical branch at Wright ADC.

I knew about Stapp, that he was the aeromedical researcher who had ridden the rocket sled at Holloman many times at speeds over 500 mph, and that he still holds the speed record for travel on land: 632 mph, which he made in an open sled ("a shoebox with a seat," he called it) on December 10, 1954.

I told Murray that I certainly wanted to see Stapp, one of the great heroes of the Space Age because he kept on with his sled work to research the effects of g-forces, even though frequently injured, with ribs and arms broken and once temporarily blinded. I was reminded that I wanted to see some of the scientists working with their bold experiments in the aeromedical labs some time today.

I wanted to ask Murray about his X-1A flights and his troubles with inertia coupling. As with Yeager, it was a rare opportunity to talk to one of the great rocket pioneers. Murray smiled at the question about inertia coupling; that nearly killing experience was far enough back now so that he could look back on it philosophically.

"Every time I got above 84,000 feet, the airplane went purely out of control," he said. "At that altitude and speed—around Mach 2 [which is about 1,320 mph]—I found that a push of as little as a half a pound would set up a yaw—the airplane was that sensitive to the controls."

I said Yeager had told me much the same thing. "But now," Murray added, "in the X-15 the stability augmentation system damps out the small oscillations."

This seemed like a good chance to get an insight into the X-15 flight schedule from somebody who really knows. Murray indicated the first powered flight should be at the end of July. And in his opinion, the Big Engine should be delivered and flying by November. But he warned that schedules in the Space Age have a way of slipping. "It takes a certain length of time to walk to Cincinnati," was his way of saying it. "Operations and developments are sequential."

I remarked that the operations and developments have lagged so far, especially the operations with the Big Engine, and jokingly suggested the testing program could be going on five years from now.

"I hate to be pessimistic," he said, taking me seriously, "but there could be crackups before that. . . . These things are flying bombs. When you store that kind of energy in such a small package, it can happen . . . rocket engines are extremely unforgiving."

Murray told me one thing about the X-15 program, however, which was cheering: he had just been to Washington to talk to his Air Force bosses at the Air Research and Development Command, to get more

X-15 funding. So the funds have been increased to $175 million; which should accelerate the progress somewhat. Maybe that walk to Cincinnati can be goosed along to a trot, if sufficient money is allotted to grease the way.

After lunch Carroll High of the public information department and I went over to the aeromedical lab again to see some of the space torture chambers in action. There was only one section of the altitude and heat chambers functioning this afternoon: it was the shiny new re-entry heat chamber, the one that looked like a shiny metal bake oven.

Around the bake oven (properly titled a heat-pulse oven) engineers and technicians were working, and one man was in the oven. He was wearing a silver suit and large cotton boots, a hood around his face—and glasses, which gave him a peculiarly patient, studious look. He was quiet as the technicians made their preparations to give him the works.

I asked the head man, a slim, youthful type wearing slacks, T-shirt, and a pair of headphones, what the operation for today was. But it was on the classified list. It had something to do with re-entry temperatures, because this hotbox is geared to conduct the kind of heat you would encounter if you were in a space ship, gingerly feeling your way into the atmosphere, and skipping back and forth into space. Possibly this test of the silver suit with the fluffy cotton boots has something to do with Dynasoar, the now-secret Air Force space ship that takes a man out of atmosphere and allows him to orbit the earth a few times before he comes back: a sort of graduate X-15 which, unlike the Mercury capsule, will be as controllable as an airplane.

The engineer in charge, Captain James H. Veghte, wouldn't say. But he did tell me that the reactions of the man in the oven were being carefully recorded during the test. His skin temperature and rectal temperature, his respiration and heartbeat were being meticulously charted.

I remember the look of the man with glasses as the technicians closed the door—a carefully cultivated stoical look. The space pioneers, always volunteers, usually seem to project the detached, scientific attitude. Probably you avoid going crazy that way.

TUESDAY, JUNE 23. This morning at the propulsion laboratory I talked with several of the engineers who are now engaged in testing one of the big XLR-99 engines here. I asked if what I had heard was true

—that there have been several explosions of the Big Engine in the course of its tests.

Willard A. Knapp, the chief of the liquid-propellant rocket section, answered without being too specific:

"There's no engine ever been built that didn't blow a few times. . . . Every engine I know about, you've had one or more major explosions which wiped out the airplane—and six or eight minor ones. A lot of these don't result in blowing the hardware around."

The story I had heard was that the combustion chamber of the Big Engine had blown out a couple of times.

But I couldn't expect three engineers to tell me, a stranger, about something that might be restricted information in some way. I would try to inquire elsewhere and put the pieces together: I would come back to the propulsion lab sometime for an engine test. Then information might be freer.

Knapp went on about the explosiveness of lox, the common oxidizer in rocket engines: "A little grease can set off lox: some people believe even fingerprints are enough to set it off."

Knapp was going on about the celebrated case of the coffee can at Edwards, during the X-1 program, when the Bell project engineer, Wendel Moore, took a piece of the gasket material, the infamous ulmer leather, out for a test. He filled a coffee can with lox, topped it with a square of the leather, then hit the ensemble with a hammer —and ended up with half the coffee can wrapped around his neck. Fortunately, he was uninjured. But he proved the hard way that the leather seals were explosive when soaked with the oxidizer.

I wasn't getting much information about the Big Engine, but general information, anyway, about the explosiveness of rocket engines and fuel. Then Knapp said something about science which I'll probably always remember:

"Like the turtle, science makes progress only with its neck out."

I had lunch with Ezra Kotcher, whom many people in the space world (including Kit Murray) call "the father of the research aircraft." Technical Director of Laboratories here at Wright ADC, Kotcher was instrumental in activating the X-1 and X-2 programs.

A kindly, mentally agile man, Kotcher told how he'd first championed the X-15 at a meeting of Air Force brass and NACA (later NASA) in July 1954 in Washington, D.C. At that meeting NACA had proposed the idea of X-15. They had been considering the idea and working up proposals since 1952. But in 1954, still pretty close to the end of the Korean War, Kotcher said, "research airplane was a dirty word. Maybe it was the economy or maybe people didn't have the vision and foresight. They were thinking in terms of practical application, trying to justify it as a potential military weapon." But at that meeting Kotcher championed the NACA presentation vigorously, and "showed that we had more technical competence than we had for the X-1 or X-2."

So again, as in 1944 when he first broached the subject of X-1 to Bell Aircraft (and had to justify it as a possible step toward a rocket fighter), Kotcher gave the big push that launched a rocket ship and our first space ship.

Kotcher told me how Scott Crossfield, who was then working as an engineer for NACA, approached him on the subject of piloting the X-15 in 1955. It was at a meeting of the Scientific Advisory Board in Brainerd, Minnesota.

As Kotcher remembers the conversation, "Crossfield said: 'I'm going to fly that airplane. Don't tell anybody. But I'd like to know how to arrange it.

"And I told him: 'When we give out the contracts, you can move out.' "

He meant that he would get the word to Crossfield so that Crossfield would know what firm would have the contract and might move there as an engineer.

After lunch at the Flight Control laboratory where the X-15 control system was designed, I heard more about Crossfield's determination to be one of the prime movers of the X-15 project. I had already heard much about his persistence in working through all the aeromedical phases of the program.

Now, at the operations office of the control lab, Mel Shorr, chief of the research branch, told me that Crossfield also had strong ideas about what he wanted in the controls. Some of Crossfield's ideas met opposition in the control section, but most came through and are in the airplane.

Before I left Wright this afternoon, I managed to catch up with Colonel Stapp, whose heroic researches into the effects of high g-forces made him famous in aviation annals. Stapp, a small, resolute man with spectacles, spoke about the X-15 program with the fearlessness you might expect from a man who would endure 38 gs on his sled, break his arm on deceleration, and have the coolness to set his own arm right afterward.

This is what this forthright aviation pioneer had to say about X-15: "The big contribution is that we can fly in space, and have control. . . . The X-15 marries aerodynamic flight to space flight."

He wasn't afraid to compare the X-15 approach to that of Mercury, the capsule which may be launched into orbit by a missile, then come back to earth by parachute, without any real control.

"I like the X-15 idea. The next step, if it can orbit. How much better than a great fleet searching for the [Mercury] capsule in the Pacific."

I'm scheduled to go on to Washington tomorrow, to Air Research and Development headquarters there, but tonight I went out to the propulsion lab in the hope of seeing the Great Beast, the big XLR-99 engine, perform. This hot night, after four hours of tinkering with the engine and instruments, the engine was ready to go shortly before midnight. But at the crucial moment it was discovered that the water supply didn't have enough pressure. This is an application of the space scientists' so-called "Murphy's law": everything that can go wrong, will go wrong.

WASHINGTON, D.C., WEDNESDAY, JUNE 24. I checked in with the headquarters of NASA and the Air Force Air Research and Development Command, to try to get appointments with the big brass. Haven't succeeded so far, but have managed to set up an appointment for tomorrow at Johnsville, Pennsylvania, to have a look at the famous centrifuge.

THURSDAY, JUNE 25. A train trip from Washington, then a subway and taxi ride from North Philadelphia, and I finally reached this Naval Air Development Center, site of the centrifuge where the X-15 pilots trained under simulated high-g conditions. Supposedly it is the world's largest centrifuge; though we don't know what the Russians may have in this line.

The Naval Air Development Center is located in modern (even modernistic) buildings which used to house the Brewster Aircraft Company, which made fighter planes in early World War II days. When Brewster folded, the Navy's Bureau of Aeronautics and then the Navy Bureau of Medicine moved in. The centrifuge is under Bureau of Medicine auspices.

I checked in with the director, Navy Captain F. Kirk Smith, a kindly and benign medic, who introduced me to the chief scientist, Dr. Carl C. Clark.

Clark is the average you expect physically in a space scientist these days: he is lean, youthful, crewcut, and intense. His look of leanness (almost nausea) was probably sharpened this morning, because he had just completed a violent maneuver in the centrifuge. The maneuver, tied to the Mercury astronaut program, involved a simulation of the physical strains and stresses an astronaut would have to endure if he got into trouble on the way out to space and had to separate from the Atlas missile that was pushing him. This would involve the firing of an escape rocket that would separate his capsule and also flip him end for end in quick order. With the missile traveling at 10,000 miles an hour, this would mean tremendous g-forces: 11 gs forward, followed immediately by 11 gs back.

Clark's intention was simply to see how an astronaut, in the approved back-down and knees-up position advocated by Mercury, and wearing a silver suit and helmet, could endure the strain. He had apparently survived the test in good order, although he was pale.

Captain Smith, Clark, and I went to lunch and Clark said he needed a martini to settle his stomach after his worst test run. I asked if the whirling in the centrifuge didn't make everyone sick, and he said: "I don't get sick unless I move my eyes or head at the beginning or end of a run." This is generally true, he said, and the riders of the centrifuge soon learn it.

I was interested particularly in the way the centrifuge fitted into the X-15 program, and how the X-15 pilots had performed here. And here, as at Wright ADC, I found that Crossfield has been the most active and persistent.

Clark told me about it as we stopped at the place the scientists humorously call The Throne Room, on the deck above the centrifuge. Here, like mummies, the plastic seats of the X-15 and Mercury pilots are lined up. These centrifuge thrones, white plastic shapes with green, nubbled seats and backs, are tailored to the measure of the fliers, and labeled with their names. I saw thrones for "F. Petersen," "N. Armstrong," and "R. Rushworth," respectively, the Navy pilot on NASA's X-15 staff, Neil Armstrong, the youngest of the X-15 jockeys, and Bob Rushworth, the Air Force back-up pilot behind Bob White.

Clark said that Scott Crossfield had come to the centrifuge first in the spring of 1957, with a group of NACA scientists. Scott by this time had become the lead pilot of X-15 for North American Aircraft.

At that point, Clark went on, the centrifuge wasn't developed to its present state. The controls were not set up with calculating machines so that the gondola in the centrifuge would respond like an airplane in flight. In those days the centrifuge was only a gadget to measure the effect of g-forces on pilots.

But within eight months the centrifuge was rigged with computers so that there was a feedback from the controls: the gondola reacted to them as if it were the X-15 in flight. It was like the static simulator at North American, with the extra advantage that it had movement, the feeling of a plane in flight.

Crossfield was the first of the X-15 pilots to fly this reasonable facsimile of the rocket ship in motion.

Crossfield, who had by this time been working for two years as an engineer and pilot for North American on the X-15 project, helped to design the X-15 gondola mockup so that it was close to the real thing in details of controls and instruments. In one of his early runs, incidentally, he shot the works and pulled nine gs on the centrifuge.

Clark bragged about the centrifuge with a kind of paternal pride. When it began giving an approximation of actual flight, he said, it also began to supply data on the aerial behavior of the plane.

"When we had an oscillation in test runs, we began to see that the centrifuge had aerodynamic uses. It seemed clear from our runs that the oscillation called for bigger control surfaces on the X-15.

"Partly because of that, North American increased the size of the tail." In other words, the gondola with the control feedback simulating flight showed up some of the extra sensitivity of the controls which might have been a problem for some test pilot to fight in the future, if it hadn't been spotted on the centrifuge runs. [North American's later comment: "The centrifuge runs had absolutely no bearing on changes to the X-15 external configuration."]

Clark and I went down to the centrifuge room, about the size of a high-school gymnasium, to look at the 50-foot, girder-like arm of the centrifuge and its gondola. Now it was equipped with the Mercury capsule mockup, with the awkward recumbent chair and the simple-looking Mercury instruments and controls.

One of the group around the gondola was an engineering buddy of Clark: a sandy-colored man who combined a native huskiness with the slightly nauseated look that most of the space experimenters can't avoid since they so often serve as subjects in their experiments.

The engineer was Flanagan Gray, an aeromedical specialist who has recently been doing some spectacular work with a futuristic space device dubbed the Iron Maiden.

The Iron Maiden, like the medieval torture device it is named after, looks roughly like a sitting statue. It has a door that opens wide so that a subject can sit within. But unlike the old torture apparatus, this door is not studded with spikes which punch holes in the victim when it is closed.

Instead, the door is smooth inside, and when it is closed, water is poured in so that the subject is surrounded by a layer of liquid insulation—insulation, that is, against the shock of g-forces. Water insulation keeps uniform pressure on the body, gives the best protection against the "sloshing of the organs," which used to play hell with a man's internal structure when in the grip of violent (acceleration, deceleration, and turn) forces.

Water insulation "will be the thing of the future" to shield space travelers against such hazards of high-speed travel, Clark said. In the future, space crews may step into chambers like the Iron Maiden during the heavy g-forces of take-off, get out during the flight, and wear normal light clothing then; and return to the protective layer of water during the deceleration as the ship returns to the earth's atmosphere or the atmosphere of some other planet.

"Gray stood 31 gs in the Iron Maiden for five seconds," Clark recalled. "And there were no effects, not even the blurring of vision."

Gray, it seemed, had been exceptionally well qualified for the experiment. Besides being educated to the necessary degree in biology and engineering-wise, he had been a summertime lifeguard in Clayton, Missouri, in the days before World War II, and at that time had been able to stay under water without air for seven minutes.

This ability was important in the Iron Maiden test, because right now there's no provision for supplying air to the subject; Gray had to hold his breath during the time of the experiment. But it must have taken considerable nerve to sit inside the Iron Maiden in the dark, in a sheet of water, holding one's breath while being whirled around at dizzying speeds—and of course not knowing whether the gadget, or one's own body, was going to hold together for the duration. It was a short enough time for someone of Flanagan Gray's capabilities, but all the same it must have taken plenty of nerve.

Crossfield had that same kind of courage when he pulled the nine gs on his first centrifuge sessions, Clark said. That time, the headrest in the X-15 mockup didn't restrain him enough, and his head flopped violently from side to side. As a result, he had a sore neck for several days, and probably more importantly, in his estimation, the X-15 headrest was redesigned to give greater support: in effect, to provide more support on three sides.

"That was the run where he went unconscious," Clark added. "His eyeballs went up."

Clark showed me the movie film made of Crossfield on that occasion by an automatic camera. I could see his head rolling wildly, and it was true that his eyeballs did roll up at the end as unconsciousness took over. It would have been a shocking film to see, except that by now I am getting accustomed to hearing about the devoted pioneers of space travel who fling themselves into this kind of voluntary suffering without any questions asked. It's the same kind of devotion I knew among Americans during World War II. But this time there's an extra element—science. These are men of special education and mental ability as well as nerve and devotion. They are a new kind of elite: scientists forced to introspect to dredge the meaning from the suffering and sacrifice of their experiments. They know their importance in the expanding world of space exploration, and so they willingly risk their necks and health. It's encouraging to know that men continue to be capable of this kind of sacrifice, in the name of science.

Maybe the way in which Crossfield referred to his experience with the 9 gs is a clue. According to Clark, Crossfield calls it "my pre-X-15 worst computation."

I asked Clark what had been his hairiest times in the four years he has been at the centrifuge. "The biggest potential hazard was this morning, with this tumbling . . . it was a complete unknown. There haven't been any really hairy times—only a few wild hairs here and there."

FRIDAY, JUNE 26. Today I went to the NASA headquarters, an ugly old office building in downtown Washington, to see one of the directing brains of our space program. He is Richard Horner, associate director of NASA. He seems a good bright engineering mind, and he is that, with a long term as chief engineer at the Air Force test center at Edwards from 1949 to 1955—so that he is familiar with most of the people and events of the X-1 and X-2 programs at the working level. It's reassuring to have such a man high up in the command echelon at NASA. He should be a good advocate of the maneuverable kind of space ship, the X-15 and its successors (such as Air Force's future Dynasoar), as contrasted with the space-apartment type like the Mercury capsule, which many of the authorities think has little future, since it is incapable of precise control. Such a capsule could orbit, but whether the astronaut riding it could bring it in anywhere near a designated area on earth with its parachute is very debatable.

The interesting thing is that NASA finds itself stuck with the management of both projects: the X-15, which it administers jointly with the Air Force and Navy; and the other, the Mercury program, representing their own funds and sole jurisdiction.

But Horner, despite his experience with the controllable rocket ships, seemed to be very cool about committing himself on the merits of the two rival systems. Perhaps he wants to be careful what he says about any comparison, because he has very recently assumed his job at NASA.

At any rate, this handsome, serious, youthful man had only this to say on the subject: "There are two categories [of space ships]: high lift, the X-15 and the Dynasoar; and high drag, Mercury. There are protagonists on both sides. And both have advantages."

It was noncommittal enough. I told the NASA public information officer, Walt Bonney, that I would very much like to see the new chief administrator of NASA, Dr. T. Keith Glennan, and the highly skilled first deputy, Hugh Dryden. Bonney says he will try to arrange audiences with these lead men, but it may take a few days.

I also talked to Colonel Pug Evans, the PIO of the Air Force's Air Research and Development Command, the top Air Force authority for space matters, about an interview with Lieutenant General Bernard A. Schriever, the dynamic new head man who made a name by spark-plugging the Air Force's missile program. Evans said that also will take some time. I hope it all can be arranged before the first powered flight of X-15.

While waiting, I decided to take advantage of a chance to ride down to Cape Canaveral, Florida, to take a look at the Air Force Missile Test Center which has been so incessantly in the news for its launching of the big rockets.

The ride was with Major Bill Coleman, of the ARDC public information office, in an old Air Force C-54 (DC-4). Coleman and his crew are heading for Eglin Air Force Base in western Florida, so they have promised to drop me off on the way at Cape Canaveral, which is to say Patrick Air Force Base, Cocoa, Florida.

I also hope that I may be able to explore the know-how that X-15 inherited from missiles: especially in the gyro-controlled space instruments and in the rocket or ballistics controls, both of which had some early equivalents in missiles. At least I can catch a glimpse of the greatest rocket range this side of the Iron Curtain.

We flew down from Andrews Field, the ARDC base just south of

Washington. Now it is dark and late and we should soon see the lights of Patrick Air Force Base ahead. Already we can feel the pleasant Florida night warmth in the cabin.

COCOA BEACH, FLORIDA, SATURDAY, JUNE 27. Last night, when Major Jim Reed met me at Patrick Air Force Base, and drove me over to the motel strip on Cocoa Beach, I was surprised to see the Miami-type boom town, all new motels, with colored indirect floodlights and neons, which has sprung up on the strength of the new missile business. The technicians and engineers have brought sudden wealth to this former quiet beach and fishing town, and the new buildings reflect the missile motif and new prosperity. The Starlight, Polaris, Vanguard, and Satellite motels have flashing, bright-colored signs that purport to show splashing rocket tails or exploding satellites.

Along the line of bright new motels are night clubs—which, when we came by last night, were in full neon glory. Night life in Cocoa Beach flourishes, since many of the 16,000 people who have come here because of the missiles are unmarried or come here temporarily without their families, according to Major Reed.

The motel where I checked in, the Satellite, has a night club with walls decorated with paintings of the mountains of the moon. Last night it was filled with dancers, a gay, noisy crowd looking glamorous because the lights were purple and fluorescent and they caught the white shirts the men were wearing and made them shine in the dark.

It was early, for Friday night, so we made a quick trip to the Koko, the flashiest and newest of the motels, and the Starlight. We found one motel, the Vanguard, where you can get food after eleven o'clock.

This morning everything in the line of missile work seemed to have shut down for the week end, and Major Ken Grine, the deputy PIO, said the missile companies aren't on any overtime these days, there's no extra work on week ends or at night, because there's no flap on, nothing like a new Sputnik to give us the national hotfoot. So it would be hard for me to round up anybody to talk about missiles, rockets, or their influence on X-15 this week end.

The beach at Cocoa was very inviting, anyway, and crowded, with many of the 16,000 missile persons; a surprising number of families in bathing suits too. The water was warm and there were several large picnics, beach parties held by contractors for employees, in segregated areas along the long stretch of beach, the picnics marked with signs such as "Pan American Party." Pan American Airways is the largest single contractor in the Canaveral area, with 7,000 employees, and they have the job of running the down-range stations, bases strung out into the Caribbean with such functions as recovering nose cones fired from Canaveral. On a sunny, hot afternoon like this duty at Canaveral and vicinity didn't seem unattractive at all.

MONDAY, JUNE 29. This morning I went down with a press group from Patrick Air Force Base to Cape Canaveral, a wide, desolate, bare area with a skyline marked only by the scattered figures of missiles, like overgrown sentinels. We stopped at the T-3 Press Observation Site to watch the launch of a Polaris missile. But in sum, I made no progress with my project of checking into the X-15's heritage of missile technology.

The Cape Canaveral facility is large in people and area and so heavily organized that it is hard for a stranger to find his way to a research source, at least on short notice. And my notice is short because I have word from Washington that appointments have been set up for the three head men of NASA and the Air Force's ARDC, Glennan, Dryden, and Schriever, for tomorrow and Wednesday.

Today was mostly filled with the stock indoctrination of out-of-town newsmen; a tour of the launching pads and several of the massive blockhouses where the engineers and technicians go to watch their birds fly, and a briefing, complete with a film that showed some fine missile shots and some spectacular explosions. It was good background for a Space-Age education, but it was not much concerned except indirectly with the subject that interests me most: man in space.

Of course, Canaveral with its asparagus-like crop of missiles is pertinent in the sense that man's future in space depends on rocket power, and here in this lowland peninsula is to be found the sheer, brute force of the most powerful rockets we can muster. The biggest of these we now have, Atlas and Titan, will be related to man's conquest of space, because engines like theirs, or clusters of their engines, will boost rocket ships such as X-15 and Dynasoar into orbit and eventually to the moon.

I guess it is probably wrong to think of these military missiles as primarily boosters for space exploration, because they are designed to be weapons in store for a possible nuclear war. But I am won over to the point of view that nearly led to Von Braun's execution when he was chief engineer at Peenemunde: that the rocket weapons are most important as a way to open up a new age of heavenly exploration.

But I had made no progress on this quick trip with the project of finding out how the X-15 got its space controls and instruments from missile ancestors. I found it's possible to write about the stable-platform (gyro) instruments of the X-15, but exactly how those same gadgets are used in missiles is sensitive (classified), because this has a lot to do with the classified subject of exactly how missiles are guided. And the secrecy again is based on the probably fatuous assumption that we know more than the Russians about the subject, therefore don't want that information leaking out.

Anyhow, I got the official tour, which was expertly put on because streams of visitors, many of them big shots, are always passing through Canaveral, wanting to see our East Coast scientific Disneyland; so the people at Canaveral have become skilled at accommodating guests from the outside worlds, military and civilian. One of the engineering types at the Titan pad showed me the separate glassed-in room in the blockhouse where VIPs can sit and watch a launching by means of six television screens, and he said:

"They can sit and hear everything, but they can't talk to us. It keeps 'em off my back."

And one of the public-relations head men told me that a touchy situation had come up recently when a controversial American labor leader of somewhat leftist inclinations had showed up with proper introductory notes from On High in Washington. There was some trepidation about how to handle him, but it was decided to give him Tour 1A, the perfectly safe one which provides an absolute minimum of military information.

Almost all of the engineers, technicians, and Air Force men I met in the blockhouses, control towers, and offices seemed to feel some excitement in their work; principally, I think, the sense that they are involved in something very important in American history and world history—the excitement of the Space Age. Even the driver who took me to the military airfield this afternoon for the flight back to Washington said what several other military and civilian people had told me: that working at Canaveral is a kick.

WASHINGTON, D.C., TUESDAY, JUNE 30. Today I had the long-awaited interviews with Hugh Dryden, the second boss man (and the leading technical brain) of NASA and General Schriever of the Air Force's Air Research and Development command. The interview with T. Keith Glennan, the politically appointed head man of NASA, is set up for tomorrow

Dryden, the chief of the National Advisory Committee for Aeronautics for many years before it became the huge government branch called NASA, impressed me as immensely competent and, for a scientist, amazingly articulate. He wasn't afraid to come to grips in words with the comparative problems of X-15 and Mercury as vehicles for the penetration of space; although he didn't want to commit himself on their relative importance in NASA's plans.

Dr. Dryden is lean, grayish, bespectacled, and a long life in science seems only to have intensified the mental sharpness of his early student years.

The crux of the problem with manned space vehicles now, Dryden said, is "maneuverability versus the difficulties of the heat problem."

Maneuverability, as exemplified in a winged space ship of the X-15 or Dynasoar type, is much greater than in the high-drag vehicle, the Mercury capsule with its primitive retro-rockets and braking parachute to control it. The heat of re-entry into atmosphere at the high speeds of space flight, though, is less difficult to handle in the Mercury capsule. It has a big heat shield of insulating metal on its bottom, to protect the pilot. Dryden pointed out that in a Mercury capsule "the heating is of relatively short duration—the rates are high, but the duration is short." He continued:

"The wing-type heating continues over a longer duration. . . . But the control is better. Our only control is in the retro-rocket. Probably the pilot can control it within 50 by 100 miles for landing —quite a substantial area. We will track him over the United States and hope to be able to predict where he'll be.

"Ultimately one would like to have a maneuverable aircraft. You will want maneuverability that improves as the aircraft slows down. Some people propose an intermediate solution—which would involve maybe only elementary wings or an unsymmetrical nose cone [to handle the heat problem]."

Dryden almost came to a conclusion when he said: "My own belief is that we will end up with some wings in the ultimate [space] ferry," which was an indication of favor toward the X-15.

But he immediately covered the other side, expounding on the advantage of choosing the Mercury capsule: "Our choice of the drag type was to get experience with men in space as quickly as possible. We accept, with that, a very limited control over landing."

Over at the headquarters of the Air Force's ARDC later in the day

I had a considerably more committing statement about the relative merits of the X-15 and Mercury types of space vehicles from General Schriever.

I saw Schriever in his office, after waiting in the anteroom for a couple of hours while bemused missile-type colonels (identified by the missile-shaped metal pins on their chests) bustled in and out. Colonel Jack Miller, the general's aide, said it's always thus with the boss man. He always works at high tension.

Schriever I found to be a tall, handsome man, with a good deal of grimness and concentration written on his face. He appears to be thirty-eight to forty, but is actually ten years older than that—forty-nine.

He speaks like a learned man on space and aviation science, he has the education you would hope for in an officer with his responsibility. He was a Wright Field test pilot in 1939, graduated from the Air Corps engineering school, and got his master's degree from Stanford University in 1942. After that, he had a long background of Air Force research. He's of the new type Air Force officer, product of a long, specialized educative process.

He said: "The X-15 will provide a great deal of information about man in his environment in space—and it will be the first experiment in which man will have to perform functions in space: more functions than in Mercury, where much of what he is doing will be either automatic or controlled from the ground.

"One of the biggest problems in space is to determine man's utility there. The X-15 has the potential of taking a large step forward in the development of man's environment—leading to his performing a useful function.

"The other thing is re-entry. It [X-15] will give very valuable information on aerodynamics and control characteristics—in the re-entry into the earth's atmosphere."

Without being asked the question specifically, he made the comparison with Mercury:

"A parachute descent with a high-drag body is not a very practical way of operating in re-entry—with passengers."

The X-15 in those two areas, man's space capabilities and the re-entry heat problem, will contribute most to man's knowledge as it pertains to space operations.

"Eventually, to get a practical system, a practical vehicle for the transportation of people in space, I think you're going to an aerodynamic [X-15 type] platform.

"I don't think you can withstand 15 to 18 g's during re-entry [as in the high-drag type vehicle]. You might expect highly selected individuals—Mercury pilots on their special couches—to withstand it. But you can't expect passengers to do it. We're going to find a better way of re-entering the atmosphere. In space you don't have to worry about aerodynamic [streamlined] shape, but in atmosphere you do."

WEDNESDAY, JULY 1. Today I was trying to arrange a flight back to the West Coast, to arrive in time to catch the next two X-15 missions —the "wet" flight on which the bird will be carried aloft with a full load of fuel for the first time, and the first powered flight, maybe two weeks after that.

It looks as if the dangerous "wet flight" may be next week, so I'd better start back.

Today I interviewed T. Keith Glennan, the administrator of NASA. He is a skilled administrator with a varied background in that field, a background that stretches from Paramount and Goldwyn studios in Hollywood, where he was studio manager, to the presidency of Case Institute of Technology, Cleveland, Ohio.

The gossip is that President Eisenhower, when he appointed a head for the mammoth, rapidly expanding space agency in August 1958, wanted to choose a man who was an expert administrator and a scientist, and also hep to big-time politics and able to handle himself skillfully in the political infighting of Capitol Hill. Glennan's experience tied in: he had been a member of the Atomic Energy Commission and the board of the National Science Foundation, and a former board member of several big corporations such as Standard Oil of Ohio and the Cleveland Electric Illuminating Company.

For one with such a background, the fifty-four-year-old administrator was surprisingly frank. In fact, I would guess that a quality of impatient, ruthless frankness, mixed with well-placed tact, is one of the personality weapons he uses to get results in his job as the space prime mover.

He was forthright in answering the Number-One question about manned space vehicles: does he favor the X-15, high-lift approach or the Mercury [retro-rocket and parachute] high-drag technique?

"When NACA became NASA," he said, "we underwent a change of function. We became an administrator of contracts, like Air Force. Mercury is our own design and development program, and we fund and build it. In a way, we are in competition [with the Air Force]."

But this well-ordered businessman type seemed to have plenty of room in his thinking for the X-15 as compared to Mercury. I noted on the mantel of his office a model of X-15 next to one of the Wright brothers airplane. There were just those two models on that shelf, and he spoke in favorable terms of the X-15 effort:

"X-15 represents one of a family of decisions. It will bring augmented knowledge at certain Mach numbers. The boys decided the frontier had to be pushed. . . . For space travel, we want to get away from the ballistic shape [Mercury capsule] to where we can have a little control. We will get some of this in the few minutes' flight of the X-15."

But, he said, Dynasoar, the next step beyond X-15, in effect an orbiting X-15, is going to extend the frontier well beyond X-15. "Dynasoar really gets to the inner face of space travel."

In good businessman fashion Glennan was thinking about costs: "It's getting to the place now where costs are going way up. It's my guess Dynasoar will cost four times this [the X-15]."

Glennan looked at his watch. It had been the kind of interview you would expect from the prime mover of our half-billion-dollar-a-year space agency: crisp and to the point.

THURSDAY, JULY 2. This afternoon I hauled aboard a beat-up old military DC-4 for the trip to California. It's been the usual long, wearing jaunt in an old vibrator, with the usual assortment of servicemen heading for West Coast duty: a crowd of airmen and swab jockies in bell-bottom trousers, and eight assorted officers.

We sat in pools of sweat in the old coffee grinder, waiting for take-off instructions, and additionally harried by a legal-minded crew chief who insisted we abide by the Air Force rule and keep our parachute harnesses on and fastened as well as our safety belts. The swabbie sitting next to me, sweltering in dress blues, started to unbuckle his harness and safety belt after we were airborne and practically at cruising altitude. The crew chief came by, glared, and said: "Not yet, Chief: safety belt and harness."

It's been that kind of trip. Most of the officers, at the tables at the front of the cabin, have been amusing themselves with a card game.

Now it's 8:25 P.M. Washington time, six hours after take-off, and we've just passed over a big river, which I think is the Mississippi.

I take advantage of the chance to talk to one of the officers, an ARDC type stationed at Edwards. He's a tall, lean lieutenant colonel with spiky gray hair named Russell, and he told me he had sometimes flown the mother ship that carried Yeager aloft in the X-1, and dropped him.

Russell seemed much abreast of the X-15 developments, and I asked him about the schedule. When did he think the first record runs, runs that would break the world records for speed and altitude, would be occurring?

"There might be some speed runs by September, with the Small Engine. The Big Engine might be flying by October—that's my guess —but really the record flights will depend on how wet the lake beds are."

He brought up a subject I hadn't thought about: that when the winter rains begin in southern California the most advanced space project can be at the mercy of an old-fashioned, antediluvian foe, the weather. Science has no answer for that one.

WEDNESDAY, JULY 8. The X-15 flight schedule has slipped again. My friends at North American tell me the wet flight won't be for two or three weeks, and of course the first powered flight will be somewhat after that.

I can't pinpoint the reason for the delay. It's the usual combination of changes and mechanical difficulties, my public-relations friends and engineering acquaintances tell me.

But my friends were failing me as sources of information—and I was not persistent enough in pursuing the truth. A catastrophe had befallen the first bird, an accident on the ground, while I was away in the East. A fouled hydrogen-peroxide line had set off an explosion, and the engine bay had been burned out before the fire could be extinguished. I didn't know it at the time, but engineers and technicians were working nights and Sundays to repair the damage. I might have known if I had been able to see the bird, but the work was kept secret.

When the hydrogen-peroxide line had blown and taken part of the engine compartment with it, a crewman had been injured, cut by the flying bits of steel, not critically. But the injury was also on the secret list. It was the first and only injury so far in the X-15 program.

Today at the North American factory I talked to Charlie Feltz, the chief engineer on the X-15 project, about the schedule of flights. I was wondering now about the record flights, and which, with the present rate of slippage, might be a long way off.

Feltz, a sane and down-to-earth man, reminded me that research aircraft programs always slip, because there are so many new, individual items that have to be checked out and made to run together. And on the record flights:

"By December 1, NASA should have the No. 1 Bird and maybe have flown three flights with it. By that time maybe they might have been to 150,000 feet, and Mach 3."

I asked about the Big Engine, and got the straight dope on that. (But not a peep about the explosion of Bird No. 1.) It has been held up by troubles with the ignition system: first, the metal was too thin, so the plates buckled in the heat and the cooling system didn't work. Feltz said the engine was scheduled for delivery in September, but it's delayed and he doesn't think it'll be flying until after January 1. A real disappointment, but the space business seems to be full of slipping schedules.

Raun Robinson, one of Feltz's two top assistants, gave me the inside story on the effect of the first X-15 landing after the glide flight. On that landing the nose came down so hard that "the struts bottomed and gave way at the pivot. We increased the resistance in the struts." This apparently is one reason the next flights have been slipping (still no word about the explosion).

TUESDAY, JULY 21. The "wet flight" has slipped some more, but I was told at the North American plant today that the engineers at Edwards have been going through a dress rehearsal with the ship on the ground and the test should be in a few days. (Looking back on this entry I can see the North American people must have transferred their efforts to the No. 2 Bird while Bird No. 1, the one that was damaged in the explosion, was being repaired.)

Today, since there is still to be a wait before the next flight, I managed to probe a little into the background of the X-15: I talked to one of the aerodynamics experts who has been with the program for four years, and I had a look at one of the North American wind tunnels where many of the bugs were ironed out.

The aerodynamics expert, Engineer Bill Johnston, a quiet, bespectacled man, told me the X-15 design hadn't been changed fundamentally since the company made its bid for the contract in early 1955. That bid was in response to NASA's request sent out to twelve plane builders. Four responded with bids: North American, Bell, Republic, and Douglas.

Johnston was one of the guiding lights of that early design, which has stood up so well thus far.

An engineer named Larry Greene, said Johnston, was the real

spark plug of the X-15 design. "He was the one who stirred up Mr. Rice [an engineering vice president] to let us do it. He could see it was elevating the sights of the company to build it." Greene was the aerodynamicist who had invented the so-called "coke-bottle" fuselage which added speed to the supersonic jets. Of the X-15 program he said: "It was a chance to get one step beyond everybody else."

Johnston said that NACA had already run wind-tunnel tests of somewhat similar designs in one-fiftieth-scale models in the wind tunnels at Langley. But these had different cathedral angles in the tail and they were low-wing instead of mid-wing; generally, they were much more like the X-1 and X-2 than the X-15. But Greene, Johnston, and another talented engineer named George Owl worked out the differential tail that slopes downward instead of upward, the elevons in it, and the stubby middle wing with swept-back front edge and straight rear edge.

"We started with two big fuel tanks, instrumentation bay, pilot compartment, and reasonable wing area, so you could get launch and a decent gliding angle, and enough strength.

"Our planning centered around minimum weight in an aerodynamic configuration that would represent the future, but not so advanced that we would get caught."

We visited the three North American wind tunnels. In one of them a good deal of developmental work on X-15 was done.

It was the hypersonic tunnel; and like many another up-to-date rocket item, it had German roots. In fact, it was a copy of a German wind tunnel built in 1939.

This original tunnel had been built by Dornberger's people in Kochel, in the Bavarian Alps, and, as one might guess, it had been used in tests of the great German missile, the A-4 or V-2.

Externally, the hypersonic tunnel building looks like two huge globes or spheres with a small house in the middle, a sort of mammoth dumbbell. The test chamber where the wind rushes through at trisonic speeds, of course, is in the small house. The wind is generated by an ingenious vacuum principle, so the cumbersome old propeller mechanism is left out.

The chamber itself is small, only about as big as a grocery carton. The models of X-15 tested in it were a foot long and cost about $20,000 each.

Bob Spangler, one of the test engineers working around the tunnel, said this kind of tunnel helped solve many of the aerodynamic problems of the V-2. When our forces overran Bavaria, he added, they brought back the design, and there are copies in England as well as here.

"Probably also in Russia," Spangler said, "because the Russians have written reports using exactly the same Mach numbers: 1.56, 2.84, and 3.24."

The North American copy was finished in 1948, and has been used for data since 1949. Besides helping with X-15, it has been used in the design of the F-100, the 107, 108, and North American's missile, the Navaho.

Tests with X-15 models in the hypersonic tunnel, coupled with runs in tunnels at NASA's Langley and Ames facilities, at M.I.T. and Caltech's Supersonic Aerodynamics Laboratory, changed many of the design details of the X-15 before the first lick of work in the factory.

Jim Kagawa, a senior wind-tunnel engineer of Japanese extraction, listed some of those changes wrought by wind-tunnel work: "Changes in the vertical tail—how much to be below and above the wind. And in the side fairings: changing the size and shape helped stability."

We went on from the tunnel to the North American model shop, where the expensive tunnel models are fabricated. Some of them, apparently of the secret B-70 and F-108, were hastily covered before we came in.

Looking at some of the less-secret models, I could see why they are so expensive: besides being made exactly to scale, they have to be instrumented with pressure taps and thermocouples and controls, so that all kinds of readings can be made during a "flight." The models would probably be a disappointment to a boy used to making scale models for decoration. These wind-tunnel models are built for instrumentation, not to show detail.

Before I left Bill Johnston I asked his opinion about the danger of the next X-15 mission, the so-called "wet flight."

"It shouldn't be especially dangerous," Johnston answered. "They've been through it on the ground in the dress rehearsal. And the B-52 has flown with a load equivalent in fuel on that side, so we know the plane can be taken off with the load."

That was spoken, I thought, like an engineer: if so-and-so is simulated, and such-and-such happens, then the test will be all right. Which, after all, is all you can say without actually making the test. But there's many a slip between the simulator and the flight. That's where the test pilot comes in, the man who puts his neck in where heretofore only the slide rule and the computing machines have been operating.

FRIDAY, JULY 24. This morning at five forty-five, checking with the North American dispatcher, I was told there would be a delay of possibly four hours in the take-off of the B-52/X-15 combination for the wet flight. Take-off had been scheduled for 0800. One of the routine delays had set in. I've concluded that in rocket tests the routine is that there shall be a delay. The unexpected and abnormal is for something to happen on time.

At any rate, by ten o'clock I was up at Edwards, and at the NASA building, where from now on the headquarters for most of the X-15 flights will be set up.

Today, for the first time, Q. C. Harvey had set up his Master Control in the NASA building. This is a sign of progress, foreshadowing the time when NASA will be masterminding the tests.

Q. C., Blake Staub, and others of the engineering high command were sitting in the master console room of the NASA installation. They sat in a row of secretaries' chairs, facing a wall of instrumentation where some of the telemetering information will be coming in from the X-15 in flight. In the middle of the wall were two charts on which telemetered information will trace the course of future flights with a stylus. There is no window, as there is at the corresponding North American installation; but the telemetering and the radio are really the window on the flight. Q. C. and several of the others wore headphones, and a loud-speaker also broadcast the calls from the B-52/X-15 combination.

A crowd of rubbernecks, some with official business and some officially attached but not working, waited around for the great event. To get out of the way, I went on up to the NASA tower, half a flight above, where two men and a woman sat and looked out through wide windows at the sky. Other buildings obscured the main runway and the B-52, which was somewhere to the south.

The woman, a small, gray-haired figure in a flowered dress, was making notes and listening to the calls with an earphone. She was Mrs. Della Mae Bolling, secretary to Joe Vensel, chief of the Flight Operations Division here at NASA. The two men, in sports shirts, were engineers Roy Bryant and Milt Thompson, both making notes on the flight from the radio calls.

I heard the voice of Bill Berkowitz, the launch operator, calling from the B-52: "We'll be taking off in about five minutes."

Then Scott's voice: "Bill, would you cut the peroxide?"

The time was 11:15 A.M. Mrs. Bolling, who is NASA's X-15 chief of communications, fiddled with a dictaphone belt. She records the radio calls on tape and later carefully transcribes them.

At eleven-twenty somebody on the B-52 said: "Airborne." And one of the onlookers at the NASA tower yelled:

"Attababy!"

We saw the B-52 climbing into the sky on the north side of the hangars. The sixth mission of X-15, the captive "wet flight," was on.

And it went well, without mishap—as Engineer Bill Johnston had predicted it would. At 38,000 feet and 250 knots, Scott Crossfield summed it up:

"We're fat today, buddy."

The vital point in today's flight was the test of the top-off mechanism, the pumps and plumbing which were to keep the lox tank filled, replacing the volatile stuff as it boiled off.

This worked well, right up to the critical time of the simulated launch—which was the requirement.

There was still one more hurdle to cross: the test of the various jettison mechanisms, including the dumping of the big tanks.

At twelve-fifteen, watching the B-52/X-15 ensemble high up, I saw a new white stream springing into life among the contrails of the aircraft.

Q. C. Harvey was saying on the radio: "Stop your jettison now."

"Stopping jettison now."

The big bomber swept in for a landing at twelve thirty-one. This had been an hour-and-a-half mission.

On the way out, through the master console room, I saw Walt Williams and Stormy Storms among the crowd. Like the others, they seemed very content.

Storms summed it up: "Best captive flight we've had yet."

THURSDAY, JULY 30. Heading out into the Pacific on a trip unrelated to the X-15 story, I called Dick Barton and asked when the first powered flight will be.

"It's off till Saturday or Monday," he said. "Maybe later."

I said cynically—and hopefully—that I would bet it wouldn't be till we got back from the trip. Dick allowed there could be that much slippage.

TUESDAY, AUGUST 18. Back from the trip, I called Barton and asked about the powered flight.

"Might be next week," he said. "But probably not till after Labor Day."

It seems the bird has been plagued with a lot of bugs—mainly in the plumbing system. With so many liquids at such low temperatures, valves and joints cause special new problems. One set of problems, Dick says, arise because for the first time cold helium (more than 290 degrees below zero) is being used to pressure the lox and the fuel, water alcohol, toward the combustion chamber. The high-speed turbopumps pick up the fuel and lox and feed them into the chamber, but the helium has to start the job. Leaky valves are a source of trouble, too, in the other plumbing systems: pipes and valves for nitrogen at 300 degrees below zero, the volatile hydrogen peroxide, and, of course, the vast quantity of 300-below-zero liquid oxygen—10,000 pounds of it, 1,000 gallons.

WEDNESDAY, AUGUST 26. This afternoon I checked with Barton about the flight scheduled for tomorrow, and was told it has slipped again—to Friday. The blasted pipes again!

LANCASTER, FRIDAY, AUGUST 28. The clan of newsmen descended on the Caravan Inn again last night, for the flight. But most of us went to bed relatively early, because we had to be out at Edwards Air Force Headquarters at 0600, and that is forty-five minutes' drive from Lancaster.

A long procession of cars, TV trucks, and Air Force vehicles took the newsmen to the 7,000-foot mark on the main runway, to watch the take-off.

But there was a hold, then another hold, and at nine fifty-five Colonel Brown announced to us:

"Fellas—there'll be a thirty-minute delay. There's a small leak in the hydrogen-peroxide system."

At ten twenty-five an indefinite hold was announced, and a few minutes later the colonel told us the flight had been canceled for today.

At eleven-fifteen Earl Blount told us the flight was now to be flown next Tuesday. And he told me the details of today's holdup:

"There was an APU leak somewhere in the hydrogen-peroxide plumbing. So they were trying to get at it with the small access door, instead of the big access door. The bigger door would take longer to unfasten, they figured. But when they started working on the small access door, they found the bolts were frozen. They worked over an hour on it."

That, it seems, is usually the way with highly sophisticated, much-automated scientific machinery such as X-15: the simplest things such as a leaky valve or a frozen bolt can stop it cold.

Scott Crossfield, freshly showered and wearing a trim business suit, came into the Air Force pressroom for a moment to be interviewed.

A newsman asked him about the defect in the ship.

"It's not a defect," he said indignantly. "It's just the debugging you do with a brand-new car."

Another newshawk asked him about his feelings when he had to abort the mission this morning.

"I'm disappointed, the way everybody else is disappointed." He paused. "This [the X-15] has been my life for the past six years."

Before I left Edwards I got hold of the mission schedule Crossfield would have fulfilled today and is now scheduled to carry out Tuesday. I turned to the pilot's card, which elaborately details all the moves he must make:

No.	Time (minute)	Event
9	4:05	50,000 feet 2 M.N. [Mach Number 2, 1320 mph] Cut three [rocket] chambers. Pitch pulse, yaw pulse, roll 0 to 45 to 0 [degrees] constant heading side slip.
10	4:45	2.4 g Constant M.N. wind up turn to burnout then 3.2 g. Head Edwards X—9 degrees. Do not exceed 15 degrees.
11		Burnout . . . jettison residual propellents.
12	5:05	Glide data maneuvers (roll and yaw modes 240 k [knots] at pilot's discretion) center stick evaluation [probably a reminder to fly on the center control stick, not the wrist-control side stick. Some of the engineers had contended he porpoised more than he had to on the glide flight, because he insisted on flying with the side stick].
13	12:00	Landing.

This kind of thing, I knew, would be much in Crossfield's mind between now and Tuesday. Also, whether the changes in the control linkage and the repairs on the SAS system would give, as the engineers promised, better control reaction than on the glide flight. If so, he would be the one who would have to prove it, at the risk of smashing up the bird and himself. I didn't envy Crossfield the time he would be thinking about all this; especially the long hours in the steaming hotbox of the cockpit, waiting for take-off—as this morning.

FRIDAY, SEPTEMBER 4. The powered flight slipped from yesterday to today, and today we of the press party were out beside the main runway at Edwards a few minutes after seven in the morning. The B-52 was off at seven-sixteen, and we went on down to the press position on the edge of the lake bed, near the agglomeration of emergency vehicles and official cars around the mobile-control van.

We watched the assemblage of contrails in the blue, the B-52 and X-15 ahead, and the trailing chase planes. At seven thirty-seven I heard the mobile-control speaker system say: "Twenty-five minutes to launch."

Lieutenant John Kirkley announced on the public-address system at the press knoll: "We're estimating twenty-five minutes to launch." And Earl Blount told me, "Everything is going well."

And so it went, through the countdown up to the "ten minutes to launch" call. But then there was no more countdown, and Kirkley passed on the word that the mission had again aborted.

At the pressroom, afterward, we were told by Blount that plumbing trouble was again responsible for the scrubbing of the mission. This time it was a regulator between the helium and lox systems, six minutes before the drop. The clue was that the helium pressure gauge was reading low. "I don't know when the flight will be reinstated," he said. "Probably no earlier than late next week."

Again Crossfield came in to face the press, not looking very worn, considering the intense strain he has been under for at least a week.

Facing the TV cameras, the radio mikes, and the fourth estate, he seemed relaxed for the moment as he explained what had gone wrong this time: "The lox tank is pressurized by the expulsion system [helium]. The regulator wasn't working properly. We decided to abort the mission . . . about four minutes from release."

I asked him about the low-pressure reading on the helium. "The gauge reads from 1 to 50," he said. But he didn't say what his reading had been (it was about 6).

He seemed to be getting a little impatient when someone asked if he had thought about dropping anyway, even though his helium reading was low.

"You don't deliberately go into emergency procedure," he said shortly, meaning that you don't launch unless everything checks out; that you wouldn't start a flight with a known hazard such as a leaky helium system. That was certainly understandable: there are plenty of things that can go wrong during the flight, even if everything checks out well at the start.

TUESDAY, SEPTEMBER 15. Today I had word that the first powered flight is scheduled again, for day after tomorrow.

And today Premier Khrushchev of the USSR arrived in Washington for his state visit. One of the first things he did was to talk on TV about Russia's recent Lunik II moon shot, which apparently hit the moon. There are persistent reports from various European cities that the Russians are going to try to fire a man or men into orbit during K's visit. Space conquest continues to be an international political issue and propaganda weapon. It's good that we have one space item, the first powered X-15 flight, scheduled to happen during Khrushchev's stay here.

THURSDAY, SEPTEMBER 17. At seven twenty-five, after the usual preliminaries of a mission, we saw the orange tail of the B-52 moving toward the far end of the main runway. We had made a mistake and gone to the wrong place, the edge of the lake bed instead of the edge of the runway, in anticipation that the B-52 would take off from the lake. It fooled us—it took off from the runway. But it didn't matter: the first powered flight after many aborts was on its way.

Soon the multiple contrails of the X-15 armada, the B-52 and the three chase planes, were curving around the high sky to the north. I edged over toward the mobile-control van and listened for the calls. At seven fifty-three:

"Disconnect the power unit from the control truck and let's get ready here . . . thirteen minutes to launch."

Colonel Brown echoed the call on the public-address system at the press knoll:

"At 38,000 feet . . . estimating thirteen minutes to launch."

At eight-four I heard the mobile-control squawk box saying: "We have estimated three minutes to drop." I watched the comb of the contrails chalking the sky over the desert to the west, about where the little settlement of Rosamond would be.

The radio speaker of the mobile-control group seemed to grow faint, possibly because the wind was shifting. The last I could get was Scott calling out his bearing temperatures. But I picked up the calls later on from the tape:

At eight-six Scott said: "Ready to go." At the same time Colonel Brown was saying on the press-knoll public-address system:

"One minute to drop."

A few seconds later Major Charlie Bock, the B-52 pilot, was calling out the countdown: "Three, two, one—*drop.*"

Colonel Brown trumpeted: "He's off! Got a light!"

Watching the B-52 with my binoculars, I saw the new white streak of a fresh contrail below it, a contrail that I knew was fattened by the surging power of the X-15 rocket engines. Almost immediately the plump white blazon began to pull ahead of the trails of the B-52 and the chase planes. Rapidly it leaped across the sky, outdistancing the others, and angling upward. But we couldn't hear the sound of the rocket engine—it was too far off and there were too many other engines in the sky.

"Heading uphill at 33,000 feet," Crossfield called in.

"Roger," the control center acknowledged.

"Looks good across the board," Crossfield reported.

"Roger."

"Mach No. 1 [660 mph] and climbing through 35."

"Roger."

Now, at eight-eight, the X-15 seemed to be leaving a double trail, a good thick track. The X-15 was pulling way out of the range of the following airplanes. The B-52 lumbered far behind, like an old mother hen. As the X-15 trail curved, a couple of the chase planes turned more sharply, trying to cut across the radius of the circle; and still they lagged far to the rear.

The rocket ship seemed to be leveling off, and about this time Crossfield called in: "There's a little buffet or sound. I don't know what it is."

Now the white trail of the rocket ship was really ahead of the others, in a whole separate sky to the east, and turning so that he would not be too far from the lake bed when burnout came—which would be soon.

In a minute Scott reported about the ominous buffet or sound, somewhat shamefacedly: "The noise I get is my head touching and getting these vibrations from the windshield." His helmet, wedged into the steep V of the glass in the canopy, was vibrating with the tremulous power of the rocket ship.

Now, suddenly, the X-15 had lost its fat white tail and disappeared somewhere in the blue: burnout had come. I searched for the ship, finally found it catching sunlight: it looked bright in the sun, not black, but it would be the X-15 in that position, angling around the northern sky and descending toward the lake bed.

Now that the landing was imminent, the chase planes curved wildly down the corridor of the sky, breaking their necks to get into position where they could talk Crossfield down to his contact with the ground. Even if the glass in his canopy is perfectly clear, visibility through the tiny panes is restricted, and the X-15 pilot needs an external check.

I missed the dropping of the lower ventral tail—for that moment the speck of the X-15 had bounced out of the field of my high-powered glasses. Then I caught the ship again, suddenly close enough so that I could see the stub-needle shape of it, coming in silently, a glider slipping toward the lake bed.

The horrid shuttering noise of two helicopters was drowning everything else: they were the two rescue choppers laid on for today's flight, knocking themselves out to be on hand for the emergency if one should develop on the landing.

One of the chase planes, the rake-tailed F-104 which would be carrying Captain Bob White, the first Air Force pilot, had managed to fall onto the tail of the black needle. His high orange tail was right on top of the X-15. I supposed that now that the rocket ship was gliding in for the landing, White at the controls of the hot 104 was having a hard time going slowly enough. Although the X-15 is probably as hot a glider as ever flew, the 104 would have trouble slowing down that much while keeping power on, and avoiding stalling out.

At right about this time White was calling out to Crossfield:

"Nice and easy, Daddy. You're showing 210 [knots]. Very fine . . . very good."

Then, a few feet from the shiny lake-bed surface, Crossfield popped down the steel landing skids under his tail, dropped the rubber wheel of the nose gear.

We saw him impact, spraying up dust like the bow wave of a boat. The nose held up high for a second, but not so high as on that wavering, porpoising first landing, then it came down into the lake bed smoothly, almost gently.

The ship slid along on a true line and seemed to slow down suddenly.

"Very good," was what White was saying at this juncture. "Very good . . . real nice."

To which Scott responded: "What do you expect from the old pro, Daddy-o?"

The time was eight-sixteen and a half, ten minutes after drop. There had been three minutes of powered flight.

Immediately the caravan clustered around the mobile-control van —fire engines, rescue crane, a flood of green North American sedans and blue Air Force sedans and trucks—rushed out toward the settling dust trail the X-15 had made on the lake bed. (It ended only about 100 yards from a drainage ditch that would have wrecked the rocket ship.)

Before we climbed into our own cars to go to the pressroom, where we would have an audience with Scott Crossfield after his debriefing, I noticed that in the settling dust two high-bowed fire trucks were standing very close to the X-15, their red blinkers glittering. I wondered if something was wrong. But no fire was visible. (Later, we found out that a fuel-line leak had sprayed alcohol into the engine bay and a hot but invisible fire was burning. It did considerable damage to the engines and the plumbing. Crossfield and the engineers were heartsick, feeling there might be indefinite delays as a result. But by dint of strenuous efforts, the damage was repaired in twenty-three days.)

I bummed a ride back to the pressroom with Colonel Brown. He was exuberant about the flight. "He was right on the money," the colonel said happily.

At the pressroom, shortly before ten, Earl Blount brought on Crossfield, in a gray business suit. He also introduced North American's X-15 project engineer, Charlie Feltz, to the nucleus of microphones, the ring of reporters, cameras, and lights.

Someone asked Crossfield about his maximum altitude and another reporter inquired about his speed.

"Speed well in excess of Mach 2," he answered. "Altitude in excess of 50,000 feet."

"Was the performance better than you expected?"

"Slightly better than expected."

"What was your landing speed?"

"About 200 knots. About like last time."

"How was the acceleration?"

"I hit higher speed sooner than I expected."

"What was the noise that bothered you—did you find out what made it?"

"Yeah—I found it. I was leaning my head against the windshield."

Knowing that Scott's insistence on flying with the side-control stick on the glide flight had caused some complaint among the engineers, I asked what control stick he used this time.

"Flew on the main stick and the side stick," he answered. He had played it safe.

"Could you hear the engines up there?"

Crossfield smiled. "I could hear the engines all right." From the ground, we hadn't been able to hear his engines once.

Someone asked what Crossfield thought of the X-15 now that he had flown it under power.

"As soon as I went supersonic, I knew this aircraft was designed for high-speed performance."

A couple of reporters wanted him to be more specific about his speed and altitude.

"Twice the speed of sound at that altitude is in excess of 1,300 to 1,400 miles an hour."

"How much faster than Mach 2 did you go?"

"Our speed was 5 to 10 per cent more than we anticipated."

He was asked when he turned on his rocket engines: "I had two cylinders going before I cleared the fuselage of the B-52—and the other six going within three to five seconds. They were turned on at one-eighth intervals. (In other words, he flicked the switches of the eight barrels one at a time.)

There were some more questions, about the landing—whether it was what was expected, whether the nose came down with a force of seven gs as expected. "Less than expected."

Then Scott was summing up: "The engineers, the technicians, the crew—they're the ones who fly the airplane." And there was a repetition of a favorite theme, that he as a North American pilot was not concerned with breaking records in the X-15, but "Our job is to mechanically demonstrate the systems in the airplane."

Then the conference was ending, Blount folding it up. I asked him about the schedule, and when the Big Engine would be arriving. He said he really didn't know yet. (No wonder, since the secret fire in the engine bay must have thrown off all the North American calculations at this point.) But one fact is undeniable: the X-15 has flown as a rocket ship. It is a going bird.

TUESDAY, SEPTEMBER 29. Since there doesn't seem to be any X-15 flight scheduled for a while, I decided to go up to Edwards and try to fill in some of the background while we're all waiting. I've been particularly anxious to find out more about the two pilots who will be entrusted with the record flights: Air Force's Bob White and NASA's Joe Walker. I've also wanted to get a sort of status report on the X-15 program, as of this juncture.

I found Bob White in his little cubbyhole of an office down at the Air Force Flight Test facility on the edge of the taxiway. White, as impeccably neat and bright-eyed as every time I have seen him, was wearing a flying suit. He's really a working pilot: today he was schooling himself again, as many times before, by flying the 104 in the dirty configuration, to simulate the landing characteristics of the X-15.

When I saw White and told him I wanted to get more facts about him, to fill out his biography, he smiled and said: "I thought we'd already done that."

I told him our last brief talk hadn't given me nearly enough background about him. I said that since he and Walker would be making the record-breaking flights, the world would be wanting to know a good deal about both of them—so a lot of writers would be eager to talk to him.

"Wasn't the last time enough?" White was incredulous. The last interview had been a most cursory outline, a kind of military summation. But White, emerging for the first time into a position of potential world prominence, doesn't yet know the meaning of this in terms of his personal life, he doesn't know how curious the world will be about his every move, when he starts flying into space.

One thing I hadn't yet inquired about was Mrs. White. Bob said she had lived in New York, came from Wilkes-Barre, Pennsylvania, and they had met through friends when he was studying at NYU for his degree in electrical engineering.

At that time, Doris Allen (Mrs. White) was working as a dental assistant. They were married in 1948. Bob was studying under the GI Bill, and keeping up his reserve status with a busy program of instructing flying students. He didn't say anything about this matter, but he must have had a strong sense of duty to keep up with such an active reserve program—especially in the slack years right after World War II, when military activity had a minimum of public encouragement in this country. Also, with the memory of a German prison camp fresh in his memory. He had been shot down and captured in February 1945, when on a strafing mission with the 355th Fighter Group.

The impression that White has a strong sense of duty is confirmed again and again through his life. He stayed with the reserve outfit (514th Troop Carrier Command) until the Korean War, and was willing to go over as one of the pilots for the antiquated C-46 transports of the outfit. But he was pleasantly surprised when the personnel officer of his reserve wing told him, as Bob remembers it:

"I'm sorry I have to pick you up and send you as a fighter pilot—because of your experience in World War II."

At this juncture, White says, "I didn't say anything, but I laughed to myself."

Bob was still happy when he went to Korea, happy that he was going as a fighter pilot, not the driver of an aerial truck.

He was assigned to the 35th Fighter Interceptor Wing, an F-51 outfit that had the mission of defending the Japanese homeland. Later the wing was re-equipped with Lockheed F-80s, early operational jet fighters. Bob served out his time in Japan—saw no combat because the wing had the mission of protecting our airfields and installations in Japan.

When the war was over, he came home and, because of his electrical-engineering training, was assigned to an Air Force electronics development center, at Rome, New York.

From there White managed to move to a branch of the service which he had decided was for him: the experimental flight-test facility at Edwards. But the way he did it was typical: "I applied under Air Force regulations."

White was shifted to the Test Pilot School at Edwards, graduated without any undue trouble in 1954, and was assigned as experimental test pilot at Edwards in 1955. He worked as a test pilot on some of the hot "Century class" jet fighters: the F-102 and F-105; "and also, partially," stating it with his usual modesty, "on the 101, 104, 106, and 107."

In early 1958, when the Air Force Manned Space Program got under way at Edwards [to fly X-15 and its successors], Kincheloe and his commanders chose Bob White and Bob Rushworth as his No. 1 and No. 2 back-up pilots. The choice was approved by Brigadier General Marcus Cooper, commanding the Edwards Test Center, and then by Lieutenant General Sam Anderson, the head man for the Air Research and Development Command of Air Force in Washington. Kinch, who was heir apparent to the throne of the Air Force King of Space because of his X-2 flights, was only a captain but he had a way with generals as well as with the flight-line mechanics and they tended to give him his head. And his choice for No. 1 back-up—I have heard this from people close to General Carpenter—was White. Besides being well educated in engineering and sharp mentally, White was, and is, a dogged hard worker and a good flier, and furthermore, as with Kinch, he looked, and looks, the part of No. 1 Space Pilot. He is handsome, clean-looking, alert, physically fit—and he has the drive a man in his position should have. The drive in White's case is strongly religious: he's a devoted Roman Catholic, his wife is the same, and they want their children to have the proper Catholic sense of duty and moral obligation.

At the time Kinch chose him to be back-up, Bob and Doris White had two children, Gregory, three, and Pamela, one. (A third child, Maureen, was born in 1955.) The White family had moved into one of a line of Edwards government houses in Thirteenth Street, one of a grid pattern of officers' and NCO's dwellings plunked onto the face of the desert near the runways and the lake beds.

I told White I wanted very much to meet his family and see his home—that the reading public would be very much interested in knowing about these things. He was puzzled, and seemed again to be surprised by this new phase of his life as premier rocket pilot.

"Does it really make that much difference?" he asked, still feeling his way along in an unfamiliar environment. I assured him that it did, that the visit would involve only a few minutes, and at his family's convenience; and he said okay, still somewhat dubiously. At least he is willing to tackle all duties involved with his job. He is openminded on the subject, as contrasted with, say, Crossfield, who has decided to use every acceptable means to curtail information about his personal and family life.

Kincheloe didn't have any such restrictive principles, and White, following dutifully in Kinch's contrails, seems willing to do as Kinch would have done if he had survived.

Joe Walker, the No. 1 NASA pilot for the X-15, seems to have the same openmindedness on the subject as Bob White (and, from what I hear, as Bob Rushworth, White's back-up). I went by the NASA installation this afternoon to see Joe Walker and to get caught up on some of the vital personal information about this NASA lead pilot, who will be one of the first men into space under the X-15 program.

Walker is already more experienced in the space business than White. He has flown many rocket flights, the first X-1s, the X-1A, and the X-1B, and the Douglas D-558 or Skyrocket, the first aircraft to fly Mach 2. Once, Joe and the crew members of the mother ship B-29 were decorated when the X-1A exploded on a flight, still attached to the mother plane. Then Joe scrambled out of the cockpit of the X-1A, and helped to jettison the rocket ship before it should also destroy the mother plane and crew. (In those days, the rocket ships were carried under the mother ship's bomb bay. The pilot mounted the rocket ship from inside the bigger plane.)

Walker is thirty-eight, with graying, curly hair, blue eyes, a flashing, quick smile, a weathered face—and, in general, the rugged look of a farm boy, which he was. He told me he had been one of four brothers on a farm near Washington, Pennsylvania. The elder Walker had a dairy and grew grain and hay and truck-farming crops.

Joe learned to fly early in his life—like all of the X-15 pilots—and was also educationally qualified to be a scientist. He earned a degree in physics at Washington and Jefferson College in his home town.

He studied flying under the Civilian Pilot Training program while at Washington and Jefferson in 1941. He had trouble getting into the flight-training program because his grades weren't high enough.

"At first they wouldn't let me do the CPT," he said, "because I had a C average. They thought my schedule was too heavy: I worked at home [on the farm] and as a lab assistant in physics. But when I had the CPT, my grades went up. It was better to do both the CPT and the other jobs than one alone. It seemed to blow the cobwebs out of my head—when I was flying."

Joe has found that combination effective ever since. The flying seems to give him fresh mental energy and clarity.

When World War II broke over the United States, Joe already had considerable experience in pilotage, and went overseas as an Air Corps second lieutenant with a P-38 fighter squadron in North Africa and later Italy.

The mission of the squadron was mostly reconnaissance for fighter strikes, specifically, getting weather and target information. "I was a seeing-eye dog on the Ploesti mission," Joe said, summing up one of his most exciting military jobs at the beginning of our bombing effort to blast Hitler's great Rumanian oil fields.

When the war was over, Walker felt the same confusion and lack of direction that befell many World War II pilots. There were too many pilots for the civilian flying jobs then available and the public had turned its back on supporting a large defense establishment.

Joe got out of the military. "I found out that the best job they had figured out for me was as a BT-13 [basic flight training] instructor."

NACA at this juncture had an arrangement with the Air Forces to screen the flying officers who might be of some scientific utility. They combed through Joe Walker's record and offered him a job as a physicist on a P-1 or junior contract.

"The salary was $2,000 a year," Joe recalls. "I'd been getting $3,600 in the Air Force."

But the job didn't last very long. Walker was assigned to NACA's Lewis laboratory at Cleveland airport, and there, during the first few days of his new job, he heard "a sound that got me right here, a P-38 engine firing up."

"I went over and there was Joe Vensel [now the head of test operations at NASA's station at Edwards]. They were doing some research in the ice tunnel. It happened there was an opening—junior pilot of the lot—ice research on the C-82 and B-24s."

Walker worked there in the research program to find out about wing icing at altitudes, both in the ice tunnel and in flight. And it was in Cleveland that Joe met the girl who was to be his wife, Grace, at one of the social functions of the Lakewood Presbyterian Church. Grace was a schoolteacher, teaching third grade, and both were members of a young professional people's club sponsored by the church. They were married in 1948, and now have three children.

In 1951, when the Walkers had only one child, son Tommy, Joe managed to arrange a chance to work on the Xs at Edwards.

"When we came here, No. 1 [*Glamorous Glennis,* the X-1 which Yeager had flown through the sonic wall] was already in the Smithsonian, and the D-558-11 [the Skyrocket] had been converted to all-rocket, and was air-launched [from a mother B-29]. The first aircraft I flew was the B-29 mother ship.

"I flew the D-558-1 [the jet-powered Skystreak], the D-558-11 [Skyrocket], the X-5, X-3—also the F-84, 86, through the 100, 102, 104—and the X-1s. The X-3 is the worst flying airplane I ever flew—and the most underpowered."

I knew that the X-3, a needle-nosed, stub-winged missile, was about the same size and configuration as the X-15, although no decent rocket engine was available for it, and it staggered along with two jet engines. In flying that difficult bird and the X-1s, Walker had an excellent background for X-15.

I asked him about Bob White's background for X-15, and Joe pointed out that although White hasn't yet had any rocket flights, he's been very active in the testing of the century-class jet fighters, which have characteristics in many ways like the rocket ships. Also, since his appointment as Kincheloe's back-up pilot, White has been practicing with the 104s in "dirty configuration" to simulate the X-15 landing characteristics, and with the 107, which has a side-stick control system somewhat like X-15's.

One of Walker's exploits, the one which was given national notice in 1955, was coping with an X-1A explosion just before a scheduled aerial launch. For that bit of quick thinking and bravery, he won a NACA citation and a NACA Distinguished Service Medal.

I asked him about it, and he told the story frankly and openly, speaking with a strange combination of country phraseology and the polysyllables of Greek derivation (like parameter and extrapolate) which the space scientists like to use.

Joe speaks with high volume, and one gathers the impression that he also enjoys using backwoods slang where he can.

"It was about in August 1955. The X-1A was in the launch check-off process. We had the propellant systems pressurized—70 seconds from launch—when kerbloom!

"I believe the operation I accomplished then was the shut-off valve. By throwing that switch, I got an unusual sort of noise. I remember being surprised, as if your pet dog suddenly decided to bite you.

"The lox tank blew out in the bottom rear. If it'd blowed out the top it would have blowed the X-1A off the airplane. I saw all the white vapor around the outside. I checked around over the gauges, to find out what happened. We'd obviously lost pressurizing gas.

"The crew was lookin' from above—wavin' for me to get out of there. I was tryin' to dump cockpit pressure—the crew wavin' for me to hurry up. I remember bein' impressed with the fact I wasn't gettin' out as fast as I should.

"I got the lid [canopy] off. I undid the straps and had trouble navigatin' out of the hole [cockpit] to the B-29 cabin with my pressure suit, helmet, and parachute.

"I came flyin' in on all fours. In a way it was a comedy. While I was strugglin' around lookin' for a walk-around bottle, I give out [passed out for lack of oxygen].

"I had the whole deal [oxygen bottle]. It just needed to be plugged in. They were tryin' to do it. [And they did, and brought Joe back to life.] Then I woke up and started all over again.

"We determined the amount of damage. The landing gear was hangin' down. It blowed the gear open.

"The bomb shackles [holding the X-1A] were out of line. It [the rocket ship] was leaking peroxide—and there was a full tank of water alcohol in the back end. They combined for an extremely hazardous condition.

"One thing was—we had an ejection seat in there that there was only one of. We thought we should save it.

"I got back in the hole and tried to jettison the fuel. We made like we were gonna remove the seat: we knew we could pull that seat up if we could arm a couple of things. But the scanner reported he could smell cooking peroxide.

"So they [ground control] told us to go over the bombing range and drop it [the X-1A]. They were worried about, one, another explosion or, two, bungin' up the B-29. There were seven [men] in the B-29 and I.

"We slowed the airplane [the B-29] in a glide and did a 1-g pull up to minimize lift. At the same time we yanked the release—we had to use the emergency release. With all that weight back in the tail, we were not particularly interested in havin' it [the X-1A] fly back up into us.

"It fell nicely. Then it came up into a loop and flipped back and augered in."

I asked Joe about the times he had trouble with another bane of the high-speed test pilot's professional life—inertia coupling.

He said this aerodynamic catastrophe had overtaken him twice once in testing the XF-102, the other time in the X-3.

"In both cases the airplane was wildly out of control for about ten to fifteen seconds," he said. "It happened because we had too high a roll rate. We achieved a roll rate high enough to trigger pitch and yaw [which is to say, inertia coupling]."

Joe found a solution in doing what the rocket pilots call a "J.C. maneuver," i.e., taking your hands off the controls and putting the aircraft into the hands of a supernatural power. Test Pilot Joe Lynch is usually credited with contriving that phrase one time in 1950 when he was flying the F-86 in a demonstration at Nellis Air Force Base, and inertia coupling had set in. Joe Lynch came out of his trouble by releasing his controls, and so did Joe Walker.

A lot of know-how has been learned from all the bouts with inertia coupling, Joe said. "Some of that know-how is in the X-15 lower ventral and stability augmentation system."

I asked Joe about the house he had built for his family and he seemed as proud of it as his valuable work with the rocket ships.

The sequence camera shows how the X-15 lands on Rogers Dry Lake bed. Instead of wheels, the rocket ship utilizes skids under the horizontal stabilizer to absorb the first landing shock. The nose gear is conventional. Photographs, starting at upper right, are in sequence from right to left. (*Courtesy North American Aviation, Inc.*)

ABOVE: X-15 in flight. Note rocket tubes functioning. White patch forward of wing is lox condensation. *(Official U. S. Air Force Photo)*.
BELOW: Three of the X-15 pilots with Richard Tregaskis, beside XLR-11 engine, with carrier-plane B-52 in background. *Left to right:* Neil A. Armstrong, of NASA; Major Robert M. White, U.S.A.F., first Air Force pilot; Joseph A. Walker, first NASA pilot; the author. *(Walton Tregaskis Photo)*

The first powered flight of the X-15, September 17, 1959. ABOVE: Just after launching from B-52 mother ship. BELOW: Later in flight, during which the rocket ship reached an altitude above 50,000 feet and speeds in excess of 1,300 mph. *(Courtesy North American Aviation, Inc.)*

Monitoring the first powered flight of the X-15 in the monitor console room at the NASA Flight Research Center. In center, wearing white shirt, is Q. C. Harvey, flight-test director for North American Aviation, Inc. *(NASA Photo)*

February 28, 1960: Brigadier General John W. Carpenter III, U.S.A.F., commander of the Air Force Flight Test Center, accepts the turnover of the X-15 from Harrison Storms *(left)* of North American Aviation, Inc. After the Air Force acceptance, General Carpenter transferred the rocket ship to Paul F. Bikle *(center)*, Director of NASA's Flight Research Center at Edwards Air Force Base. *(Official U.S. Air Force Photo)*

X-15 Bird No. 3 after explosion of Big Engine, June 9, 1960. Panels were removed from forward part of ship for inspection. *(Official U.S. Air Force Photo)*

The X-15, piloted by Joseph A. Walker of NASA, drops to a landing after setting a new world's speed record of 2,196 mph, August 4, 1960. Chase plane is seen above and beyond the X-15. *(Official U.S. Air Force Photo)*

NASA test pilot Joseph A. Walker in the cockpit of the X-15 just after landing from the world's record speed flight on August 4, 1960, when he reached 2,196 mph. *(Official U.S. Air Force Photo)*

The X-15, piloted by Captain Robert M. White, on its flight into the fringe of space and to a world's record altitude of 136,500 feet, August 12, 1960. *(Official U.S. Air Force Photo)*

"I started from the ground and built it," he said. "I fought the whole battle."

Joe said he had even designed the house himself. I asked how he knew enough to make his own design.

"I patched up a lot of features from a lot of houses," he replied. "The building was what took the time. It cost me three years of accumulated vacations, holidays, and week ends."

I asked Joe if I might sometime meet his wife and family and see his ranch house, and he said sure. He already understands the light of publicity that comes to the rocket pioneer—something Bob White is in the process of learning.

Leaving the NASA building, I was glad that there are two such good, devoted, and highly-skilled men at the head of the X-15 assault on space.

WEDNESDAY, OCTOBER 1. Trying to catch up with information on the men who will be taking over the X-15 birds after North American's manufacturers' tests are completed, I sought out Joe Vensel of NASA today.

Vensel is the slight, nervous, intense man who is NASA's chief of flight test at the Edwards facility. He is an old aerial pioneer type—a polite, gentle man, too—with a technical experience that runs inclusively from the old Navy biplanes of pre-World War II days and the first of the X-class rockets to the X-15 and the next controllable space ship, Dynasoar, now in the design stage.

Vensel, who was a NACA test pilot way back in 1939, also has the formal education to go with his job. He's a graduate of Carnegie Tech with an engineering degree.

I was anxious to ask him how the early X's linked into the present effort to probe the fringes of space. But I got more than that—an exciting account of some of the dangers that had to be overcome on the way. Vensel was an eyewitness to many of them.

"I came here in April of 1947. The first X-1, No. 1, was here. Yeager was here and Bell [Aircraft Company] was on demo flights. Slick Goodlin [Chalmers Goodlin, the Bell Company pilot] was doing the demo flights. He had a deal to get $5,000 from Bell for the first sonic boom. He produced the sound at .8 Mach. He got sonic velocity over the top of the wing in an eight-g pull-up. It didn't take him long to get to a phone."

I asked Vensel what had happened to Goodlin after Bell refused to meet his bonus terms (rumored to be $100,000) for breaking the sound barrier and Yeager took over the job. Vensel said he'd heard that Goodlin was working in Turkey on some kind of aircraft sales franchise. He'd done the same kind of job in Asia before. Goodlin, it seems, has been making the kind of money he likes.

Incidentally, there has been a rumor that Crossfield was paid a bonus of $100,000 by North American for the first glide landing. I haven't been able to get any comment on this story from any of the parties concerned.

The motivation of the test pilots in taking the ferocious chances they endure in the X program continues to fascinate me. Some of the pilots, such as Yeager, who took over the X-1 from Goodlin, seem to be interested in the challenge itself, aside from the money that might eventually come with fame—or might not. Kincheloe was once asked why he took the risks of the X-2 program on a captain's pay when he might at almost any time have shifted to a civilian test-pilot job for five times the money. Kinch said cannily and honorably that he would do the job with the X's first, and if it were done well the ultimate financial rewards would be a lot larger than he could imagine. He was doing the job well when death cut him off.

Skip Ziegler, the X-2 pilot for Bell Aircraft, and "Wheaties" Welch were both earning handsome salaries when their occupation of testing high-speed birds killed them.

But many test pilots in the Air Force tackled the job of testing the X's for the same reason Yeager did, primarily because, like Mount Everest, or the Matterhorn, it was there to be conquered. Most of them survived the experience and gained fame if not money. Kit Murray, as we have written earlier, is holding down a major's desk at Wright Air Development Center, as project officer for the X-15. Pete Everest, the X-2 pilot, is a colonel in charge of an Air Force gunnery range in North Africa. Yeager has his squadron of F-100s at Victorville. All three of them have had at least the glory of contributing importantly to space progress—more than most men could hope to achieve.

Vensel recalled that there was a lot of trouble with the landing gears of both X-1 and X-2.

"On ten or twelve occasions the nose wheel of the X-1 was busted when the pilot came in for a landing. It would start to skip. It was divergent—the nose would bounce higher each time. The gear would break off, and it would start ripping up the fuselage and all the propellent lines. And the controls were such that the pilot couldn't get out of the skip. There was sufficient lag [in control reaction] so that you were always too late. The secret was to get real close to the ground and hold it—then stall in."

Of the X-2 landing difficulties, Vensel said: "There was only one belly skip, and the aircraft was directionally unstable. Finally we added two outriggers."

These outriggers or whiskers, I knew, hadn't solved the problems of landing the X-2. Pete Everest cracked it up twice in landing, and the solution came in shortening the strut to the main landing skid.

The X-15 landing skids and nose wheel, I remarked, had given considerably less trouble. Except for the need to reinforce the shock absorbers, after the rough first landing, it has worked as the engineers estimated.

There were plenty of troubles in the cockpits of the X-1s and X-2s, Vensel said, some of them leading to the solutions incorporated in the X-15.

"Pete Everest was the first man to fly the X-1 in a pressure suit. It was the old capstan type. The suit blew up on him—the canopy frequently cracked.

"One time Pete's canopy cracked before the launch—and they decided to try it anyway. The canopy blew out. We could hear him on the radio—'ehh!' It squeezed hell out of him. He got down fast."

One of the persistent cockpit troubles with the early Xs, Vensel said, was the fogging of the canopy glass. "We used a canister of lithium oxide to absorb the body moisture. Same in the D-558 [Skyrocket]."

I knew this problem—the fogging of the glass because of the pilot's body moisture as he came down to the relatively high temperatures of the lower altitudes. It had beset Yeager several times in the first X-1s, and he had made practically blind landings, guided by his chase pilots, when he couldn't see out. An enterprising ground crewman had discovered that an administration of ordinary shampoo to the windshield would cut the misting.

In the later Xs, Joe Vensel said, the engineers used nitrogen nozzles blowing against the glass—and that is the solution of the problem in the X-15; although, as we have seen in this book, it has taken a lot of labor to make the nozzles perform efficiently. The greater purpose of the X-15 as with the earlier Xs is to provide the tedious kind of trial and error that leads to smooth-working mechanisms: the mechanisms, in sum, which future space travelers will take for granted,

not thinking what agonies and discomforts and dangers produced
them.

Later this morning I went out to the concrete apron of the NASA
hangar to witness the first tryout of some reaction, ballistic, or rocket
controls (all three adjectives mean the same) installed in an F-104 to
provide practice for the X-15 pilots.

I had watched the NASA crews working on these rocket-control
jets in the wings and nose of the 104. The rocket jets are a good deal
like the ballistic or space-control jets in the X-15 with the main difference that they are more powerful! They'll put out a 300-pound thrust
where the X-15 rocket-control jets average 100 pounds. This difference is good because the 104s with the rocket controls will be flying
at lower altitudes where the air is thicker; they'll need the extra power
to overcome the air pressure, where the X-15 rocket jets will be
working in the void of space, with nothing to push against except
themselves.

On the apron with Stan Miller, the NASA public-relations officer
at Edwards, I watched the curly-haired Joe Walker in the cockpit as
he prepared for the first ground test of the rocket controls.

He was wearing a checkered sports shirt—no need for a silver
suit or even ordinary flying clothes this time. A generator was putt-
putting beside the plane, supplying auxiliary power for the experiment. And a couple of firemen were spraying the concrete under the
nose and wings to cut down on the explosion hazard: hydrogen
peroxide, the fuel that supplies the energy for the control jets, is un-
pleasantly combustible.

Miller was explaining that in flight the rocket-control jets would
be invisible. The superheated steam that makes up the rocket blast
would look like air. But the first blasts, before the mechanism warmed
up, might be cool enough to make visible white steam like a loco-
motive.

The ground crew checked the hydrogen-peroxide vent lines to see
if there were any bubbles, which might make backfires. The mechanism of these controls works like this: the hydrogen peroxide is
passed through a silver catalyst screen, and the resulting chemical
reaction produces steam, and the steam blast moves the plane. But
bubbles could make the system back up or explode.

A group of us rubbernecks stood on the lee side of the plane to
stay away from the rocket blast, and a fireman with headphones
clamped over his ears played water underneath the rocket jets at the
wing tips.

There was a rough, rushing sound as white steam shot from the nose and wing tips in short, separate blasts.

The rocket jets were small, leaping out perhaps only 10 or 12 feet from the wing tips. Joe was evidently feeling out his controls with small movements.

Then he hit the ballistic controls hard. The shots were loud and crisp, and the white steam geysered up in sudden structures 25 or 30 feet above the nose and out of the wing tips, a healthy blast.

A split second later we heard Joe laugh heartily—happily as a kid with a Fourth-of-July toy. But I would wager that laugh was mostly satisfaction that the controls were working well. Here in thick atmosphere, with the nine-ton weight of the fighter pressing against the concrete, the rocket blasts hadn't moved the ship. But it was easy to imagine how they might change its course abruptly at altitude.

TUESDAY, OCTOBER 6. The Russians have a new space triumph going for them on the international propaganda front. Lunik II is circling the moon, getting pictures to be televised to earth so that we can see the unknown far side.

I checked with Earl Blount at North American for dope on the next flight of the X-15. It will be the second powered flight. Blount says it's scheduled now for Friday.

THURSDAY, OCTOBER 8. Checking with North American, I'm told that tomorrow's flight has been postponed. It might be on Saturday —and I know how anxious they must be to make it go, if they fly that day, because pay rates for all the technicians and ground crewmen go up on week ends. I've heard estimates that an ordinary weekday flight (or an abort, which costs the same) totals out to about $100,000, including all the Air Force and NASA facilities involved. A Saturday flight might be 15 or 20 per cent more. Fortunately for the contractor, the engineers don't get paid for their overtime, it's only the people on hourly scales who get what you might call hardship pay. Some of the engineers at the North American installation have told me that an 80-hour week is getting to be routine.

SATURDAY, OCTOBER 10. I flew up to Edwards with a group of North American engineers for the second powered flight—which turned out to be another abort.

I went to the North American tower to watch the flight. The B-52 had already taken off. On the radio I caught the usual chatter about pressures and temperatures—Crossfield reading his instruments aloud: "No. 1 bearing is 50, No. 2 bearing is 60, one source is 2,750, the other is 2,200, lox tank pressure cycling between 22 and 24." He makes these readings lickety-split, too fast even for an expert secretary such as Della Mae Bolling.

After the "fifteen minutes to launch" call, it was decided to abort the mission. Again it was plumbing trouble that caused the cancellation—a helium valve in the lox system.

As they were coming in for a landing after so much accumulated tension, so many aborts and postponements, the chatter of the flying crew seemed a little punchy. I know that Crossfield feels that at a time like this he should try to liven up the scene with a wisecrack or two.

Crossfield made his effort: "I think we ought to make a glide flight into LA International."

Someone in the B-52 picked up the remark as well as he could: "Do you think they'd file a violation on us?"

A few minutes later Q. C. Harvey inquired:

"You okay, Scott?"

"Oh, yeah, just catchin' a little shuteye."

Then, after dumping his hydrogen peroxide, Scott reported: "I feel kinda naked up here with these APUs jettisoned."

No one picked up the remark this time, so Crossfield added: "Okay—just so you know my modesty problem. . . . The tank is flattened out to 80 and the source is a normal zero."

Q. C., all business, announced: "I would like pictures of the landing-gear extension cycle."

A chase plane (Al White) replied quickly: "Okay, we'll be in position. Just give us the word."

Blank space on the radio as the X-15 aerial cavalcade was sweeping in for a landing, then:

"How's the chase?" Crossfield wanted to know.

"I'm sittin' right here lookin' at you, Daddy."

Crossfield hesitated, then: "Yeah. I was going to retort in kind, but I wanted to maintain the dignity of this flight."

He was getting ready to drop his gear and gave a countdown: "Okay—three, two, one—now."

White, on the radio: "Wait'll I get my store teeth back now and I'll have a look at the nose."

"Every time I see that thing [the nose wheel] come down, I can't believe it," Scott said.

It seemed laudable to me that the crew, led by Crossfield and Al White, could take this good-humored escape route toward diminishing some of the accumulated tensions—even if they could have used a better gag writer.

After the mission, I flew back to Los Angeles in a little Apache light twin, with company pilot Ray Niles, Stormy Storms, the chief engineer, and Shorty Holland, the highly-skilled lead man I had met at the North American factory during the completion of Bird No. 2.

Shorty was grousing a little about the rapidly advancing state of rocket technology.

"We used to be able to go with steel valve seats. They were okay for ambient temperatures—you know—40 below. Now we've got teflon valve seats—for the helium at 400 below. You get a fingernail scratch and you can have a leak."

Niles, a grizzled, veteran pilot who flew with the Canadians early in World War II, pulled the Apache off the lake bed and turned the control column over to Storms, who wanted to get some flying time on the way back to Los Angeles.

"You can go right down Scotty's runway and start the climb out," he told Storms. The biggest lake bed, in North American lingo, has become Scotty's runway.

We flew down the nine-mile stretch of lake bed laid out for the X-15, with three long black lanes marked for direction, and the large letters L and R so there would be no confusion about ground instructions when they called left or right. In a few days, maybe Tuesday or Wednesday, that runway should see another landing of the rocket ship, after Powered Flight No. 2.

Stormy was studying the runway, apparently thinking back to today's aborted mission, "Goddamn," he muttered to Ray. "You can't win every time."

WEDNESDAY, OCTOBER 14. I was on standby for the North American flight to Edwards this morning—and finally hooked a seat when one of the engineers canceled out.

We piled into the company DC-3 and as we were settling for take-off, Bill Johnston asked the other engineers in general:

"How are the lox leaks today?"

"L.L. in code," appended another engineer.

It was only a rhetorical question: all the engineers know that the troubles with valves, pipes, and switches have continued, despite the new teflon valve seats.

Roy Ferren, chief engineer of flight test, was sitting next to me, reminiscing about the first powered flight, which is already becoming history. "Q. C. Harvey was having kittens," he said. "It was one minute to drop and he said: 'Oh, God, I think I'll have a heart attack.'"

When we landed at Edwards, I managed to hitch a ride out to Mobile Control on the lake bed. The B-52/X-15 combination had already taken off, precisely on time, for once, and someone was announcing on the public-address system: "To all personnel: the B-52 is now at 25,000 feet."

I saw Cooper Lindley and asked him the question which was on many engineering minds:

"How are the valves today?"

He grinned, and silently lifted his hand with two fingers crossed for good luck.

A few seconds later I heard some conversation about a leak from the B-52. I asked Storms, when he had a free moment, what was the story on the leak.

"I think it's in the B-52," he said.

But in a few minutes the leak must have subsided in importance, because the launch operator was saying from the B-52: "Fifteen minutes to drop—now."

Then the trouble evidently came back with a rush, and the L.O. reported: "The cruise tank will not cut off. It's acting the same as last time: when I cut it off, it goes to zero." (The cruise tank in the B-52 keeps the X-15 lox tank topped off.)

Q. C. was instructing him from Central Control: "Try the bypass to build up the pressure."

The X-15 drop was put off twice while the launch operator fiddled with his switches. Then another difficulty came up: Crossfield's cabin pressure wouldn't behave.

The drop was aborted, and the flight was finished as a captive mission—using the air time to check out an accumulated miscellany of detail in the various systems.

I asked the knowledgeable Cooper Lindley about the flight:

"Was it the lox climb tank this time?"

"No. This time it was the cruise tank. All the valves were frozen."

Lindley was philosophical about it, and articulate as usual:

"We're in the jewelry business. There are 150 changes [engineering modifications] in this part alone.

"The systems are extremely simple. The parts are very complex.

It's not really a science, it's an art. You cut and try. The people that do it, do it by ear."

I checked with Blake Staub, the stability augmentation system expert, about the schedule of flights. To make the question exact, I asked him when the stable platform (space instruments) would be installed in X-15.

"They're in Bird No. 1 now," he said. "The bird should be turned over to NASA by November 2."

Despite a little leaky valve trouble, the X-15 schedule seems to be progressing fast. But the second powered flight has slipped again to Friday or Saturday.

SATURDAY, OCTOBER 17. The second powered flight finally came off. This time all the valves and all the plumbing held together.

Much of the credit for this, I am told by Engineer Bill Johnston, belongs to a young engineer named John Gibb, who wouldn't give up in the search for materials that would work. To fashion a tighter valve for the helium system, which pushes the lox and fuel toward the engine, he used serrated metal for the valve, and made a tighter seat of mylar plastic.

The recording tape of the mission showed that there were a few small items that gave trouble, but they were the kind of thing Crossfield is used to by now.

At one point, running through the check list strapped to one knee pad, Scott said: "Oh, damn, I've lost my place. Never mind, found it again."

Scott made a speed run that wheeled the X-15 up to 2.4 Mach—just short of 1,600 miles an hour. And Joe Walker, flying chase and trying to be helpful, narrowly missed ramming Scott.

"There goes my chase," Scott reported, "right across my bow."

Coming in for a landing, Scott was alarmed at the presence of a plane sitting near his touchdown point in the lake bed—when he was on his final approach, gliding in and twenty seconds from landing.

He said on the radio: "There's an airplane down on the lake."

But it was only the rescue helicopter standing by for his landing. Scott had to drop his lower ventral almost directly over the chopper. "I hope that helicopter didn't get hit," Scott said. And it didn't.

After the landing Q. C. Harvey asked: "Everything all right?"

"No sweat," was Crossfield's response, and evidently, to someone used to the dangers of a test pilot's job, it summed up the mission accurately.

THURSDAY, OCTOBER 22. Scott Crossfield tried for his third powered flight this morning—and the mission was aborted. This time it was an oxygen switch that wouldn't function: a mundane, time-proven gadget that nobody expected would give trouble.

Minutes before the launch, Crossfield tried to switch his oxygen supply from the B-52 to the internal system of the X-15. But the switch wouldn't budge. On the tape, you could hear Scott thumping at it, to no avail.

TUESDAY, OCTOBER 27. Saturday's flight slipped—and today's try at the third powered flight aborted again. The dread disease that afflicts research aircraft programs, cancelitis, seems to be setting in.

I flew up to Edwards for the attempt. At the mating area right after we landed, I saw Cooper Lindley standing by, watching the servicing operations with a jaundiced eye.

"There's a leaky valve in the H_2O_2 system," he said. "We don't know whether it's in the APU or the reaction controls—or it could be a leaky bladder. Chances are two to one we're dead. We have to find out."

I went over to NASA with a busload of engineers, to wait for final word on the mission. It was scratched—didn't even get as far as take-off.

At NASA I had a chance to check into the X-15 telemetering equipment, which I knew had been giving trouble. I had a firsthand report from sandy-haired, slow-spoken Norm Hayes, the chief of instrument operations.

"We had a new beacon developed for this project. But we finally went back to the old one. The new one had more power. But it also had more parts and was more sophisticated. The old one proved to be more dependable."

The NASA people, like the North American engineers and craftsmen, are also in what Lindley calls the jewelry business, slowly working the bugs out of their machinery by trying different parts.

There's been one other notable bug developing in the X-15 program at NASA. The reaction controls being tried out in the F-104 have blown up.

Joe Walker was in the cockpit at the time of the explosion, but fortunately he was not flying. The blast blew out the side of the 104 well behind the cockpit, and Joe wasn't hurt. But it'll take several weeks, my friends at NASA tell me, to repair the damage.

THURSDAY, OCTOBER 29. I checked with Blount today about the much-anticipated third powered flight. He says it's on for tomorrow, take-off scheduled for 9 A.M.

FRIDAY, OCTOBER 30. As I drove to the Los Angeles International Airport, and reached the North American hangar, I saw Scott Crossfield walking out to his own plane, a Bonanza, and so I ran after him and bummed a ride to Edwards.

The flying-weather prophecy on the radio was correct—overcast and windy.

The air over the mountains was terrible. We hit one bump which shoved us up abruptly more than 1,000 feet and indicated 2 gs on the accelerometer. Scott said it was the worst his Bonanza had ever taken.

There was enough give in our safety belts so that the bump banged both of our heads against the cabin ceiling with a solid thud. But though stunned, 1 was impressed again with the quickness of Scott's reactions. He saw some sign that the bump was coming—maybe a ragged cloud sloping our way. He hauled back on the wheel just before it hit—and certainly saved us some trouble.

I had a chance to ask Scott some of the questions which I have been accumulating. One was how he manages to stand the strain of waiting in his uncomfortable cockpit, in his uncomfortable flying suit, for the endlessly delayed take-offs and frequently-aborted launches, then starting all over again the next day. Today's effort marked Scott's fourth try to make the third powered flight happen. The last try was aborted because of the heavy cloud cover above the desert.

Scott said: "I'm not worried about my own nerves. After all, I've been in the business a long time and I'm used to it. But I'm concerned about the line crew. They have to keep trying—and you have to repay it in kind."

We landed at eight forty-five under a lowering cloud bank. The air below the clouds was smudgy with dust, a cold wind blowing.

Scott ran in to see Cokeley at the engineering department, and Cokeley shook his head. The cloud cover was much too thick. The mission would be scrubbed.

Scott was anxious to get back to the plane. "I want to get out before it closes in."

Cokeley said: "We'll try for tomorrow."

Scott and I hurried for the Bonanza. He told me why he was in such a hurry to get back to the city: "My eleven-year-old daughter gave me an ultimatum. She said: 'This time you *have* to be back for the Halloween party.'"

We skimmed low over the mountains, following the Soledad Canyon route which is about the last resort when the weather is unspeakable. Scott said he has made about 350 flights over the mountains, commuting between his home in Los Angeles and Edwards. He said it gets a little expensive—it runs about $15.00 or $20.00 over and back and he has made four trips in the past week.

Scott told me about one accident I hadn't heard about in the course of the X-15 program. He was flying NASA's F-107, getting practice with the side-arm stick, when he blew four tires taking off and set his landing gear afire. As a result, the 107 will be side-lined for quite a while. There are only two 107s, and parts are scarce.

SATURDAY, OCTOBER 31. Another abort today. I flew up with a plane-load of engineers. At seven fifty-two, just before our take-off, one of the engineers wisecracked: "Fifteen minutes before they abort."

He was wrong about the time, anyway. We waited around at Edwards for the X-15 take-off until twelve-eighteen, hoping moment by moment that the clouds would clear away. The X-15 can't launch unless the pilot can see the lake bed and pick his landing spot. But the clouds only grew thicker. And the take-off, a fling in the face of bad weather, didn't bring any magical clearing of the overcast.

The B-52 came back and landed, and probably, like many of us on the ground, I wondered how long the disease of cancelitis will afflict us. The rainy season is growing closer now, and the cloudy wintry weather is going to be more and more troublesome. When the rains come, the hard-surfaced lake beds can become real lakes for weeks at a time, and end flight operations effectively.

Earl Blount told us the third powered flight will be scheduled for Wednesday now, if it doesn't rain.

THURSDAY, NOVEMBER 5. I waited for two hours at the North American dispatcher's shack this morning, trying to hitch an aerial ride up to Edwards for the sixth attempt at the third powered flight.

I saw Scott Crossfield's red-and-black Bonanza parked near the shack and asked Chuck Hughes, the dispatcher, if Crossfield was flying his own plane up to Edwards today. Hughes said Scott had already flown up on a company plane.

I waited around, hoping that a place would clear on one of the three North American planes ready to take off. But no opening developed.

Roy Ferren came in at 7 A.M., and I tried to get aboard his Apache, but no dice. He had a full load of engineering talent.

Roy was his usual polite and debonair self, but there was just no room. I chivvied him about the fact that this was the sixth attempt to make the third powered flight go, and he smiled and said: "If we don't go this time, we'd better give up."

I saw Gordon Gray of the North American public-relations office as he got ready to board one of the aircraft. He said his place had been reserved for several days.

I asked him about the schedule for today's flight. He said:

"Launch from 41,000."

"Then what?"

"Then everybody . . . prays he lands at Edwards instead of in the mountains somewhere."

By eight-thirty I knew I'd had it—wasn't going to catch my ride to Edwards today. All the planes had gone.

I went on home, and at 2 P.M. heard the shocking radio bulletin on KLAC: "The rocket ship X-15 made an emergency landing after an explosion on its third powered flight. The craft was damaged but Pilot Scott Crossfield was unhurt."

I quickly called Gordon Gray, who had returned to the North American plant by this time. He said the ship seemed to be pretty badly damaged after the landing: "It's bent on top and ruptured on the bottom. The fuselage is broke just aft of the cockpit. There's extreme damage—no doubt about that."

He said nobody knew exactly what had happened. Crossfield had made an emergency landing on Rosamond Dry Lake and he was surprised to find any damage. He thought the landing had been all right. "Scott didn't know it was busted until he got out and looked."

I asked if Scott had hit a crack on the lake bed.

"No," Gray answered. "The lake bed was smooth. He just hit hard. Scott said he wished there had been a hole—it would have explained things."

Gray said the repairs could probably be done "in several weeks." The break seems to be at one of the few bolted joints in the plane, just aft of the instrumentation bay, between the bay and the big lox tank.

The thing that most concerns Gray and apparently the other North American people, from what he says, is that they don't know what caused the break and they're afraid it'll slow up the program. They'll have to find out, and probably the other bird that's been flying (No. 1) will be grounded until they make whatever changes are needed.

"Until they can find out what caused this," he said, "they can't take a chance. It's got 'em snowed."

I asked Gray if he had listened to the radio calls during the mission, and he said he had:

"Bob White [flying chase] said: 'It looks like you've got a small fire.' He said he had heard the explosion.

"And Scott said: 'Yeah, I got a fire-warning light.' He said, 'I'm slowing down and starting to jettison.'

"White said he couldn't see a fire any more.

"Scott said: 'The fire-warning light is out. I'm going into Rosamond [Dry Lake].'

"It took maybe a period of ten seconds for all this—right after the launch and the light-up. White talked him into Rosamond: '100 feet—50 feet'—like that.

"White and Walker [chase pilots for today] both said it looked like any other landing. But White said when he flew over: 'It looks like something wrong with the fuselage—a hump?' But Scott didn't hear him. His radio was out."

I asked Gray when the bird would be hauled to the factory. He said he didn't know yet, but "Gene Ricketts [a general foreman] will put it together." I knew Ricketts was one of the devoted craftsmen who had built the slick ships, and that his loving care would restore it if anyone could.

Gray didn't seem so much excited as depressed. The crash is a real monkey wrench in the progress of the program—especially now that the rainy season will be coming along and even if the bird is repaired in a few weeks, the rains may make the lake beds useless.

I told Gray I'd like to take a look at the bird and also talk to Crossfield. Gray said the bird should be down here at the factory in a day or two and he'd see if he could set up an interview with Crossfield.

I checked the film of the crash tonight. The film, made from the North American F-100 chase plane, showed a thick trail streaming from the X-15, but you couldn't tell how much was fire, how much was rocket, and how much only fuel jettison.

The landing looked smooth until the last second, when the X-15 seemed to belly down onto the ground. The stills showed Crossfield in the foreground, the bird behind him with a very noticeable broken back, the belly dragging on the ground: ignominy for the once beautiful and powerful beast.

FRIDAY, NOVEMBER 6. No luck at contacting Crossfield. However, somebody got a quote from him, in this morning's papers: "I had complete control all the way. I'm just sorry the run couldn't have been completed as planned and sorry for the delay this will cause."

The broken-back X-15 will be trucked into the Los Angeles plant tonight and I plan to make at least part of the trip with it.

SATURDAY, NOVEMBER 7. Early this morning, in the dark of the big San Diego freeway, I found the bird on a flat-bed truck moving slowly toward Los Angeles.

The cavalcade spread wide across the almost-deserted road: the big truck at the center with the X-15 standing high above it, the wings marked with yellow and red lights. Three pickup trucks and two company police cars rode herd on the procession.

The bird seemed to be little damaged. The break in the fuselage showed only on the bottom, the top looked only slightly swaybacked. Some of the side paneling had been removed around the engines and the uppermost tube of the lower rocket engine was missing. That must have been the one that exploded.

The cavalcade didn't seem tragic or depressing. The pile of lights on the X-15 truck and the blinkers on the other cars gave the X-15 centerpiece a carnival look, like a float on parade.

The flat bed turned at the gate to North American's factory reservation at the airfield. The truck rolled on toward the West Bay where it was built, like an injured child returning to momma. It will be repaired there. But probably the work won't be starting until Monday. Today the engineers will come to survey the damage and confer about plans.

MONDAY, NOVEMBER 9. With Dick Barton I went down to the West Bay section of the North American factory to look at the broken bird, which is still sitting on the flat-bed Air Force truck which brought it from Edwards. Sports-shirted technicians were working nearby amid the big metal and wood ribs of the jigs on which the X-15s were built. The cracked-up bird will be put into the jigs for the repair job.

Another group of engineers were watching as two yellow fork lifts and a tall, rubber-tired crane moved near the flat bed. These machines would pick up the bird, very gingerly I was sure, and place it on the whale-like ribs of the jigs.

"Stormy came in Saturday to work on the bird," Barton was telling me. "Feltz, Benner, Ricketts, and Mellinger, too, I think.

"I guess they don't know the answer yet about what happened. They know one thing, though: the lox tank wasn't empty when the bird landed: it hadn't all been jettisoned and maybe there was 500 pounds of lox in it. The nose came down hard, with that extra weight —they estimated it hit with 21 or 22 gs.

"The break was right at the joint between the nose and the lox tank —right at the splice joint where the front of the fuselage bolts. It doesn't look as if the lox tank was bent much—a pretty clean break."

Barton was enthusiastic about the way the two chase pilots, Bob White and Joe Walker, had stayed right on top of Crossfield to watch him, on the day of the explosion—not knowing whether the smoking X-15 might blow up at any moment.

"If it were our company policy, we'd have made a couple of heroes of 'em," he said.

We looked at the bird. Its broken belly was propped up now on big cushions. A crowd of engineers stood around the break: Raun Robinson, Dick Stacey, and Cooper Lindley, down from their usual beat at Edwards, and a dozen others.

One of the crowd was Fran Mueller, one of the pilots who fly the little Apaches and the other transport planes for North American. Fran was examining a fat bundle of instrument wires near the break, in the upper part of the fuselage.

"All those wires," he said ruefully. "They'll have to be disconnected and hooked up again."

I knew that each of the python-sized wire bundles is composed of hundreds of tiny wires, many of them running out many feet into the fuselage and wings.

Mueller had been flying an Apache on the day of the crash, and was one of the first on the scene. In his Apache, he flew some of the engineers from Mobile Control to the spot where the X-15 had pranged.

"When Brian Laufer [an engineer] and Toby Freedman [the flight surgeon] ran up to the X-15," Mueller said, "Scott was still sitting in it, trying to work the canopy. Laufer yelled to Scott to get out, 'The damn thing's gonna blow up.' Laufer and Freedman helped to open the canopy.

"Brian's beanie blew off," Mueller went on sadly, "and Scott said:

'Don't worry about that twenty-five-cent beanie. We just creamed a 50-million-dollar airplane.' "

I noticed that Cooper Lindley was studying a series of photographs of the damaged bird. In the pictures the skin had been torn from the fuselage, apparently by the blast. I said it must have been quite an explosion.

He demurred: "The side panels are designed to blow out to prevent bigger explosions. As soon as an explosion occurs, lox and water alcohol are all sprayed around. Confine it, and you might have a big bang."

I asked Coop how you differentiate an accidental rocket explosion from the purposeful explosion that gives rocket power.

Lindley smiled. "The power of a rocket engine is a *controlled* explosion. When it's not under control, you're in trouble."

A group of shirt-sleeved men were moving steel girders into position on the fork lifts so the X-15 could be picked up. The tall crane or cherry picker was moving closer to lift the bird from the top—and one of the heavy traveling cranes that line the roof of the factory rumbled slowly, carefully toward the X-15.

Sam Richter, the assistant test director, was sitting on a bank of lockers, with an electronic bull horn in hand, ready to call out instructions to the crew. Cooper Lindley had climbed up on the front of the yellow fork lift as it moved into position to support the X-15. He was talking through a mike into a public-address system:

"C-1 [a crane] . . . I want you to move just a little . . . C-2 just a little bit—a little bit more . . . cherry picker up just a little bit more."

Fabric slings had been rigged under the two parts of the broken X-15, attached to the crane, and the bird was supported by them and by the girders riding on the fork lifts. Without fuel, the X-15 weighs six and a half tons, and holding the two parts in position while it was being moved was a touchy operation, but with their mammoth tools the engineers handled it like a fragile toy, edging it gently but firmly toward the assembly of jigs.

Richter was checking the movement closer to the jigs. "Easy does it," his voice boomed through the bull horn. "Go forward slowly."

Richter and Lindley both suddenly yelled: "Whoa!" as the bird almost collided with a steel support.

Lindley was squatting at the level of the truck bed, squinting at the belly to make sure that nothing was going to scrape. "Okay, you're clear."

Dick Barton and I decided to leave the engineers and technicians to their work. At this rate, each movement only a few inches, it would take at least three hours to move the ship its own length.

As we were leaving, Lindley was patiently warning on the public-address system: "Take it inch by inch. Let's play it safe—even if it takes all night."

I asked Barton, as we walked out of the West Bay, if he'd had any luck setting up an interview for me with Scott Crossfield. He said maybe tomorrow.

4   The Big Adventure

FRIDAY, NOVEMBER 13. Today I got the appointment with Scott Crossfield.

This morning, while waiting for a chance to see Scott, Barton and I went by the engineering section and heard about the detective work the engineers have done in finding the roots of the explosion and the crack-up.

In the office of Charlie Feltz, the engineering head man of the X-15 project, we found Bud Benner, one of Charlie's two assistant chiefs, and were starting to ask him about the explosion when one of the girl secretaries came in holding a small model of the X-15. "Have you seen the latest X-15 model?" she said. We looked and saw that it had a broken back. And a passing engineer told us the latest gag—that the X-15 is the only space ship with the Ivy League look: it has a buckle in the back. The engineers are capable of laughing at their troubles. But I rapidly discovered that they have also tackled the problem with fantastic seriousness and thoroughness. When I asked Bud Benner about the cause of the explosion, he said:

"We expect it was in the ignition. Right now they have it [the ignition] in a cold box. They take it down to zero degrees—which is what the engine was at—to see if one of the valves was hanging up.

"What we expect happened is that when he turned on his switches this one went out prior to igniting, so once the chamber was loaded with lox and walc [water alcohol, the fuel] the result was a gelatine-like substance in the chamber, at that temperature. It was like napalm —just as explosive. Maybe the adjoining [rocket] tube set off the napalm bomb."

I asked if there was any connection between the explosion and the structural failure when the fuselage broke. Bud said no connection, except in so far as the explosion led to an emergency landing in an unfamiliar lake bed, which wasn't fully marked.

"He dropped off a lot of speed during the last few seconds and ended up with a pretty nose-high attitude. The nose came down plenty hard.

"Afterward we took the accelerometer off the nose gear. It was calibrated to 12 gs and the indicator was well beyond that, maybe to 19. How much of the load was transmitted back to the fuselage I don't know. All I can say is, it was enough to break it."

Bud said the impact was enough to break 30 to 40 per cent of the bolts joining the two sections of the fuselage, to pull the heads through. He added: "There were the intangibles of the side tunnels [the bulges on the sides of the fuselage] and the wire bundles, which helped to give it strength."

I asked what Scott's chances would have been if the two sections had broken apart and the section with the cockpit had flipped away from the other one.

"It's a very good restraint system [in the cockpit]," he said. "If he'd taken the g-forces, he might not have had anything but a bruised knee." That, I thought, was spoken like a true, confident engineer.

Bud said that when the cracked-up X-15 is repaired, the bolts that gave way will be replaced by heavier ones, with bigger heads. The same will be done with the No. 1 Bird—the bolts at the same splice joint in that one will be replaced with heavier stock.

I chivvied Bud about the final size of the modifications—despite all the elaborate analyses and intricate calculations, the main improvement will be bigger bolts with bigger heads; that, I said, sounded more like Old MacDonald's farm than the last word in space ships. He took the kidding in good grace.

Charlie Feltz came by and said things didn't look bad: he would estimate that the No. 2 Bird, the one that had pranged, would be completely repaired and ready to fly by December 5.

Charlie and Bud, both looking tired and pale after the week's night-and-day exertions, told me about a wonderful metal craftsman, a German, who had solved some of their pressing problems in a hurry.

"This guy works on the day side," Benner said. "But last night he hung around because we were straightening out the dents in the lox tank. We pumped water into the lox tank at 90 psi, and it worked—the pressure straightened out most of it. But there were still some dents in the bottom. This guy [his name is Ernie Kalash] was hanging around. He kept asking Charlie [Feltz] for a crack at it. Charlie finally let him try.

"He came up with a sheet of metal and a special crowbar and hammer. He had it all figured out—just what he needed for it. He wanted to get at it so much he could taste it. He would have hit Charlie on the head and done it anyhow, if Charlie said no.

"He went up there with a buddy, put it all in place, and gave it a couple of cracks, and it was all fixed."

I couldn't catch up with Scott Crossfield until after five. Barton and I had been trying to track him down, getting occasional reports about his whereabouts, but missing him. We finally found him at Robb's, the local large restaurant and bar.

By this time I'd been over the accident so often with various specialists that the events were growing familiar. But there were some personal questions that only Scott could answer—principally, did he consider ejecting when he heard the explosion and saw the fire-warning light?

He said bailing had crossed his mind, but "it was only a matter of five seconds, when I heard the bang and White called the explosion, and I knew from the gauges that one of the engines was damn sour. The explosion—it felt as if it was right behind me."

I had touched on a philosophical point which is important to Crossfield: in crude terms, his honor as a test pilot. And now he was in a strange mood: wound up tight as a clock, the way he usually seems to be, but mellow enough to talk about it for once.

"I've never left an airplane. I've had a few fires and I've brought a few of 'em back bent. Once I had a fire in the D-558-2 [the Douglas Skyrocket]. There was a leak in the engine. But the fire was out when I landed. I did think about getting out, but you couldn't get out of it, anyway.

"It's a matter of professional integrity, if you please—to get it home—that's what I'm paid for. An airplane is like a good horse—you don't shoot it."

Crossfield had led himself to an important point in the philosophy of a test pilot:

"In all of this business there's a requirement of intense concentration—if you can train yourself to be self-disciplined. If you close the car door on your finger, your impulse is to put it in your mouth and curse. But you train yourself to wait. It's part of the profession—to avoid an emotion or a reflex reaction."

This was a good time to ask a question that I had been wanting to ask Scott for some months. It was a vital one, and something he was especially well equipped to answer: with his high-strung temperament and his rigid mental discipline, his philosophical bent and his fondness for categorical judgments. And now he was in the right mood,

I thought, to answer the question: how did he feel about the possibility of violent death, likely more than a possibility in his line of work?

"It isn't suicidal . . . but . . . I have no fear of dying in the airplane if it serves a useful purpose. . . . Somebody else would be doing it." I thought that was a pretty brave statement for a *pater familias* with five children, just recovering from what might easily be described as a brush with extinction.

WEDNESDAY, NOVEMBER 25. I called Blount this morning to check on a news story about the X-15—that it would fly December 1. Blount said yes, the bird is scheduled for delivery at Edwards by December 1, flights should be starting again shortly after that, if the rains don't start.

MONDAY, NOVEMBER 30. Checking with North American public relations, I find that Bird No. 1 won't be delivered tomorrow. Dick Barton says the engineers are still working over it, still beefing up the fuselage, and the landing gear, too—to conform with what was learned from the crash of No. 2.

TUESDAY, DECEMBER 1. I flew up to Edwards today, mainly to look at Bird No. 1 and get an idea how soon it will be flying again after the modifications.

What I saw wasn't very encouraging. I knew that the broken-backed Bird No. 2 was still being repaired at the factory. But I didn't know that Bird No. 1 is still far from ready to fly.

I looked down from the engineering deck at the North American hangar, and saw the bird with a huge section of skin off—and the usual knot of checkered-shirt technicians and white-shirted engineers around the cockpit. Five men were working around the tail and inside the skeleton of the tail, and this area seemed to be in the midst of considerable remodeling.

Bud Benner dropped by to tell me that the stable-platform instruments, the first true space instruments in any man-carrying vehicle, were being installed in Bird No. 1. That will be the first one to be turned over to the Air Force and NASA. Watching the work around the cockpit and in the instrumentation bay behind the cockpit, I could see that a lot of the equipment had been taken out to make way for the new stable-platform gyro. I would guess the job is a long way from completion now, especially since the beefing up of the main and nose landing gear is still very much in the process.

The picture is discouraging, because Bird No. 3, the one that will eventually have the Big Engine, looks as much out of commission as Bird No. 1. It is still, of course, without its engine; the tail is only an empty frame. In general, the prognosis is bad: even if the work could be completed on No. 1 and No. 2 in a week or so, the rainy season may come with a rush to make the base useless to the X-15s and turn the lake beds into real lakes or seas of mud.

This afternoon I sought out Joe Walker. I was anxious to see something of his family, to meet his wife, as he had agreed I might.

Joe's house is in a part of the desert encompassed by the city of Lancaster. Although a bare, open wasteland with a sprinkling of stubby joshua trees, the section has the optimistic name of White Fence Farms.

Joe's do-it-yourself mansion had gracious, pleasing lines much like what you'd expect in an eastern, woodsy suburb such as Wellesley Hills, Massachusetts, or Basking Ridge, New Jersey. The house is a low, rambling cottage with wide, white-framed windows, Cape Coddish in effect, except for the fact that there is only one tree, a knobby joshua, in the yard. The house lives up to the zoning requirement of its neighborhood—it has a white post fence around it. The garage is evidence of the do-it-yourself character of the house, like many others in the neighborhood; it is skeletal, and Joe is working on it in his spare hours, with the assistance of a contractor for extra-difficult items such as wiring and plumbing.

In back of the house is an open lot which, Joe says, is often filled with kids playing football.

"I maintain the football field for the street," Walker said. "Sometimes it gets funny. An insurance man coming by to make a check on me said he was tryin' to figure how many kids I have. He was puzzled."

In fact, Joe has three children: Tommy, nine; Jimmy, seven; and Joey, six months.

Joe introduced us ("us" being Julian Hartt, the aerospace correspondent for the Los Angeles *Examiner,* and his photographer, Russ Lapp) to Jimmy, and to Mrs. Walker, in the living room.

Mrs. Walker (Grace) looks like a bit of Old Ireland: fair, fragile skin, red hair, and bright blue eyes. Jimmy is endlessly active, with a sun-bleached crewcut.

Joe proudly showed us his dining room, paneled with lustrous rich wood. "It's hand-rubbed," he said. "I have the fingers to prove it."

Grace came in, carrying the baby, and smilingly announced: "This is *my* racket."

Russ Lapp made photographs of the family—Joe, Grace, Jimmy, the baby, and Frisky, the dog. Tommy, the oldest boy, wasn't home this afternoon.

Lapp wanted to get a shot of Joe saying good-by to Grace as he does in the mornings, going to work.

We walked to the skeletal garage and Joe backed out his 1956 Mercury for the picture. "I expect a 1960 Merc for this," he said, with his usual big grin.

I said I had expected his car would be a Mercedes 190 SL, and he indicated the Ford pickup parked there.

"You'll get my 190 SL in that," he said. He added that he very often drives to work at NASA (25 miles away) in the pickup truck, rather than the Mercury.

There wasn't much time to talk to Joe and his wife. It was gracious of them to allow this much of an intrusion. But I had a chance to gather a few personal facts. There wasn't time to ask what she thought about being the wife of one of the country's first space pilots. But at some later date, I hope, we can get her to talk about it.

Joe was saying something about the dog, Frisky. "He's All-American," he said. "Part beagle and part Dalmatian."

There was one question I did want to ask, even in this short time: is Jimmy interested in Joe's job as a test pilot?

"For a while he didn't give a damn, but now he's interested," Joe answered.

I asked Jimmy, playing around the white fence, if he wants to be a pilot when he grows up.

"Yes," he said swiftly.

"What kind of pilot?"

"A jet pilot."

"Not a rocket pilot?"

The boy did a little dance, kicking his leg up high. "No-ooo." He practically squealed it out.

"Why not?"

"They go *straight* up," he said, illustrating with a violent gesture of the arm.

Joe laughed. "He's already decided he wants to be in *control* of this vehicle."

Joe was kidding, but I knew he was touching on the largest, most formidable unknown of the X-15—the time at some point in the near future when in the Black Rocket he will be arcing in a ballistic curve, like an artillery shell, out of the atmosphere and into the emptiness of space, when the old controls men have learned will be useless, when he'll rely on rocket controls to trim his ship as it sails free: and the time just after that when he'll be coming back into atmosphere at bullet-like speed which will make the nose and underside of the wings glow red with the heat of friction that may drive the metal temperature as high as 1,200 degrees Fahrenheit—or a lot hotter than that if the rocket or ballistic controls haven't been handled correctly during the high portion of the flight into space.

FRIDAY, DECEMBER 4. Today NASA announced that for the first time a primate has made a space flight in the Mercury capsule. The animal was a seven-pound rhesus monkey named Sam, fired up to 55 miles altitude on the nose of a Little Joe rocket, from Wallop's Island, Virginia.

This "monkey in a ball" experiment foreshadowed, NASA hopes, the day when one of the seven Mercury astronauts will make a similar ballistic flight on the nose of a short-range rocket, blast his capsule away from the projectile with retro rockets, and come down in the capsule under a parachute to be recovered somewhere in the Atlantic Ocean. After many such flights, a bigger flight on a more powerful rocket will, hopefully, send the astronaut into a brief global orbit.

The Mercury shot which carried Sam was of limited thrust and speed. Sam was lucky that his capsule was found in the ocean, though recovery of such a capsule after a short ballistic flight is a lot easier than finding a capsule after a world orbit, where a mistake of a millisecond could put the space chamber hundreds of miles off course. It looks to me as if the Mercury astronauts have a long way to go before they can take a ride in space.

Meanwhile, the X-15 people have a relatively maneuverable, controllable space ship in being, already carrying a man. Soon, within months, it will be carrying a man out of atmosphere and into space, and bringing him back to a predetermined spot, the Edwards lake bed. That is, if the engineers can finish their repairs and modifications and if the winter rains don't interfere with the schedule by inundating the lake beds.

TUESDAY, DECEMBER 15. The next flight of the X-15 (Bird No. 1) is scheduled for tomorrow, right on the mid-month schedule Barton promised. He says if the next couple of flights go well, the bird may be turned over to NASA within a month.

WEDNESDAY, DECEMBER 16. This morning I checked with Stan Miller, the NASA public-relations officer, preparing for today's scheduled X-15 flight, which, to come to the point, was aborted.

It was supposed to have been the first test of the Inertial Platform, the first true space instruments, now installed in Bird No. 1.

I bummed a ride out from NASA headquarters to the lake bed with Paul Bikle, the new director there. Bikle, a former adviser to General Carpenter of the Air Force command at Edwards, is probably a good choice to take over the NASA installation because he understands both the Air Force and NASA points of view in the X-15 program. He has had experience on both sides.

Besides having a long background in research aircraft, Bikle is incidentally a champion glider pilot who has competed in many international soaring competitions.

He doesn't look the part of a soaring eagle. He's chunky and not athletic in appearance. But his light eyes have the clear, sharp-edged look you might expect.

A shuffle in the NASA high command transferred Walt Williams, the former head man at the Edwards facility, to Langley Field, Virginia, where he is now associate director of the Space Task Group.

The name of the Edwards NASA installation has been changed, too, from NASA High Speed Flight Station to NASA Flight Research Center. The work seems to be roughly the same as it was, though the meaning of the term "high speed" has changed since missiles started flying 18,000 miles an hour.

Today, Walt Williams was back at Edwards on a visit from his new post at Langley. Two other NASA engineers from the East were in the car with us, and Matt Portz, the West Coast public-relations chief for NASA.

We wheeled out to the lake bed in the NASA sedan, with Bikle driving—to see the red-tailed B-52 with the black sucker fish climbing into a clear, sunny sky. We could hear the radio calls very well on Bikle's high-powered receiver. At nine fifty-nine Captain Jack Allavie, the B-52 pilot, gave the warning: "Five minutes to drop." But just thirty seconds before drop, Allavie reported: "He's saying hold. We will make another pattern."

After the pattern, Allavie's voice: "He wants to launch in one minute."

The B-52 crew were hearing Crossfield's transmissions better than we on the ground.

Q. C. Harvey said: "Let's make that minute and launch from there."

Allavie reported: "The system is armed. . . . Ready to launch. . . . Forty seconds. . . . Twenty seconds. . . ."

Then, a letdown in his voice: "Prepare-to-launch light is not on. . . . He wants to go home."

Matt Portz summarized the sad history of today's mission: "So near and yet so far."

I went by the North American hangar to check up on the cause of the abort. The verdict, after the engineering debriefing: a hydrogen-peroxide valve stuck. "Next week," was Cooper Lindley's laconic comment.

I took advantage of being in the Edwards vicinity to visit with the Air Force's No. 1 X-15 pilot, Bob White, at his home—to finish the interview I'd begun when I mystified him by saying that the world wants to know all about the first men into space, White and Walker.

Bob's promotion to major has come through since I saw him last, but he still lives in a plain-looking captain's dwelling on one of the numbered streets in the Edwards military housing tract. It's in the Wherry housing section, which the Edwards people call "Weary Housing." The home has an unromantic designation, completely in terms of numbers: 116 Thirteenth Street. And it's undistinguished among a line of similar desert-worn dwellings in the dusty street. It's even difficult to find that particular house in the close-packed row. And the traditional badge of Bob's profession, the old, unpainted Model-A Ford which marks him as Edwards' premier test pilot, must have been shut up in the garage.

Plain and ordinary outside, the Whites' house inside is individual, it has an unexpected elegance. The living room gives an impression of richness—of leather, mahogany, and polished brass—as you might expect of a couple with Bob's and Doris's educated, big-city (New York) background. There are mahogany tables with polished leather inserts, and brass plates and oversize, shiny brass keys as decoration.

Doris and Bob are a handsome couple, with an inherent air of quiet sophistication—quite a contrast to the more informal and ebullient Walkers. Doris, like Bob, has a patrician leanness and is well spoken. This afternoon she was very trimly dressed in a tailored slack suit: black capris, a white blouse, and a red-checkered vest, and black shoes with white laces.

I expressed admiration for the house furnishings, and Doris said they had been bought for the apartment she and Bob had in Hicks Street, Brooklyn Heights, when Bob was studying at NYU, in the days before the couple had their first child. Now there are three, a boy and two girls.

The Whites' oldest child, Greg, aged five, came into the room, a well-instructed youngster who was on his good behavior in the presence of the stranger.

It was a little early in Greg's life to ask about his career intentions, but I did want to ask the same question I had put to Walker's nine-year-old offspring Jimmy. I asked the parents if Greg had expressed any desire to follow in his father's footsteps as an engineer-pilot.

"At first he wanted to be a garbage man—the usual thing," Bob said seriously. "We asked him if he wanted to be an engineer, or a doctor. He was confused as to which type of engineer—we'd told him about the engineer on a train."

Bob said there's one indication, though, that Greg is fond of aviation: the boy loves plane models and wants every kind of model he sees. He's had a big yen for a miniature Steve Canyon cockpit and helmet he spotted in a toy store. "He'll have it for Christmas," Bob told me in an aside.

I asked him about the social life of a test pilot at Edwards, and he replied that it centers around the group who fly the experimental planes here, and the milestones in their lives, their accomplishments, and defeats. The social life is tame, since the pilots have to keep in good physical shape. "During the week we stay out only till eleven o'clock," he said.

To keep in trim, Bob dons shorts and goes running, or works out at the Edwards gym. "Sometimes we get a group and play basketball," he said.

It seems clear that Bob and his family have a duty-bound life. They are faithful church-goers. Bob is an usher at the Roman Catholic church, a measure of his regularity at services. He was brought up a Catholic and Doris was converted.

Doris's father was a trainman on the Delaware and Hudson Railroad. He died in 1941. Bob's father works for the National Biscuit Company, in New York.

Before I left Edwards, I checked with Charlie Brown, the Air Force chief of public information, to get a reading on the next flight of the X-15. Charlie said it should be within a week, barring rain or other acts of God.

SUNDAY, DECEMBER 20. The X-15 flight is scheduled for tomorrow, but showers have been falling. I called Stan Miller, the NASA public-relations officer at Edwards, to inquire about the mission. He said the flight is on for tomorrow, and the birds, B-52 and X-15, have been mated—but it's rainy and cloudy at Edwards and the prediction is bad.

Later today the rain began to fall heavily, and it's still falling. I called Earl Blount and learned the mission has been canceled.

MONDAY, DECEMBER 21. On this, the day before the winter solstice, the beginning of winter, the rain fell hard. And it fell still harder at Edwards, Blount told me, where they had a half inch of water.

"It might slow us up a bit," Earl said. "The bed was so dry, and hard as a rock. It might hold the water for a while. About 50 per cent of it is covered with water now. It looks as if they won't be able to fly for a couple of weeks."

The rains have arrived with considerable vigor for southern California, and it's still drizzling.

TUESDAY, JANUARY 12. This morning I called Dick Barton to ask if there is any report of resumed flight operations. It didn't seem likely, since there was rain again last night here, and probably out on the desert, too.

"We are saying three weeks' delay and the Air Force says four weeks," Barton answered. "That was before yesterday's rain. So I'd say it's off for six weeks, maybe."

He added that there is a proposal to move landing operations up into Nevada or Utah, where the climate is drier and lake beds like those at Edwards are available. The beds near Salt Lake City, where auto racers try for speed records, are the best known.

"We're looking for an alternate lake bed that's dry," he said. "But they're all inaccessible. We'd have to have all the emergency equipment [fire trucks, ambulances, cranes] wherever we'd go. And the B-52 could take off from here and launch up there, but after the X-15 landing, we'd have to pick it up and truck it back to Edwards for the next flight. Also, there might be some snow areas."

"Which lake bed do you think it'd be?"

"Any of the lake beds that run up into Nevada. Maybe Mud Lake or Crater Lake. There's lake beds all the way from Salt Lake down here."

"What's your prognosis?"

"That they won't go as long as there's no push."

"A push like the Russians putting a man into orbit?"

There have been reports from several European capitals recently that the Russians have been preparing to fire a man in a capsule out into space on the nose of a missile.

"Yes," Barton answered. "Something like that."

We talked about the four Russian scientists reportedly launched and lost in space-travel attempts in the last month.

"The decision about the X-15 is up to the top level," he said. "We're proposing the alternate lake-bed landing sites to the Air Force. They have to decide."

THURSDAY, JANUARY 21. Checking with Charlie Brown at Edwards by phone, I found that the X-15 committee—the group of Air Force and NASA officials managing the space ship's flights—hasn't yet decided whether to try a landing at Mud Lake.

At two-thirty Brown called back to say the bet has been hedged: the take-off will be from Edwards as usual, but the launch and landing will be wherever the weather looks best: at Mud Lake if it's raining or overcast at Edwards, or at Edwards if it's clear there. I decided to go to Edwards and take a chance on finding clear weather.

FRIDAY, JANUARY 22. Another long day of preparing for a mission, ending in an abort. I was up at 3 A.M. It was raining and windy as I drove up into the San Gabriels, but a telephone check with the North American control center indicated the mission was still on.

I checked in at NASA and went up to their monitor console or Master Control room, where Bikle, Joe Vensel, Norm West, Norm Hayes, and others of the NASA staff were waiting for the weather to clear. The B-52/X-15 combination was still sitting out in the servicing area, and there was a two-hour hold on the schedule.

There was occasional phone conversation between monitor console and the NASA High-Range station at Beatty, Nevada, 75 miles from Tonopah, to check on the weather.

While we waited, Norm West showed me the rooms full of radar tracking equipment which will give exact readings on the X-15's speed and altitude when it eventually flies the record runs, arcing over the High Range, the chain of radar stations that will follow it automatically all the way from Beatty to Edwards 150 miles to the southwest.

On the NASA roof Norm showed me the massive 10-foot aluminum radar dish, which will automatically track the X-15, the southernmost of a series of similar radar dishes along High Range. Each reaches out 80 miles to pick up the bird, and they automatically interlock.

At nine-thirty this morning the weather washed out at Mud Lake—too overcast. Stan Miller said: "Now the flight depends on the weather here at Edwards. The lake's been certified to be hard enough so they can land on it—if the weather will cooperate."

With Norm Hayes, a NASA instrument specialist, we looked into the roomful of telemetering equipment—high-voltage rectifiers, banks of electrical machinery in green metal cases, batteries of dials, screens, recorders, barographs.

"It can't be overemphasized how important the radar system is in a research project," Hayes said. That was undeniable: radar was the key to any exact measurement of course, speed, and altitude.

But today the equipment wasn't to have a chance to perform. The orange-red tail of the B-52 was still sitting in the service area at Edwards when the mission was called off at 11:30 A.M. The program had slipped again, but not much: now it is set up for tomorrow.

SATURDAY, JANUARY 23. Another early morning, another interminable series of holds that dragged into the day. The last maddening X-15 delay was a broken electric wire in an elevator. It had been broken by accident in the fueling process, and the only way to locate it was to examine every one of the wires in that particular fixture.

But at last, well into the afternoon and as the sunlight was running low at 3:44 P.M., the bird was off, in an almost frantic hurry, as if for once everybody was determined to make this flight happen, or else.

Q. C. Harvey, the test conductor, was far jumpier than usual. "These late take-offs make me nervous," he muttered. "That's the way it was with the No. 3 X-1A when it exploded."

Q. C. was sitting at the NASA Monitor Console panel, in the blind room where the only windows are the charts at one side where radar traces the flight path of the plane.

Scott Crossfield's voice showed a little more tension than usual, though, as always, the strong brake of his will power was operating. His voice sounded consciously firm and unemotional.

As Q. C. gave the word to start the mission, Scott said: "We don't need any briefing. Let's get to the operation."

Q. C. was rushing through a series of last-minute instructions.

Crossfield held him back: "Gently, gently, my friend."

Fitzhugh Fulton, the B-52 pilot for today, reported: "We're topped off. We're puttin' the last of the screws in the elevator." (Where the wire had been broken.)

Stan Miller and I went up to the NASA tower to sit behind the neat little communications secretary, Della Mae Bolling, as amid a group of engineers and technicians she tended the spools of the recording machine monitoring the radio calls.

Beyond her, through the panoramic windows, I saw the tall orange mast of the B-52 moving into position for the take-off.

"It's a beautiful day," said Mrs. Bolling, and she, too, was nervous. "I'm afraid it's going to get dark before they get off."

A technician next to her said he hoped the light lasted long enough for the landing.

Miller was asking Roy Ferren, North American's chief flight test engineer: "What does Scott do when he waits all day like this?"

Ferren said: "He sleeps in the trailer."

Crossfield must have unbelievably good control of his nerves.

Mrs. Bolling was listening intently to the loud-speaker, and also through the single earphone clamped on her head, and, like the others, she seemed to want to talk to relieve the tension.

"It's funny to have the sun coming in from that direction," she said. "Usually it's right in our eyes."

"I hope Fitz is goin' the short way," said one technician in our room —he also was worrying about the lateness of the day.

"Oh, boy, what a lot of dough in one place," said another, as the B-52 at last was airborne and climbing up with a smoky tail of water injection into the soft afternoon light.

As the plane spiraled up, Fitz Fulton checked in quickly: "Ten thousand—260 indicated."

Q. C. acknowledged. "Rog. . . . Scott—everything look okay?"

"Like a million bucks," Scott answered calmly.

The B-52 accelerated toward its launching position in the sky. Over our heads in the tower the mammoth dish antenna of the radar thumped heavily, alarmingly, as it turned to follow the B-52 sky train.

Scott was running through his pressure and temperature checks, reading his instrument panel with machine-gun rapidity, and trying to get his space (stable-platform) instruments ready for a performance check on this, their first flight. The ship is Bird No. 1, and it is the first man-carrying vehicle to be equipped with the space instruments tested in missiles. But it takes time to get the gyro of the stable platform to take correct position. Scott was hurrying along with his regular re- ports on the plumbing system of the ship, the pressures, and temperature readings across the board, and also fitting in stable-platform checks.

"... indicator says 125 degrees ... linear ball saying about 195 ... It's erected—however, it's kinda backward ... comparison ball and azimuth will help here. ..."

Fulton was saying: "Forty-three thousand."

Q. C.: "Rog, Fitz."

Fulton: "Ten minutes."

Q. C.: "Scott, items three through six?"

Scott: "Completed items three through six ... be sure to call me on that landing instrumentation. ... This ball's gone a little ape in *pitch*." [The artificial horizon was out of whack.]

Q. C. "Items seven through ten are complete, Scott. Is that affirmative?"

Q. C. was still talking fast, like everybody else.

Scott: "Through twelve."

Scott flung into his temperature and pressure readings: "Both APUs are in business ... hydraulic pressure 3,250 on No. 1, 3,250 on No. 2 ... No. 1 370 on governor, No. 2 is 360 on governor ... 545 No. 1 tank, 550 No. 2 tank ... electrical power is off ... upper engine preheat is on now ..."

"One minute [to launch], Scott," a voice cut in. It was probably Fulton. "... 30 ... 20 seconds ... 10 seconds ... five, four, three, two, one—*release*." The time was four-seventeen.

We all craned close to the windows to watch the new contrail blooming above the multiple white tails of the B-52 aerial cavalcade.

Scott's voice came with surprising clearness on the radio. He was singing—one line, on key:

"Back in the saddle again."

The firm white trail of the rocket blast forged fast ahead of the sky train, curving toward the south and east.

Our little group in the tower was practically cheering:

"He's goin' up!"

"Boy, isn't that pretty?"

"That's him out in front."

"I hope it is."

A bright dot, the hull of the X-15 catching the sun up high, pierced the blue ahead of the billowing rocket trail. It was climbing, probably nearly at 60,000 feet, circling wide, heading into the eastern sky. Among the group now in the tower I saw Bikle standing beside Ferren, his face bright with enthusiasm.

He was saying to Ferren: "As far as I'm concerned we're about 99 per cent over the hurdle right now."

He meant that the X-15 had practically proved itself, and that the turnover to NASA, which everybody anticipates, can't be far off.

The X-15 was turning back toward Edwards, curving around the eastern sky, power still on. At four twenty-one the power trail disappeared—engines off.

Scott was coming back through the sonic walls—Mach 2 and Mach 1—as he decelerated, and reporting a little buffeting:

"A pretty good buffet—not a good buffet, a mild buffet. . . . I'm just passing Highway 466, due north of the station. . . . I'm on a high initial . . . coming up on 20,000 feet, about 270 [knots] . . . the vertical is armed and the tank pressurized."

At four twenty-seven the lower vertical had been jettisoned and the black cigar was falling swiftly, heavily toward the lake bed, then hitting the surface with a rooster tail of dust, rolling fast.

"It does steer real good," Scott said enthusiastically.

Mrs. Bolling said: "Better look out, or he'll bring it right into the hangar."

And in a second, as if he were on the same psychic wavelength, Scott said: "I'll put it right in the NASA hangar."

The 104 chase plane flown by Bob White zoomed up from above the X-15 as it came to a sudden halt, apparently okay and certainly upright.

"I'm in the mud," Scott said.

Q. C. was still preoccupied with more important things. "Would you turn off the stable platform, Scott?"

"Stable platform off."

In a moment what Crossfield had said about being in the mud got to Q. C.

"How deep are you?"

"I'm just kiddin' you, buddy."

Joe Vensel came into the tower room and joined the mob standing beside the window, watching the helicopter and the emergency vehicles and the official cars gathering around the X-15. One of the engineers called enthusiastically to Vensel:

"Damn—even the damn engine worked."

Joe nodded, and I would bet, from his expression, that he felt as I did, and probably most of us in the room did then, that the X-15 was running in the clear again: that the incubus of the crack-up has been dispelled. It is dispelled by the hard work and stubborn courage of the

hundreds of men and women who make up the X-15 task force—
especially by those traits in the pilot who stuck his neck out again in
the same place to make the flight happen.

Of course the research objectives are far from achieved, and as I
passed through the monitor console room where Q. C. had directed
the flight, a knot of engineers were already talking about the next
problems. I stopped to ask Blake Staub, the stable-platform expert,
how the stable table and space instrumentation had worked out.

He wagged his head negatively: "You have to erect the platform—
we didn't have time enough today. It takes forty-five minutes. You
have to have that before you can get results." Setting up the gyro of
the space instruments takes time.

Driving over the desert toward home, while the sun went down, I
heard the Lancaster radio station with a news bulletin: ". . . the
X-15 was dropped at four-seventeen, touchdown was at four twenty-
seven. It reached 65,000 feet altitude and speed in excess of Mach
2."

KLAC, a Los Angeles station, quoted North American as saying
the speed today was more than 1,400 mph, more than Mach 2.3—a
record for the Black Rocket so far.

TUESDAY, FEBRUARY 9. The weather has been bad—drizzly, windy,
and overcast. But most of the lake beds at Edwards are dry enough
for landing, and a flight is scheduled for tomorrow. It will be another
check on X-15 systems: a North American flight with Crossfield still
the pilot.

A more important piece of news: North American will probably
deliver the No. 1 Bird to NASA and the Air Force soon after the next
mission—so that the really high-powered flights can begin. I talked
to Dick Barton about tomorrow's mission: "There are high winds but
they are expecting them to die down. They may mate the birds at 8
P.M. tonight, or hold it till 4 A.M. tomorrow."

While I had Barton on the wire, I asked if he might arrange an
interview with Crossfield—since we have now reached a new stage in
the X-15 program: the near completion of the manufacturer's demonstration flights and the turnover to the customers, NASA and the
Air Force.

WEDNESDAY, FEBRUARY 10. A check with North American Control
Center this morning revealed that the flight was canceled because of
the rainy, stormy weather.

THURSDAY, FEBRUARY 11. Today, the flight finally got off, and was successful. It was Bird No. 2, the first time this bird has been flown since the repairs after the crack-up. Bird No. 1, I find out, is being readied now for the turnover to NASA.

The flight went almost on schedule: take-off at nine-seven, landing at ten twenty-seven, a ten-minute free flight for the X-15 with four minutes under power. Today the rocket ship went higher than ever before: to 86,000 feet. These manufacturer's demonstration flights are restricted by Air Force instructions to a maximum of 100,000 feet altitude, and Mach 2 speed—although almost every time he flies it, Crossfield, despite cutting his throttles long before burnout, exceeds the Mach 2 limitation. There has to be some elasticity in this speed limitation. It is hard to hold the bird back that much. On the last mission, the flight in the late afternoon, he went to 1,400 mph because he wanted to have power on for the final turn that would bring him back to the lake bed. He was afraid he might not get a restart if he chopped power on the eastward leg; might, therefore, not have had power to get back to base. He's certainly entitled to this kind of discretionary judgment where his own safety and the safety of the bird are concerned.

With today's flight and the last one, Crossfield has killed two nagging dragons: last time, he flew an X-15 successfully for the first time after the crash. This time, he laid the ghost of the crash by flying the repaired bird, the same one he'd cracked up, without mishap.

In today's test, all the systems checked out well—all the valves and pressures and temperatures, the engines, the stability augmentation system—everything with one slight exception: Crossfield's oxygen ran out at ten twenty-seven and a half, just as the bird was completing its landing roll. On the radio we could hear his breath getting short as he read his instrument panel aloud, and he said:

"I gotta get out of here. I'm not gettin' any oxygen out of this thing."

Q. C. Harvey was quick to respond: "Rog—APUs off and open the canopy."

As we filed out of Monitor Console, Stan Miller waxed enthusiastic about the mission: "Things look real good. There wasn't any horsing around. They just took him up and dropped him."

Over at the North American hangar I heard the same opinion. Gordon Gray, of the North American public-relations staff, said enthusiastically: "I never saw such a gleeful bunch of guys. Everything went well—even the SAS worked. They were saying everything was going too good."

I also sought Joe Walker, who had flown the 104 chase today, just before the debriefing began. He looked tired.

"How'd it go?" I asked him. He extended thumbs up.

"He did a lot of roll and yaw?" I knew Scott was still checking control response and the reaction of the ship to stresses and maneuvers.

"He was doing a lot of pulses—side slip, roll, yaw."

"Look good?"

"What I could see of it."

"He left you far behind, didn't he?"

"Far below—I was lookin' up."

I asked him the really important question: "When are *you* going to fly it?"

But Joe ignored it. He rushed off to the debriefing. It would be up to the top brass, such as Bikle, to give me the dope about the beginning of the NASA flights.

I passed Scott Crossfield going into the debriefing with Q. C. Harvey, Cokeley, and Roy Ferren, and Crossfield said he'd told Barton he'd accede to the request for an interview: he'd see me tomorrow.

FRIDAY, FEBRUARY 12. Barton and I finally caught up with Crossfield after tracking him over the lot, at about four o'clock. He came into Barton's office, saying he was due for an appointment with Storms in eight minutes.

I had a lengthy list of questions. One topical one was: why is he so shy about reporters, especially in protecting his family from the press?

"I don't want my family to be involved," he said decisively. "Once you get it started, you're in for it. A few times the reporters nearly got it broken down."

I surmised that at some time he must have had an unpleasant, perhaps even traumatic experience with the press. Or maybe his attitudes come simply from mistrust, perhaps even from ignorance of the press. I could see that I had touched on a sore point. I asked how many boys, how many girls, in his family.

"Three boys and two girls." He was still exercised. "I've got a strange feeling that the boys should fight their own battles. They're going to have to get there by themselves—not riding on the X-15's coattails. I don't want to be in the position of ever having let them arrive at this condition."

I assumed he meant a position of public note for them because of his flights in the X-15. I told him I didn't think his accomplishments in the X-15 would bring enough publicity to spoil the kids. He said he didn't want to take a chance on that. He said his oldest boy, Thomas Scott Crossfield, aged ten, had already been challenged by a toughie at school who wanted to fight and prove he was as good as the son of Scott Crossfield.

In the short time available today I was able to extract only a few more answers from Crossfield. I asked him about the most dangerous moment of his career with the X-15. "We've never had an emergency, a real tough situation. You're not in a dangerous situation until you run out of alternatives . . . unless you panic—and we don't do that."

I was surprised by this because his *Saturday Evening Post* articles are quite vocal about the dangerous moments of the program, facts I'd had to dig out the hard way after Crossfield's noncommittal answers when questioned by the press on flight days. There were, of course, the loss of stability and near crack-up on the first glide flight, the fires and explosions, the near collisions, the injury of the crewman when the bird exploded on the ground, the pranging of the bird on the day of the big explosion.

I asked Crossfield about the best moments of the program so far and he fought the idea.

"We don't feel elated because the airplane will fly. We made it to fly." He was working himself around to some acceptance of the question. "Maybe the glide flight. There had been a considerable uninformed negativism about the landing qualities of the aircraft. We got away with a very fine landing under adverse conditions."

He fought clear of comment on the causes of the instability on the first flight: "It was purely mechanical. I won't go into it any more than that."

I asked him for another appointment in the near future when he might not be so pressed for time; certainly he had been uneasy today, with the interview with his boss coming up. He said maybe an interview could be arranged after the next flight.

WEDNESDAY, FEBRUARY 17. Crossfield made another flight in the No. 2 Bird today, to make a few checks of the way it responds to stresses. He was scheduled to make a 6-g pull-out, something like the record pilots will make when they pull out of a ballistic flight in space. But he couldn't carry out the maneuver today because his upper engine quit shortly after launch.

FRIDAY, FEBRUARY 19. I had another interview with Crossfield today. Barton and I met him in his office, one of many semi-enclosed cubby-holes in the North American engineering department. It's semi-en-closed in that the frosted glass walls come up only part of the way to the ceiling. It's really more of a compartment than an office; but in the hierarchy of engineers it's luxury and distinction. Only the upper echelon have these private chambers: the lower ranks have to share offices, and most of the men work in the huge auditorium-like main room amid fluorescent lights and angled drafting tables set in close rows like shingles.

Scott is now chief engineering test pilot for North American; he has succeeded Bob Baker in the job; Baker is leaving the company, going to Air Research, where he has a selling job. Thus Scott is of-ficially in charge of North American's test pilots—though 99 per cent of his time is given to the X-15.

We had another wait for Scott. We talked to Marian Brown, his pretty secretary, while we waited; and had a chance to look around the office, which looks mostly like a shrine to the X-15. Above Scott's desk are a triptych of large portraits of the X-15: attached to the B-52, in flight and landing. On the left, the handsome model of the X-15 which Storms gave him. On the right wall, a chart of space and the planets, and one of the atmosphere listing air pressure at the vari-ous altitudes.

On the desk top stand miniature photographic reproductions of two X-15 instrument boards: the one at the right is the panel with the old-fashioned pressure instruments. The other carries gyro-driven true space instruments for speed and altitude, the stable-platform dials which are so revolutionary and new. At the center of the left-hand board some wag has mounted an extra small panel, red with a black button at the center, and bold yellow letters: PANIC BUTTON.

Near the desk is a glass-topped conference table. Under the glass, an original (not printed) cartoon evidently drawn by one of the North American draftsmen—a man of talent. It shows the B-52 in flight, the pilot sticking his head out the window, consternation in his face as he looks toward the X-15 under the wing and notices that there's nobody in the cockpit.

"4-3-2—?" he's saying. "Hey—where's Scotty?"

Another drawing inserted nearby has the title "Meanwhile, back at the office." The picture shows a desk labeled "Chief Engineering Test Pilot," with stacks of papers piled on it. Scott, wearing the silver suit and helmet, with a hose connected to an oxygen tap at deskside, is immersed in the paper work.

On top of the glass-covered table lay a drawing tablet on which Crossfield had been making a crude sketch of the X-15, showing the tankage. In the fashion of most engineers he had been quick to make a drawing to explore or exhibit some design question. Scott thinks like an engineer and the X-15 is his favorite subject, so here was an expected phenomenon.

As Barton and I were looking at his cockeyed sketch, Crossfield came in, and Barton kidded him: "With your talent in drawing, you should win an art scholarship."

"That's what I want—recognition for drawing ability," Crossfield said, smiling. He set about lengthening one wing that was palpably too short in the sketch, while I asked him some questions.

I got him to talk frankly and at some length about the beginnings of the X-15. He said he had worked on the X-15 concept as far back as 1952 when he was working as a research engineer and pilot for NACA at Edwards. In fact, "Walt Williams and I—simultaneously with other people—invented the X-15. It was when the Navy was negotiating about a D-558-3 with Douglas. I was with Williams, Truszynski, and Vensel, coming back from a fishing trip. We heard on the radio news that a Redstone had been launched with 75,000 pounds thrust, from Rocketdyne.

"We started putting figures together—mundane physics. You have an engine with so much thrust and weight—can build an airplane around it that would weigh 25,000 to 30,000 pounds . . .

"Williams passed it over to Drake [Hubert Drake, then assistant chief of research at the NACA High Speed Flight Station at Edwards]."

At the same time, Crossfield said, the Langley facility of NACA in Virginia had also been doing some calculations about an X-type rocket plane to follow on the heels of the X-2 (the X-2 was first airborne in 1952, in glide tests. But for lack of a proper rocket engine, it didn't make a powered flight until the end of 1955). "In 1953 NACA's study came out, giving views on an advanced version of the [X-15] airplane. The specifications were laid out for it."

So, Crossfield continued, he asked Ezra Kotcher, at the Scientific Advisory Board meeting in 1955, to give him a boost into the job as X-15 test pilot. But he had been associated with the X-15 from the earliest days, and had actually worked on it as an NACA employee.

When I got Crossfield going about his favorite subject, that rocket ship, he went on for a while with some frank opinions; he was very violent about those certain people who had opposed the project. I could see how much like his own children the three X-15s are to him; he's violently protective about both broods. But when I tried to steer him to talking about something more personal, the dangers he faced in this test program, he shied away: he said I was wrong if I insisted that he must feel tension.

"I don't consider flying the X-15 especially dangerous unless I goof."

He added matter-of-factly, "I memorize the flight plan and I know these engines intimately"—these being the main steps he takes to avoid what he calls goofing because "if I do something wrong, it's because I missed something." But that was the end of it; he shifted the conversation to Q. C. Harvey, who as test director "has the toughest job in the world . . . Q. C. is a sort of copilot on the ground."

I said I certainly agreed about Q. C.'s importance and ability, and I steered back to his flying—especially his plans for flying the Big Engine, the power plant that should take the X-15 well into space.

He said he was very restricted on what he could do with that engine because of the NASA and Air Force instructions.

"If NASA and the Air Force have their way," he said, "we'll barely get to light that engine."

I asked if he didn't feel like shooting for greater performance even with the Small Engine, and he said yes, looking quite assertive about it now. "All I'd have to do is leave the switches on a little longer." He summed it up: "We're jealous of this airplane, and we're proud of it."

After we left Scott, and were walking out of the factory, I asked Barton about the expected turnover of Bird No. 1 to NASA. He said it should be soon, in the next few days. He added that the NASA and Air Force people want to start their tests, naturally, but that Scott has been opposed to the turnover without some more checkouts, and he also worries about some of the pilots not having enough training yet. That figures, with a man as single-minded and as emotionally involved with this bird as he is.

WEDNESDAY, FEBRUARY 24. Checked with Marion Kent, the administrative head at NASA, in Edwards, to see when the turnover of the first X-15 (Bird No. 1) is going to be.

He said the big yellow NASA stripe has already been painted on the tail of Bird No. 1, and the NASA dark blue circular shield of space and stars emblazoned on the nose (the large letters U.S. AIR

FORCE and USAF, and the white star insignia of our country, have been on the birds since the beginning).

"We're not going to be making a big thing of the turnover—no speeches. They're just going to be making pictures—pictures to make the turnover official, that's all."

Then, he said, the first flights of Joe Walker and Bob White should be occurring within a few weeks. Maybe as quickly as two weeks. From then on, if things go well, the program will be stepping up toward maximum performance runs.

A North American flight of Bird No. 2, with Crossfield at the controls, is still scheduled for tomorrow. Barton tells me there will be three or four flights more for Crossfield in this bird, to run more checks on the systems (such as the Ballistic Control System) and do a few more pull-ups, rolls, and turns to prove the design is structurally strong enough.

This time I've fixed it up to go down to the North American tower at Los Angeles International Airport to watch the flight. I'm told that on a clear day one can see the contrails of the B-52/X-15 sky train 75 air-line miles to the north, and also see the big trail the X-15 makes against the sky as it flies under rocket power. Also, you can hear the radio calls except at landing and take-off when the mountains get in the way. Barton said it's a small room, the North American tower, so only a few people can be there to watch the flight. But he can set it up for me for one time. He said some of the X-15 engineers who can't get up to Edwards for the flight watch from the tower. So does Marian Brown, Crossfield's secretary. I'll be interested to see their reactions as their X-15 baby flies.

THURSDAY, FEBRUARY 25. This morning, after a series of holds because of high winds and overcast weather, the flight was at last canceled, shortly after ten o'clock. It's set up now for tomorrow.

FRIDAY, FEBRUARY 26. I checked the North American control center at six forty-five this morning and the unusually sociable company cop on duty said:

"There's a holdup—because of the weather. It's about in the same situation as yesterday. I just heard Scotty talkin' to somebody and sayin' there's no hurry. They're holdin' up on servicin'—and you know it's three hours after servicin' before they can take off."

At nine-fifteen I checked with Barton. "They haven't started to service yet. The chances don't look very good. I think Scott is still down here. The weather is still against flying up there—it's overcast and the wind is starting up now."

I said it seems impossible there could be strong winds *and* a heavy overcast, too. But Dick said it happens often at Edwards this time of year.

At a time like this, when there's one hold after another *ad infinitum,* I think about Crossfield and the strain of build-up, overtraining, and anticlimax and letdown that must badger his nervous system. It must be especially vexing when he has to wait around in the miserable, muggy silver suit up at Edwards in the suit-up trailer. Today he was waiting around at the North American plant, knowing that if the weather at Edwards began to clear, he could fly up and be on deck before servicing was finished.

Crossfield always says the strain isn't hard on him—he worries only about the ground crew, he doesn't want them to get overstrained, because that's when accidents happen. One thing seems certain: Crossfield has remarkably good nervous control; he's been in the X-15 flight program for eleven months, and made 19 flights, not counting twice that many attempts canceled before the birds were airborne. The strain shows in his pale, somewhat peaked and drawn face. But the face was that way before the flights began—the worn visage of the test pilot.

Probably the strain will be worse on White and Walker, because they have had less experience in adjusting to the ordeal; also because they will be working with vast governmental agencies not so well geared to making life passably comfortable for the rocket test pilot as a faster-moving and probably more efficient private company. Often, in a long experience with the military and the government, I have thought that there seems to be a dedication toward making life as uncomfortable as possible for government employees. When you start with an occupation as basically uncomfortable as a test pilot's job, and multiply it by the slowness and impersonality of a government agency, you can come up with considerable physical misery for the pilot. But I know that neither White nor Walker would give up the honor of their jobs—not even for all the money and comfort and security they could garner as salesmen for one of the major aircraft companies. They are in this X-15 program and they have what to me is the most admirable kind of philosophy; what Nietzsche called "an over-going and down-going," the tremendous, driving will which is the mark of the Superman. Probably neither White nor Walker ever read Nietzsche and maybe never even heard of him. But if I invoked the motto of the

238

X-15 DIARY

Nisei troops in our heroic Japanese-American 100th Infantry Battalion in World War II—"Go for broke"—both Walker and White would know exactly what I meant. Both would no doubt deny that they were taking that kind of chance, they would say their jobs are scientific and as safe as possibly can be. But their necks will be out as much as Crossfield's has been and perhaps more—and their measure of protracted discomfort and even misery, and their need for rapid skill and dogged courage and inventiveness may also be greater. That is, if they survive.

MONDAY, FEBRUARY 29. It's been raining hard yesterday and today—not good for the flight schedule. I called Barton and he said of course the next North American flight would be put off for a while. He doesn't know how much because "we haven't found out how much water there is on the lake beds yet."

I checked with Matt Portz at NASA and he said their first mission will probably be two or three weeks off. "The plan is Joe Walker will make the first flight." He let it rest there. Portz is a man of few words, not very voluble as you might expect of a public information chief; perhaps it's his long training as a Navy flight instructor that shows through. Words come cautiously from him. You can almost see him being judicious, as if he were commenting on a student's flight.

"Then Bob White will take the next one?" I asked.

"Yes."

"And White and Walker will alternate flights?"

"Yes."

One very good thing about Portz as a public information man: the dope he gives you is accurate.

MONDAY, MARCH 7. The weather has been sunny, and Blount says the lake beds should be dry enough for a landing by Friday—although the next flight will likely slip till next week.

He told me one great piece of news: "We're expecting the Big Engine soon. Maybe next week. Some of the engineers have gone to Reaction Motors for inspection. We might know tomorrow." He said that the 900-pound hunk of convoluted metal will probably be sent to Edwards by Air Express.

FRIDAY, MARCH 18. Up at two-thirty this morning and drove to NASA headquarters for a quick repeat flight by Crossfield, which was supposed to take off at 0800, was airborne at 0808, but didn't launch. A leaky fuel prime line caused the abort.

I saw the old familiar North American engineering faces at the NASA Monitor Console room—Q. C. Harvey, Blake Staub, Bud Benner—and the new group of NASA engineers breaking in: Tom Finch, Norm West, Norm Hayes. The men were working side by side with the North American engineers in command. Next time, in a flight scheduled for next Tuesday, the NASA engineers will be in charge and the North American men only looking over their shoulders as consultants, when Joe Walker of NASA becomes the first man other than Crossfield to fly the X-15. He'll make a powered flight, then maybe a week or ten days after that Bob White will follow for the Air Force. But the North American people are far from washed up on X-15 as yet: there are still some flights Crossfield must make on Bird No. 2, system checks. And sometime, perhaps in midsummer, the Big Engine will be flying in Bird No. 3, or 66672, Crossfield at the controls. The Big Engine still hasn't arrived at Edwards. It should be here next week.

LANCASTER, TUESDAY, MARCH 22. I drove to Lancaster, 25 miles from Edwards, yesterday, and spent the night at the Caravan to be on deck early for today's first NASA flight. The history of today's effort wasn't much different from what happened often on a North American mission: the start of servicing in the dark of night, under floodlights—the rush of mechanical problems and solutions, the breakneck efforts to meet deadlines, the radio problems, the frustrating long holds after the mechanical problems are worked out. And at last, an abort because of the weather—in this case, clouds.

I had arranged with Stan Miller of NASA to pay a visit to the X-15 servicing area before the flight; to have a look at the NASA service crew now for the first time preparing the bird all by themselves. We had to start early, in the dark, for this.

I picked up Miller at 5 A.M. at his home in Lancaster. Besides being involved as public information officer in NASA's critical first flight, Miller was facing a personal problem today. I knew his wife was pregnant, and now I found out how acute the problem had become.

He was looking even more serious and intent than usual as he came out to the car.

"Mom's in labor," he announced as he climbed aboard. He said he'd go out to Edwards, and to the servicing area with me, but he'd probably break away to come back to the maternity ward at Lancaster and wait for the impending blessed event.

At NASA headquarters Stan and I climbed into a NASA truck with an equipment man hauling a parachute out for one of the B-52 crewmen.

The servicing area was the same as I had known for the year of the North American test program, an Air Force service facility: the same elongated yellow Air Force tank trucks were drawn up in the dawn light, labeled "Water Alcohol—No Smoking," "Liquid Oxygen—No Smoking," and there were the smaller trailers, the liquid-nitrogen and helium chilling units, the hydrogen-peroxide cart, and to one side the huge freight-car-like suit-up trailer for dressing the X-15 pilot in the silver suit. We arrived too late to see the hooded Hot Papas doing their fueling work in fireproof suits. The floodlights were out now but the generators still whirred, bringing emergency power. And the same security cordon, a rope with a guard, kept rubbernecks away.

One conspicuous difference was in the people clambering around the black dart shape under the B-52 wing, and up and down the steps of the metal workstand. They still wore fatigue suits and rough jackets against the morning chill, but now they were different people, and they had a new uniform badge, a red, sharp-billed baseball cap with the blue-circle shield of NASA on the front.

Now the red caps with the blue shields were visible in the X-15 cockpit and around it, too. The man in the cockpit, Miller told me, was Ralph Haley, a lead man, and bending over to talk to him was Ted Rasckowski, a crew chief. Near the foot of the workstand a tall man in khaki pants talked to a shorter one in a flying suit—respectively Jack Russell and Jack Moise, launch panel operators.

I walked around to the side to see the X-15 in its new war paint: the old white AIR FORCE lettering on the fuselage and USAF on the wing, and the number of this first of the three birds, 66670 on the tail, all are still there. But there are big bright new yellow stripes on the tail, too, and the blue-circle shield of NASA on the nose. The black, slick dart is getting quite garish.

Rasckowski walked away from the plane for a moment and Miller introduced us. Rasckowski is a tall man with wide shoulders and steady gray eyes. I asked him how the NASA ground crew could take over the job so easily, and he smiled.

"We've been at it a year," he said, "training for it. Six or seven of us—the crew chief, lead men, supervisors—went to North American in April–May of 1958, that far back. Then a lot of us have been do-ing actual work, mechanics and observers, here for a year."

I hadn't known the NASA people had been so close.

Rasckowski (pronounced Raz-kowski) said the hardest problem the NASA boys had was learning the workings of the APUs, the Auxiliary Power Units. That was surprising to me because it seemed that the bigger systems, like the engines, the turbopumps, the nitrogen and helium systems and the telemetering and instrumentation, would be tougher to learn. But Rasckowski reminded me of a fact I had disregarded: that many of the ground crew had worked on rocket ships for NASA for years before, when it was called NACA. He, too, had worked on the X-2 as a crew chief, but for Bell Aircraft. And the APU system was brand new.

Stan Miller wanted to get back to the NASA headquarters to make a telephone check on whether he was yet a father, and whether the arrival was male or female, so we trundled back in the truck.

We found there was still a hold on take-off: the delay was not mechanical, it was caused by an old enemy, a recalcitrant radio. And a still older foe, the weather, was beginning to look bad—the winter clouds deepening and spreading overhead, blotting the vision the X-15 pilot would need to pick his landing spot on the lake bed as he glides in after his powered flight.

We sat in the NASA cafeteria talking to the boss man, Paul Bikle, while Stan Miller fidgeted—a phone call to the Lancaster hospital had revealed that Mrs. Miller was still in labor. And he didn't want to leave Edwards as long as the first NASA X-15 flight was still on. I was ask-ing Bikle about the Big Engine, whether it had been delivered, and he answered:

"For three months they've said it was ready to ship. But it hasn't arrived yet."

Bikle spoke without much enthusiasm about the Small Engine; he referred to it as "the little engine" with almost pitying condescension. He said that if the Big Engine arrives soon and tests out well, "we might drop it [the Small Engine] and shift over."

He did say, though, that until the Big Engine becomes a workable quantity, speed and altitude runs will be made with the Small Engine, and the world records for both speed and altitude can be and probably will be broken. That means that even with the Small Engine, White or Walker will be going beyond atmosphere, into space, and beyond the altitude Kincheloe hit that day in 1956 when he climbed higher than any man had ever been, to 126,200 feet, in the X-2.

At nine fifty-three Matt Portz announced to the correspondents hanging around the public information and security office at the NASA building that there was an indefinite hold on take-off. The weather was getting worse, he said, and there was a three-tenths cloud cover, too much to allow an X-15 landing.

It began to look as if the mission would slip another day—and by now the can-do Marine type, Stan Miller, was at last satisfied that his duty for today was fulfilled, and he had slipped off for the Lancaster hospital maternity ward.

The flight wasn't definitely canceled yet, but Portz announced that he had arranged a press conference with both White and Walker, and they met us in the NASA debriefing room in a few minutes, both freshly showered and changed out of their flying clothes, so it seemed likely that the flight wouldn't go today, unless late in the afternoon by some miracle the clouds cleared. White had been scheduled to fly as a chase pilot for Walker's mission today.

White and Walker faced a barrage of questions, mostly about the NASA and Air Force program, and when the record flights would be happening, the world's speed and altitude records broken. Joe Walker said unhesitatingly: "The next step—we'd put Bob White on the same flight—then we'll extend up to the maximum we can get with this power plant. We've planned increments of five hundredths of a Mach number, but we're gonna have to jiggle the increments depending on launch availability." (Bikle corrected this to "five tenths of a Mach number" instead of five hundredths.)

Someone asked about the Big Engine, when that program would be happening, and Joe answered: "I've thought we'd be under way by September or October with the 99 engine."

About the altitude and speed records that can be hit with the Small Engine: "We're pretty sure we can beat the X-2."

Several of the newsmen wanted to know how Walker and White had been preparing for their rather daring current job: taking the X-15 up, launching, making a powered flight, and landing without ever having been at the controls of the aircraft.

White said both he and Walker had checked out in the X-15 simulator, and for two years they had been landing the F-104 in the dirty configuration, with flaps down and power off, to simulate X-15 landings. Also they both have been flying chase for Crossfield, and from this they learn "the action of the airplane as it comes off the shackle and during the climb out—and how he makes his approach."

Someone wanted to know if the two pilots had arranged consultations with Crossfield, and White answered:

"We got the reports, and we've gotten together and just bulled the thing out—not just once but several times, at the convenience of the personnel involved."

What he seemed to be saying was that there hadn't been very many consultations with Crossfield.

Joe Walker was questioned about his attitude toward the flight. He was a little noncommittal and someone rephrased the question:

"What is your personal reaction to it—are you excited, anxious, worried, hesitant about it?"

Walker laughed and said, "Yes!" But then he saw that he had missed something that needed tending, and he added seriously: "The word 'hesitant' does not apply in any way . . . I'm kind of disappointed that we got clouded out. I was really cranked up to go."

I asked Bob White how many flights he thought it would take to get to a maximum altitude mission. "Eight or ten," he said.

"How long will it take to get eight or ten flights off—two months?"

He smiled. "We'd like that very much."

Portz closed up the conference and the corps of newsmen headed back for Lancaster, there to wait for final word about today's mission —whether it would be canceled or not.

As I reached the city limits I saw a dusty brown sedan following me and tooting his horn. I pulled over and as the car passed I saw that it was Stan Miller. He yelled:

"It's a boy!"

About noontime we were still waiting for word about the mission. Julian Hartt checked with Edwards and passed on the word:

"The birds are being kept mated but the mission is canceled for today because of the weather."

Hartt, who is a very able aerospace, aviation, and rocket correspondent, said he is concerned about the danger Walker faces on his first X-15 flight.

"He's the first man except Scott and he's going to start cold and go right into powered flight. He's got no time to get used to it as Scott did."

I agreed: Scott had a glide flight and five captive flights before he tried power. But it seems to me that the transition will be even more violent for White, who's never flown a rocket. At least Walker has piloted several of those.

WEDNESDAY, MARCH 23. Telephone calls in the wee hours of the morning revealed that there was an indefinite hold on today's schedule because of the cloudy weather, and at nine-thirty it was canceled. Also, the prophecy for tomorrow's weather is bad. The correspondent corps shoved off for the big city.

FRIDAY, MARCH 25. After one more day's slippage because of the weather, the mission was on for today—and it went.

I drove up from Los Angeles to Edwards in the small hours of the morning with Matt Portz, the West Coast public information chief for NASA. It's a long pull, about two and a half hours up into the mountains and desert, and we had plenty of time to talk.

I said I thought this must have been a tough week for Joe Walker, full of tension and buildups to anticlimaxes.

"Yes, but he's used to it," Matt answered.

I said: "It's going to be tougher for White than Walker. White's never had rocket time."

"Time in a turbojet fighter is a lot like rocket time," he said, as concisely as usual.

Portz had just come back from a NASA policy meeting in Washington and I asked him rather bluntly:

"What is NASA's emphasis going to be? Are they going to downplay the X-15 and build up Mercury?"

But he didn't want to answer that directly. I was treading on confidential material from an agency conference.

"X-15 is the last of a long line of research aircraft," he said. "It's the last of the flyboys." And I could make my own interpretation of that.

We arrived at NASA's Edwards headquarters about seven-fifteen and found Miller waiting for us.

"There's a two-hour delay," he said. "A ruptured lox hose. They have to purge the lox, replace the hose, and refill."

At nine-thirty Bossman Paul Bikle came by and passed the word that the flight might get off by noon. The weather was fine. It was just the lox line that was holding things up.

Colonel Charlie Brown, the Air Force P.I.O., took a group of us correspondents for a tour to Rocket Ridge, to pass some waiting time—and to look at a new test stand being built for a new rocket engine of one and a half million pounds thrust. It's the F-1 power plant for the big Nova rocket scheduled to be sent in the 1970s to an orbit around Mars. Nova is the biggest announced NASA rocket—a thing of the far future: 2,400 tons at take-off, 220 feet long, 44 feet in diameter, with a thrust of four F-1 engines totaling 6,000,000 pounds thrust. But probably a space taxi related to the X-15 will ferry people in from Nova to the far planet.

When we got back to NASA headquarters, we heard the flight was postponed till 2 P.M. But then it slipped some more. Portz said that the lox line was fixed and take-off scheduled for three-fifteen with launch at four. This was getting perilously close to the end of the daylight.

We dropped by the servicing area and saw that the work, as one might expect, was going on at an urgent pace. Now the North American mobile-control wagon was drawn up near the plane, and I saw familiar faces of the North American engineers hovering about to help if they should be needed: Harry Gallenos, a power-plant engineer; bulky Bill Berkowitz, the launch operator of the company flights; Pete Barker, of human factors; and the dependable, prime-mover engineer, Cooper Lindley.

Lindley said tactfully: "We have done nothing. NASA has done it all. We're just a sort of backstop in case something goes wrong."

I asked him how he felt about the new pilot about to take over his bird. "Every time you put a new pilot in a bird you get a little edgy," he said.

As we were talking we could see Joe Walker, in the silver suit, climbing into the X-15 cockpit.

Lindley said: "It's really not the first time around for him. He's had a lot of time in the simulator—that gives him the feel of the X-15."

I asked how Lindley felt about his own job on X-15 now that the turnover is a fact. "It feels like another flight except I don't have any responsibility. Most of the fellas seem a little lost—they're walking around as if they don't know what to do."

At two-fifteen the black lid of the cockpit was down and we could see a white object dimly behind the slits of the dark windows: Walker's helmet.

At two-twenty the public-address system announced: "Starting engines." The B-52 engines barked, then began to scream. The screaming keyed the feeling of excitement higher. Stan Hall, the tall UPI correspondent standing near me, muttered a kind of prayer: "Good luck to you, Joe."

Our press cavalcade of Air Force cars rumbled out to the main runway to watch the take-off. We saw the tall mast of the B-52 tail moving

as it taxied, then the smudge cloud as the pilot poured the coal on
with water injection, the moving, shimmering mast in the heat. At
two forty-two, a little earlier than the last schedule, the big bomber
was climbing up into a bright sky. There was no weather problem
today, at least not yet.

Our caravan streaked across the shiny lake bed to the tufted dune,
near Mile 2 on Scotty's runway, which is now known as Press Island
or Press Knoll.

Colonel Brown took charge of the press delegation. He had sent
an Air Force communications crew out earlier to string a field phone
connecting with Mobile Control on the lake bed, so that he could
supply the press with bulletins on the progress of the flight.

Now Brown picked up the phone and talked into it, and reported
to us:

"We're in contact with the world."

"What's it say?" one of the newsmen wanted to know.

"Go home, American."

"Where's Scotty today?" someone asked.

"In the F-100," said Colonel Brown. Crossfield was one of the
chase pilots for Walker. A newsman added: "His [Crossfield's] mother
died last night." She had been ill for some time. This was one of the
personal matters Crossfield had tried to keep to himself.

I looked up into the northern sky, where the fat vapor trails of the
B-52 unreeled. A slim, small contrail followed it closely. That would
be Crossfield in the F-100, the closest plane in the sky.

The mobile-control vehicles—the van, the suit-up trailer, the ambulance, fire trucks, and crane and Air Force cars—were only a few
hundred feet from us, at the next dune ridge. We could hear the blatting of their public-address system and see the crowd of engineers
(and doubtless many rubbernecks) clustered around the van now
borrowed from North American by NASA. But we couldn't pick out
the words on the public-address system, they were just too far off.
It was maddening almost to hear but not quite make it. Mobile Control didn't want the press clogging up their act.

At three-six, we had a bulletin from Charlie Brown: "Twenty-five
minutes to drop."

But in general there seemed to be nothing to report. Brown's in-
formant at the other end of the wire, at Mobile Control, was Matt
Portz, and though Colonel Brown kept asking for "quotable quotes,"
the taciturn Portz was living up to his reputation as a man of few
words.

Colonel Brown, like the local reporters who came from the desert area, was now watching the sky worriedly as the contrails of the B-52 sky train spiraled higher. I noted now that the rough grass on the dunes was moving in the wind, and Charlie Brown said:

"The wind seems to be freshening a bit."

The sudden springing of the wind was ominous. In the afternoons, the Mojave Desert breezes frequently reach gale force—far more than needed to cancel an X-15 flight.

The B-52 group was circling toward the east. Charlie Brown squinted apprehensively at the sky.

"That desert wind!" he said. "All of a sudden—it's nice and quiet —and boom!"

Bill Solberg, a news commentator from the Lancaster radio station, agreed: "It gets worse, too—from this time of day on." The time was three-nineteen.

Charlie Brown called out via the public-address system: "Eleven minutes to drop."

I moved a few feet to the scraggy dune where four Air Force cameramen, veteran sergeants in fatigue pants and T-shirts, had set up their Big Bertha movie cameras, the long fat barrels on heavy tripods. All the barrels pointed to the same area in the northern sky where they knew the launch would probably take place. They, too, were jumpy, partly because picking out a fast-moving rocket plane in flight with a telephoto lens and holding it is a feat, and partly because they, too, knew the suddenness with which the desert gales can spring up in the Mojave.

The sergeants had the patient, long-suffering manner of the average "rocker boy," the noncom who has learned over the years to roll with the inertia and impersonality of the service, but now they were keyed up, pulling for the man in the sky.

"He's gonna drop on this one," said Master Sergeant Chuck Lewis, squinting into the sky. "He's just gonna make his run, level out east, and drop."

But the wind was getting bad. In gusts, it seemed to be 20 or 25 miles an hour. We all knew that a crosswind or downwind landing could be very tricky and dangerous with the skid landing gear of the X-15.

The B-52 was churning across the northern sky with its chases, heading toward the spot where the drop is usually made. Chuck Lewis, judging by the previous radio calls about drop time, gave us a time hack:

"One minute and fifteen seconds."

Colonel Brown didn't have any bulletins to relay on his mike—Matt Portz at Mobile Control wasn't passing any along.

"Give us a countdown," Sergeant John Morgan called out to Lewis. Morgan and the others were fiddling tensely with their cameras. Lewis obliged:

"Twenty . . . fifteen . . . ten . . . nine . . . eight . . . seven . . . six . . . five . . . four . . . three . . . two . . . one—*drop!*" But there was no new contrail springing out of the sector of sky where the B-52 moved.

"No drop," said Lewis, crushed. And in a moment Colonel Brown came up with a new call:

"Returning to a five-minute drop warning." There had been some trouble up there and a delay. We had no word about it from Mobile Control.

"Tell him to come on in—we'll work tomorrow," Lewis offered. It was quite an offer for a salaried military worker; tomorrow would be week end, Saturday.

Now, with five whole minutes before drop, time seemed to hang heavy. And I watched the tufts of coarse grass moving on the dune top in the gusts. You could hear the wind blowing now.

Chuck, the talkative one, was working out some of his tension by summarizing one of the choice passages in Errol Flynn's book, *My Wicked, Wicked Ways.* "That's my kind of man," he said.

Charlie Brown announced on the public-address system: "One minute and a half . . . one minute."

Chuck said to Carmie Zaccardi, one of his sergeant cooperators, as Carmie bent over the barrel of his camera, correcting his aim to the north: "You gonna catch him, Carmie?"

Chuck was counting down: "Thirty seconds . . . twenty . . . fifteen . . ."

The camera barrels had a uniform alignment, something these old motion-picture operators had learned in years of covering the Xs. They and the eyes of the press corps stared at the same spot in the northwestern sky.

"Ten, nine, eight, seven, six, five, four, three, two, one—*drop.*"

We saw the new fat white wake of the rocket jump into the sky below the B-52, immediately surging ahead of the other contrails.

The photographers were bending over their cameras, they were working and had him, but they were talking, too. It was a moment of excitement, a kind of baptism for the latest of the Xs, because for once somebody besides Crossfield was hitting those rockets.

"That's him with the thick contrail."

"He's goin' now."

"We ought to hear the boom-boom now."

It really was too soon to hear a sonic boom from that distance—and as a matter of fact I had never yet heard one from the X-15 as it went through the Mach. It was usually so far away you couldn't hear any sounds.

"Goddam, he's movin'."

The rocket tail was way ahead of the B-52 to the chases, now, curving south and east.

Zaccardi said: "New record, man, new record."

Morgan: "He's kind of movin' out today."

But it was no record. Only the relatively slow speed of Mach 2—1,320 mph.

The trail seemed to be ending far to the east: no more white against the blue. The rocket engines were shut off.

"Be comin' down soon."

"Yeah—he's out."

Carmie was in trouble finding the ship: "Where is he? Can you see him?"

"He must be in that area."

"He has to make a complete 360."

"The 104's just passing him now."

"They dropped out of the vaporization zone—or whatever they call it—the twilight zone."

The long cameras had all swept around now but their orientation was different. The blackbird had vanished. But Morgan still had him.

"Stay with him, Jack."

"I got him, Dad."

Then Morgan had missed. "Damn it, I lost him."

But now everybody on the Press Knoll could see him, he was low, coming in from the southeast, dropping like a plummet as usual, but higher, streaking toward the east: so high that he would still be way up above the ground when he went by us. Perhaps the wind was edging him faster than he expected, or maybe he was playing the landing on the safe side, overshooting rather than undershooting, as Crossfield had on his first landing.

The black cigar went by us, still well up above the lake bed, past

Mile 2, and it seemed from his altitude that it would be about Mile 6 before his skids hit. To the dismay of the photographers, as he came low enough for the landing, a dune to the north had intervened and we didn't see the touchdown.

Morgan lamented: "Six-thirty in the morning till now for nothing."

Now we could see something very cheering: the high dust feather of the X-15 as it rolled along the lake bed beyond the high dune, and stopped, upright and steady, though far to the north. The time was four-twelve. With a great commotion, the vehicles of Mobile Control were cranking up and starting across the lake to hurry toward the plane. The orange-tailed chopper was settling in beside the X-15, and there were no visible signs of a fire or other trouble.

Our press cavalcade of cars fell in behind the vehicles which were racing across the lake bed, churning clouds of the familiar tan dust. We rolled on interminably, for several miles—seeing the crowd of vehicles in the dusty spot where the X-15 must be—the flashing rubies of the fire-truck beacons, the blades of the helicopter flicking at idle, and already a crowd of rubbernecks standing in the thinning dust beside the high black ship.

We came up to the edge of the jam of vehicles and stopped, and we were held back by our escorts from going over to join the rubbernecks. Portz, however, hurried in to look, and he came back in a few minutes to report:

"The airplane's fine, Joe's fine, and he's in the trailer getting ready to desuit."

Portz was impressed with the safe landing, his face glowed with it, but as usual articulation lagged: "You should have seen the grin on Joe's face when he climbed out of the plane." We could have used some more exact statement on just how it happened. But Portz is a man sparing with words and this was also a time of great excitement, with the Air Force, NASA, and miscellaneous people charging in all directions, the chopper taking off with a great commotion, cars and trucks revving their engines.

The big yellow suit-up trailer was churning dust, rushing across the lake bed toward the Edwards base buildings, and our motor cavalcade followed in the muck like blind bugs.

We came to a halt at the edge of a runway, stopping by the high wall of the truck side, where an air-conditioning fan whirred at the level of our window.

Matt Portz came hurrying by to tell each carload of reporters: "We'll get Joe when he gets out of the truck."

We gathered at the tail-gate ramp of the truck to attend Joe's appearance. At four-seventeen Portz came out, ushering the freshly scrubbed Walker, whose big-toothed grin seemed to be a searchlight of happiness.

"Well, fellas," said Matt by way of introduction, hesitating, and finishing quickly: "you know him."

He stood aside, and the questions began.

Someone asked the usual question about whether Joe had landed where he expected.

"A slight tail wind helped boost this thing down the lake bed," Joe answered. And I knew he was being conservative. It had been more than a slight wind, and to try his first landing in it took courage. But it was plain that by this time, with all the delays, Joe had been determined to make the mission happen and show that the X-15 really could be flown by somebody besides Crossfield. (I found out later that he had landed at 240 knots, 275 miles an hour, and that in this he had come dangerously close to the maximum stress allowed by the engineers on the landing gear—250 knots or 287½ mph.)

"How'd she handle, Joe?" This question, too, I remembered hearing after Crossfield's first flight.

"Handled pretty good."

"How'd you react to it?"

"I was busy—I felt good as soon as I got it on the ground. I would have landed a little longer in the 104." He seemed to mean that the gliding of X-15 was very steep.

I asked him whether the flight had seemed like the simulator. I knew this was a familiar comparison to him after so many simulator missions, and the feeling of flying by those instruments was one I knew slightly, too. He said:

"When I made my first turn I could have kicked myself for saying it was like the simulator."

Correspondents asked the questions about what speed he made and the maximum gs he pulled: Mach 2 and 2½ gs on that turn.

There was also the question of the delay in launching. "I had an overspeed started in the upper engine but got that thing fixed up again so it wasn't the worst kind of trouble."

Then Portz was guiding him away, the interview finished, and Joe had one last word as he walked off: "Next time it'll be Bob White's turn." But there was no doubt that today was a day of glory for Walker. He had started the X-15 research program for NASA and the Air Force in a veritable blaze, a blaze of rocket power.

TUESDAY, APRIL 12. Bob White's first flight in X-15 was scheduled for today, but when I reached NASA headquarters at 7 A.M., I heard the mission had slipped to tomorrow.

Joe Vensel told me the reason: high winds. "The B-52 boys don't like to take off with more than a 10-knot tail wind." Today the winds were gusting between 20 and 40 knots in the Mojave.

But I was glad I had driven up to Edwards, because I picked up two bits of information: first, Stan Miller's new son is to be named Eric. Second, when I sat in the cafeteria talking to Jim McKay, a NASA landing-gear engineer and the brother of the test pilot, I heard something startling about the influence the X-15 will likely have on the design of future space ships: that the future rocket ships will probably use steel skis for main landing gear, mounted right under the tail as in X-15—and probably with spikes on the surface that will touch the ground!

The reason for this is that coming in with such small wings at such speed you want to slow down very quickly. Or in McKay's wordage: "The ski gear is probably the gear of the future for re-entry vehicles. You need a high drag coefficient and a C.G. far aft, and probably you will have skis with spikes. The reason is the pilot has no control when he hits the ground."

WEDNESDAY, APRIL 13. Today was another big date in the history of the X-15—when still another pilot, Major Bob White, was to fly the X-15.

I reached NASA at six fifty-eight, a beautiful, clear, calm morning. Miller said the preparation for the flight was going well. For once everything in the X-15 check list was on schedule—although an outside event threatened the flight. A B-58 Hustler, a supersonic bomber undergoing flight tests at the Edwards AFFTC facility, was in trouble: a part of the landing gear, including one wheel, had been broken off at take-off. Sometime this morning the fast jet would have to be either brought in or abandoned in the air; and there was this emergency to spur the X-15 testing crew to make their mission happen promptly.

Somewhere in the air near Edwards the B-58 was circling slowly, conserving fuel until the experts could decide whether to chance a landing or bail out and let the $40-million airplane crash. The trouble had one extra link with the X-15—besides impinging on the X-15 flight schedule: Fitzhugh Fulton, who often flew the B-52 carrier plane, was piloting the B-58 on its research flight today, Captain Jack Allavie subbed for him on the X-15 job, and another bomber test pilot from the Edwards Air Force facility, Captain Kuyk (pronounced Cook), had taken the second pilot's chair in the B-52.

The B-58 had enough fuel to hold if the X-15 flew promptly, but not enough for one of those all-day, protracted, indefinite, marathon-type holds that sometimes have happened.

We went down to the servicing area, seeing that at seven-fifty White was in the cockpit, his helmet on. Before eight his cockpit lid was down, the streaming cloud of lox rolling out behind him as the top off was finished.

We piled into Air Force cars and rolled toward the lake bed where the take-off would be today. The B-52 taxied by, screaming and rattling stones, and following right after it the blue Air Force sedan that carried General Carpenter. Major Ruth Dudley, Charlie Brown's No. 2 officer in Air Force public information at Edwards, told us that General Carpenter had been on leave, but he interrupted his vacation for this, an epochal mission in the Air Force X-15 program.

At eight twenty-six the B-52 was rolling down the lake bed, heading almost due south, the cavalcade of vehicles racing along the edge of the bed, the banana-shaped rescue helicopter flapping along overhead, for a few seconds at least keeping up with the accelerating B-52.

"It's the first time I've ever seen a chopper used as a chase plane," a newsman wisecracked.

As the B-52 picked up speed, we saw the general's Air Force sedan stopping farther down the taxiway. He got out and stood at salute while the bomber screeched by and lifted into the air. The general was doing honor to Bob White's courage and devotion.

We went on out to Press Island and there saw some distinguished visitors also paying homage to the occasion. Standing near us as Colonel Brown unlimbered his field telephone were two Norwegian Air Force colonels with an escort of United States liaison officers—and two young Catholic priests: Father John Dolan of Notre Dame, with Chaplain (Lieutenant) Paul McDonald, the Edwards Air Force Base Catholic father, showing him around. Father Dolan and Chaplain McDonald were old friends who had been ordained at the same seminary. Chaplain McDonald had come out to pay respect to White, one of his devoted parishioners at the Edwards Catholic services; and Dolan, though only a visitor, did the same.

I talked to the two Jesuits for a few minutes in the desert glare as we watched the B-52 moving slowly in the northern sky, gaining altitude.

I asked Chaplain McDonald if White ever missed church, and he replied in the negative. "He's an usher," he said as if that answered the question. And he looked up at the B-52 and said: "Two of those boys are ushers at church." He meant White and Captain Jack Allavie, the B-52 commander.

Chaplain McDonald is slim and serious. "This must be a most critical time," he said. I agreed it was, especially for White, on his first X-15 and first rocket flight.

Now Lieutenant Don Rhoads, the young public information officer just checking in from duty in Korea, was relaying the phoned information usually put out on the public-address system by Colonel Brown. Colonel Brown was baptizing the lieutenant with a big mission.

"All the systems are checking out including the stable platform," the lieutenant said knowledgeably. "Everything's going on schedule."

A minute later, at eight fifty-four: "Chase Two and Chase Three now airborne . . . twenty-two minutes till launch."

"The B-52 is approximately in the position where the launch will take place on the second turn around," Lieutenant Rhoads said, still efficient and exact, fitting into the new job well. Next: "They're topping off lox . . . ten minutes to launch."

The B-52 moved in a big circle, the thin white lines of three chase planes following below it.

"The lox check valve is closed . . . four minutes till launch." The time was nine-ten, and the sky with the B-52 fleet curving around into launch position seemed calm, bright, sunny. The Press Knoll seemed calm, too, sun-baked and lazy, probably because little information was being forwarded from Mobile Control to Lieutenant Rhoads.

But excitement began to reach us as Rhoads made the "Two minutes to launch" call and he said: "All temperatures read out good, the launch light is lit."

Now we all watched the spot in the northern sky where the heavy contrail of the B-52 unreeled. And Rhoads called out: "Five, four, three, two, one—drop!"

We saw the plump trail of the rocket starting well below the B-52 and he kept sinking farther than Crossfield usually did; but Crossfield is used to it.

"All chambers lit," Rhoads called out. "Everybody keeps saying it looks good." The thick, wavy rocket trail was angling up and turning.

"Now starting his first turn," said Rhoads. The rocket was really leaping ahead now, as it always did, leaving the fast jets as if they were standing in a far corner of the sky.

"He's really tearing it up," one of the spectators said enthusiastically.

And the dutiful, firm-voiced Rhoads still had a good grip on the proceedings: "He's preparing to start maximum acceleration and reach Mach 2."

The first hurdles were behind now. Crossfield has said the critical moments for explosions are right after launch, and that time fortunately was past for today.

The rocket trail wheeled far around the sky, to the south and then into the east. It was long enough now so that the high-altitude winds were twirling and smudging the tail end of the rocket trail into crazy patterns.

Then the healthy white rocket trail rolling out so fast against the blue cut off, it ended abruptly. Up there ahead of the white trunk somewhere the glinting black dot of the X-15 flung fast on its momentum. I couldn't find it.

"Burnout," commented Rhoads. To be exact, it probably was not burnout, because White was no doubt doing as Walker had done before—shutting off his rocket barrels before the ship gathered too much momentum.

I missed the black glint of the X-15 in the enormity of the sky. And the chase planes, too, were still having trouble overtaking the rocket ship. Their contrails angled sharply in several directions as they tried to cut across the sky and get into good position for the landing.

I caught the X-15, the gleaming black dot gliding well, moving west on his landing approach. At last we had a word from Rhoads: "Lower ventral jettisoned." But I had lost the ship at that moment in my field glasses.

At nine twenty-two the X-15 was close enough so you could see the shape of nose and fuselage; in a second his tail was held expertly down as he flared out, and he was shooting up the usual healthy squirt of lake-bed dust as his skis struck. We saw the mobile-control caravan hurrying toward the X-15, the chase plane zooming up, the helicopter thrumming in for a landing, a split second before the X-15 stopped.

There was the usual rush of newsmen, too, toward our press cars, and Charlie Brown was announcing that there would be an interview with Major White at the Air Force altitude chamber building as soon as the pilot could change from his silver suit to street clothes.

As we wheeled in toward the altitude chamber building, we saw throngs of people lined up on the rooftops along the flight line. They would be base people waiting for the approach of the disabled experimental bomber, the B-58. Colonel Brown said the decision had been made to land the broken bomber. Beyond the hangars we could see a line of fire trucks moving. They had come in from Palmdale, extra help to spread foam over the runway so that it would be slippery, safer for the landing with one wheel missing. Now that the X-15 was landed, the mission safely ended, the emergency facilities of Edwards could be turned toward the new pressing issue, the B-58.

At the altitude chamber building we filed into a classroom with folding desk tops and waited for White's arrival. Although they were not properly part of the press group, the two Catholic priests came with us, to get a closer view of the church usher who had acquitted himself so well today.

Some of the newsmen took this chance to phone in their stories to the Los Angeles offices. I heard Ralph Dighton, the Associated Press man who is a familiar at the X-15 tests, in the middle of his call from an adjoining room:

". . . This was the first time that Scott Crossfield, the test pilot for North American Aircraft, builder of the airplane, was not aloft for a flight." It was a thought: today Scott wasn't even flying in a chase plane, for the first time in over a year of X-15 missions. Times were certainly changing.

At last Charlie Brown bustled in with Bob White, now obviously refreshed with a shower and wearing a summer uniform.

Facing the newsmen from the front of the classroom, White began somewhat uneasily:

"Well, it was a very fine experience. As you know, I've been waiting for it for a long time."

Then came the questions, which started the same as before. But this time it became apparent that we were dealing with a quite different personality type than the other two X-15 pilots.

Bob White seemed to blame himself for not going as high as he planned to go on this first flight. "I just didn't get up there. . . . I was about 8,000 feet lower than I expected. I was so interested in control pulses."

"Did you have any problems?"

"Nothing more than my own inadequacies—in doing some of the things I wanted to do." I saw that Chaplain McDonald was watching his church leader with rapt attention, probably as proud as I would have been, in his place, of the pilot's humility. White was saying nothing about the dangers he had faced in today's bout with the unknown, only berating himself for not having done more.

It was only on further questioning that some of those hazards began to come out.

"How'd it feel?"

"It was a little different than I expected."

I saw in this a lead to more particular information on the control problems he had faced in this hot rocket. I asked him if the controls were touchy.

"It was a little more sensitive than I expected," he said. "There was a little more yaw and oscillation and rolling. . . . The nose was hunting slightly, on the turn."

"On the landing, how did it compare with the 104 in the dirty configuration?" White had made more than 50 of those practice landings.

"The sink rate was the same. The handling was about the same. The landing was not quite what I expected. The aircraft rose a little before touchdown."

But the unexpected things had not interfered noticeably with White's performance. If he hadn't mentioned his self-criticism, the newsmen would have thought he had done a perfect job.

"What did you do last night?"

"Wrestled with the kids, as usual."

"What did you eat for dinner?"

"I think it was meat loaf."

"What did you think just before the launch?"

"The clock was moving very rapidly about five minutes before the launch. I was very busy."

"Did you pray last night?"

"No more than I usually do—which is normal."

"What is normal?"

"We pray every night."

I asked him if he knew that two Catholic priests, including Chaplain McDonald, were on hand for the mission today. He said yes, he knew, and I asked how he found out.

"I saw them on the lake bed," he said. He must have spotted them as he came in for a landing.

The interview was over as Major White hurried off for debriefing with the engineers. As we were leaving the building Charlie Brown summed up Major White's behavior today: "A cool young man." I nodded, but I was thinking that White is a lot more than that: a smart, dutiful, and religious one, too.

With Ralph Dighton and Colonel Brown I went down to the flight line to watch the B-58 landing which the X-15 mission had delayed.

There must have been several hundred watchers strewn along the rooftops and even along the wings and fuselage tops of the aircraft, as the fire trucks sprayed foam on the runways, and the B-58, having dumped some fuel and jettisoned the cockpit canopies, came in for an attempt to sit down.

Fitz Fulton brought it in as smoothly as if the landing gear were all there. He kept the right wing up a little, the side where the wheel was missing. The fire trucks stood by at several sections of the runway but there was no need for them. The broken gear on the right side shot up a shower of sparks, and a fire burned briefly and bright where the sparks had started. But by the time the plane had slid to a straight stop, the fire was out: no damage and no injured, and a valuable airplane saved for further research experiments.

The next research mission of the X-15 is scheduled for next week. I'm told at NASA that it will be a familiarization flight for Joe Walker. Then a similar get-acquainted mission for White. Then, if all goes well, they'll be beginning to reach out toward what the engineers call maximum performance, or, in every-day language, the world records.

TUESDAY, APRIL 19. This morning Joe Walker made his familiarization flight. It was on schedule, and Joe flew the bird faster than it has gone so far—not by much and not a record, but a step in the direction NASA wants him to go. The Los Angeles *Mirror-News* carried a two-paragraph story—and no correspondents were up to cover this one because a familiarization flight is not very newsy.

The story doesn't take cognizance of the fact that the X-15 with the present engine is able to go beyond the X-2 marks for both speed and altitude, and into space—and that this will happen, if NASA and the Air Force have their way, within a few weeks.

I hear that the Big Engine has arrived at Edwards and the North American engineers are preparing for a ground run. I called Matt Portz and asked when the first ground test of the new engine is supposed to be. He says he doesn't know yet.

MONDAY, MAY 2. Bob White's familiarization flight, scheduled for tomorrow, has slipped to Thursday. He's had a siege of flu. North American has a test flight scheduled for Crossfield for tomorrow; it's supposed to be the first firing of the ballistic (or reaction or rocket, or space) controls in the air. Joe Walker has made a couple of flights by now in the NASA 104 with these rocket controls, and they have been fired at the test stand, but never in flight.

Tuesday, May 3. The flight by Crossfield has been postponed to Thursday. The NASA flight for Bob White has been put off till Friday, since there is only one B-52 carrier airplane in commission for the moment. The holdup with the reaction controls is the usual rocket ship holdup—leaks in the plumbing, the system of pipes and valves.

I talked to Blount for a moment about the flight plan for the BCS, the Ballistic Control System test. "It's to fire off the BSC at low altitude," he says; "50,000 feet." Perspectives in flying are certainly changing fast. Five years ago flying at 50,000 feet was still quite a challenge, except for the advanced experimental test pilots. Now it's a low altitude for them. And of course in another five years anything below 100,000 feet, 20 miles, will seem very low for rocket ships because it is in atmosphere.

Thursday, May 5. Scott Crossfield's BCS flight has slipped again; there are still leaks in the peroxide bladder feed system that powers the controls. The NASA flight—Bob White's second—is still on for tomorrow.

Friday, May 6. Today Bob White carried out his familiarization flight and it went off well except for one incident. The incident came a few seconds before landing. Then there was real trouble that could have cracked Bob up, but didn't, thanks to his quick action. We probably wouldn't have known about that if it hadn't been for the sharp eyes of Ralph Dighton, the AP man, who saw the evidence.

At ten-three the black cigar, after a successful flight, was landing and the Air Force public-address system was informing the press: "He's just touched down about a mile from us, ladies and gentlemen." A sizable delegation of newsmen were at the Press Knoll: a group of journalists from all over the country had come up from Los Angeles, where the Aviation Writers' Association is holding a convention.

And Ralph Dighton, the most faithful of the news corps when it comes to being on hand for missions, said to me:

"Did you see that vertical?"

I hadn't been able to see the ventral fin as it was jettisoned during the X-15's approach to the lake bed.

"Right there's the dust from it," Ralph said, pointing to a faint tan plume delicately close to the spot where the X-15 flared out for the landing.

I agreed with Ralph that we must ask White what happened. It looked as if the ventral, the vertical fin on the lower part of the tail, had been hung up till the very last minute. Usually an explosive charge separates the ventral fin from the airplane during its landing approach, maybe 7,000 feet up, and a parachute brings it to earth. The ship can't land with the fin attached—that is, without doing considerable damage to itself. The fin is invaluable in maintaining stability in the thin air of the high altitudes. But it sticks too far down to permit landing. In case the explosive charge doesn't work, there is a button by which the pilot can knock the heavy fin free electrically; then, as a last resort, the landing-gear lanyard is set to drop the ventral. But that would be at the very last moment before landing. At the rapid sink rate of the X-15 as it comes in for a landing (it is falling at about 9,000 feet per minute), there isn't much time to find out whether the fin is gone and do something about it. (The chase pilots have to tell the X-15 pilot because he can't see behind or below.) Then if the fin's still there, he must act fast.

Later in the morning Dighton asked White the question. About 100 AWA writers had filed into the auditorium of the Edwards Test Pilot School and had been briefed by General Carpenter and De E. Beeler, second in command at the NASA station. Finally White came on the lectern and told us generally:

"The flight went pretty much according to our plan—to get stability and performance information . . . it was rather routine in my opinion."

One of the newsmen asked if he could be more specific about the mission.

"The mission was to fly to 45,000 feet—prepare the propellant system . . . we launched at 45,000. . . . All eight chambers were lighted. . . . Then I proceeded to climb to 60,000 feet. . . . I made a turn, I increased the angle of attack. The roll-and-yaw dampers were turned off to get some stability information."

He went on in this fashion, almost as if he were dictating a report to the test-pilot facility: "Burnout occurred at approximately 2.3 Mach number. At this time a turn was initiated toward the lake. Again I turned off the stability augmentation system to get a pulse on stability."

Bob said he had "some minor difficulties" with the roll dampers—but still said nothing about the last-minute release of the ventral fin a few seconds before landing. It seemed probable to me that with so many mechanical chores and readings to make, so many control movements and measurements, he thought of the narrow escape with the fin jettison as only one of many movements he had to go through—any one of which, bungled, could have piled up him and the ship. These were all routine to him, though to one less qualified each could have been dangerous. In this way a test pilot can miss mentioning something very dramatic to an outsider.

"You dropped your vertical fin quite late?" It was Dighton asking the question.

"The procedure is to drop it at 7,000 or 8,000 feet. But the ventral did not jettison. Since the first means didn't let it go, I released it manually." Bob said nothing about the fact that the release occurred only a few seconds before his skids hit the lake bed, so close to the landing that the fin's parachute didn't open. (He told me later that he had hit the button twice but the electrical emergency system was shorted out. So he had to depend on the last-minute action of the landing-gear lanyard.)

"What would you have done if it hadn't released?"

"I would continue with the landing," said Bob steadily. "That is procedure." Of course, there is nothing else he could do at that altitude except pile it in and see what gave way. That is all part of the X-15 pilot's job. But I would bet that he gives thanks tonight for this and other of his deity's blessings today, when he makes his prayers at bedtime.

THURSDAY, MAY 12. Scheduled for today was Joe Walker's first speed run—and the X-15 had its first flight outside of the Edwards area. The B-52 launched the black baby near Silver Lake, California, 110 miles east of Edwards.

I drove up from Los Angeles, starting in the dark to arrive at 7 A.M. Take-off was scheduled for 0800. When we checked into NASA headquarters, we heard that there was only a slight hold—fifteen minutes, practically nothing by the standards of space operations.

And the take-off was only eleven minutes behind the original schedule, not even fifteen. And from then on everything in the flight worked perfectly.

But the rocket trail, dashing so spectacularly into the blue, didn't last very long. It had traveled a long way in the high overcast, and now, halfway across the huge blue backdrop, it suddenly came to an end, the white, soft trail truncating.

Without the rocket trail to mark it in the sky, the X-15 was gone. I knew the gleam of the black dot was out there somewhere against the glaring sky.

Time seemed to hesitate as we all swept the quiet sky with our binoculars. We knew the bird was coming close, because the violet smudge of a smoke signal eddied over the gray mirage of the lake bed where the ambulances and fire trucks floated.

Somebody called out: "There he is."

The silent black bird was falling in toward the lake bed, declining a mile a minute downward and 350 miles an hour forward, making the landing approach.

At eight fifty-nine the bird was in the clear over the lake bed, flaring out, with the nose struggling upward as the tail settled, landing with a heavy brown smudge, while a chase plane swooped overhead and zoomed steeply up into the sky.

The X-15 trailed its usual dense triangular dust plume on the ground, sloping up from its tail skids. It came to a stop, the rescue chopper came fluttering, and vehicles rushed from all sides, smudging the desert with their progress—a projection of dust streaks all aimed at the settling murk where the bird had stopped and the helicopter was beginning to sit down.

Ruth Dudley was quoting Miller: "It looks like a very successful flight. There were no malfunctions."

We still didn't know whether Joe Walker had achieved his goal—gone faster than the X-15 had flown before. Back at NASA security office, which doubled as a public information headquarters, Stan Miller appeared from the Mobile Control. He read us a tentative estimate on Walker's speed from the Mach meter as Joe read it in flight. The space instruments, giving true speed from the gyro platform, haven't been installed in the bird yet.

Joe's instrument readings and the estimates from radar are subject to confirmation when the NASA scientists wade through the data gathered today.

Meanwhile, Miller was reading: "Altitude, 75,000. Mach, 2.8. Launch altitude, 45,000. Launch, 8:47. Touchdown, 8:57. Time, 10:10. 110 miles."

Someone asked how much 2.8 amounted to. Stan did some figuring, checked himself, and announced 1,848 mph—which is well beyond the previous mark of 1,700 Joe had made on his last flight. But it was also quite a way below Captain Mil Apt's world record of 2,094.

(A later authoritative check through NASA's complex instrumentation showed that Walker had equaled or perhaps slightly exceeded Captain Apt's record. The Apt record was never exact because his fatal crash right after the record run had cut off much of the data—such as the temperature and exact altitude at which the run was made, important in translating a Mach meter reading precisely. The Air Force finding for Apt was 3.189 Mach, which their engineers converted to 2,094 mph. Walker's final count, NASA announced two weeks after the day it was made, was 3.2 Mach, with the tentative conversion of 2,112, "give or take 30 miles." It was never clear why you had to give or take 30 miles, except that perhaps the computing engineers didn't know what the temperature or altitude was exactly. So there was no official claim of a record. It would take a speedier run to break the Apt record by a clear margin.)

Checking to see what the next NASA flight will be, I find it should be next week—another mission for Major Bob White along the 110-mile Silver Lake course. It will be in quest of altitude as Joe Walker's was after speed. Now it seems clear that the X-15 NASA Air Force flight will be following the pattern of the earlier Air Force programs of the Xs: one pilot flying speed runs, the other altitude, just as Murray and Yeager did with the X-1s, and Everest (and Apt) and Kincheloe on the X-2.

THURSDAY, MAY 19. With Bob White at the controls, the X-15 flew to 107,000 feet today—the closest a man has come to the world record of 126,200 feet hung up by Captain Kincheloe in the X-2. We don't know whether the Russians have been trying to surpass this record.

I was briefly out of the country on a flying visit to the South Pacific at this time, so asked Vic Boesen, a good writer, my friend and a space and aviation authority, to fill in. Vic has written a good deal about Kincheloe, Apt, Bridgeman, Gene May, and other rocket types. He kept a diary on the flight for me:

"Kinch, who was to have been the Air Force's No. 1 man on the X-15, was on my mind as I checked in at NASA headquarters soon after sunup for Major White's flight. Stan Miller handed me a fact sheet on it, along with a diagram showing the course to be followed . . . it was the same run as Joe Walker had flown in hitting Mach 2.8 a few days ago (the mark that NASA revised to Mach 3.2). The altitude mark Major White would reach for was 110,000. The highest an X-15 had been to date was 88,000 feet, reached by Crossfield on February 11.

" 'He'll accelerate in level flight at 60,000 feet, then pull up in a 15-degree climb, pulling about one and a half gs,' Miller explained. 'He should hit 110,000 somewhere over Three Sisters Lake.' "

White apparently didn't get quite as high as he hoped. But he was well over the 100,000-foot mark, and so, according to many authorities on the subject of where space begins, he was in space as Kinch had been in space on that high flight in 1956; that is, above the atmosphere. Boesen, who knew well the fantastic effort that went into pushing the X-1A and D-558 to altitude marks that didn't even reach 100,000 feet, was impressed with the ease of White's mission.

He was especially impressed with White's nonchalant radio call wafted to the NASA press knoll from Mobile Control, as the X-15 arced up toward the top of its flight. About that call Boesen wrote:

"White adds a sight-seeing note: 'It's clear up at San Francisco today.' The Bay City is 350 miles away. 'Quiet, isn't it?' He is far outrunning the thunder of his rockets."

Boesen also remarked on the nonchalance of the NASA and Air Force people about this pioneering flight to altitude. "Thus," he wrote, "a non-routine undertaking, to make the second highest probe toward space ever tried, had been accomplished in remarkably routine style. As Major Ruth Dudley, of the Public Information Office, had remarked in a fitting epilogue as we turned toward our car at the finish, "It sure goes a lot smoother these days.'"

SUNDAY, MAY 22. Back from the quick air trip to the South Pacific (French Polynesia), I took the liberty of calling Joe Walker at home, even though it was a week end, to find out about the X-15 schedule—also to ask about his reactions to his speed run on the day before I left for the Pacific. We hadn't been able to talk to Joe on the day of that flight.

Joe was cautious as I asked him what his maximum Mach meter reading was: did he hit 2.8 Mach on that mission? He hesitated. "You've got me over a barrel," he said finally. I knew he must be under pressure on the subject: NASA headquarters would do the announcing about the official speed: the data investigations of the NASA scientists must have revealed more speed than Joe had first estimated.

He gave me a hint: "It looks like more than 2.8. It looks like it might maybe kinda have snuck over that." An afterthought, a decision to be more exact: "I think it will be closer to three than 2.8."

I asked about White's next flight to altitude. Would that also be an attempt at a record? "White will run the same length [from Silver Lake], but run his engines longer."

I knew Joe was trying to give me an indication, through a screen of restrictions, that Bob White's next mission would be a record run. (The official position of NASA is that such flights are research missions, not record flights.)

I took advantage of the chance to inquire of Joe if the bird was beginning to feel easier, if he was more at home in it these days. He said yes, on the first flight it was something special to have flown it, but "now it's getting to be like another airplane you fly."

"It felt better last time," he said. "I seemed to get better damper action." He said with a chuckle that flying the bird still seemed like the simulator to him, and he flew it by the instrument panel as if it were the simulator. "Sometimes I don't look out the window." But of course, he added, he does when the time for the landing arrives.

MONDAY, MAY 23. I called Matt Portz at NASA to set the detail on the schedule for this week. He said there are two flights scheduled for sometime later in the week.

"There's the North American flight with the ballistic-control test, and Joe's [Walker's] flight, which will be a speed run."

The North American ballistic-control test is the one they've been trying to make happen for about a month. They've been having trouble with leaks and valves—the usual plumbing difficulties.

I asked Portz if Walker's flight would be an attempt to break the X-2 speed record.

"Yes," he answered, still the man of few words.

THURSDAY, MAY 26. The ballistic-control test of the No. 2 Bird was on for today, a North American mission with Crossfield at the controls. And Joe Walker's speed flight for NASA is put off till next week.

Today's ballistic-control system test was an important one—to show that the BCS really does work, that the plumbing for these space controls will stand up in flight. The flight was also an epochal one for North American, because it is the last of the company tests with the Small Engine. Next they'll start tests with the big one.

The Big Engine has been run several times on the test stand by now, and it is already installed in Bird No. 3. There will soon be some test runs of the engine in this bird. And after today's successful test in Bird No. 2, technicians and engineers will start right away to take the Small Engine out of it and prepare it for the second Big Engine, which hasn't arrived at Edwards yet.

When the X-15 was safely landed and the pilots came in to the

North American hangar for the debriefing, I had a chance to talk to Bob White, a chase today, about how the BCS controls looked when they were fired.

"It was real solid steam coming out," Bob said.

"Could you see the X-15 move when the controls were fired?"

"No—because of the Q." He meant that at 50,000 feet the Q, or air pressure, is still thick enough (though only about a tenth of sea-level pressure) to hold the ship against the action of the steam-rocket controls. Out beyond the 100,000-foot level, where the atmospheric pressure is almost gone (a hundredth of the sea-level pressure), the rocket controls should be a lot more effective.

I asked Bob, while he moved toward the debriefing, if his reaction controls were working in the No. 1 X-15, when he flew it to 107,000 feet.

He said no, "They're not connected, they probably won't be for a while."

I know the reason: the engineers still have problems with leaky valves and peroxide bladders. Without the BCS didn't he have trouble controlling the bird on the last flight, up there where the air is just about gone?

He said, "No—there's enough dynamic pressure if you keep your speed up." He meant that even among those residual shreds of air there was enough wind blast at speed to get some action out of the old-fashioned, earth-bound rudder and elevons.

"The response of the controls is limited," he said. "But the small amount of control is adequate."

Of course, he added, "You have to be real easy with it—you don't plan on upsetting the airplane. . . . But I got into the murk and back without trouble."

White was hurrying toward the debriefing room, but I wanted to ask him about something which I believe would bother me considerably if I were in his shoes, waiting for a flight that would take me beyond his 107,000 feet and beyond Kincheloe's mark of 126,200 feet up and into the void—without any form of space controls.

"Are you worried about the control situation on the record flight?"

"It'll be a little less [control] than last time. But we'll have enough speed so we can leap out and get back without any real problems."

I hope he is correct.

Before Bob takes his first record leap into space, Joe Walker has to make his attempt to break the speed record. That flight, I found at NASA, is still scheduled for tomorrow.

FRIDAY, MAY 27. Today's speed attempt by Joe Walker was aborted when the telemetering system failed. As De E. Beeler, the acting chief, told us: "When we lost the instrumentation, we lost the research portion of the flight. If anything went wrong, we wouldn't have the information so we could go back and see what happened."

The meeting of the press at NASA headquarters did have one positive effect. The NASA and Air Force people had firmed up their views on Captain Mil Apt's world speed record, which has been variously quoted from 2,040 to 2,260 mph. Colonel Brown of the Air Force had gone to the engineers for a definitive figure and they had come up with 2,094.

FRIDAY, JUNE 3. Joe Walker's speed run, which was to be the ninth flight of Bird No. 1 (seven powered, one glide), and the eighteenth flight for Birds No. 1 and No. 2, aborted less than four minutes from drop. The cause this time: low hydraulic pressure linked to one of the auxiliary power units. De Beeler told the press: "One ground rule we observe is if there's anything wrong with either APU, it's an automatic abort." That's sensible enough, because there should always be a source of power for controls, landing gear, and other systems—and a functioning back-up or stand-by system.

The next try at the mission is to be next week, probably Tuesday.

MONDAY, JUNE 6. Latest progress report from Earl Blount of North American: "The Big Engine has been static-tested once in the bird, and it will be tested tomorrow. It will be run three times before the first flight. That flight is scheduled for mid-month." All of which really is rapid progress. The NASA speed run, with Bird No. 1, Joe Walker at the controls, is now set for Wednesday.

WEDNESDAY, JUNE 8. Joe Walker's third attempt to bring off his speed run was aborted today. Vexed by a thickening high overcast that made it hard for the B-52 to get lined up for its launch run, the mission was scrubbed at ten forty-three by something else, when Master Control told Walker: "Joe, we've been discussing your source pressures, and the consensus is we'd better abort now." It was five minutes to launch.

Joe had been reporting low helium pressures, important because the pressure of helium is used to push the fuel toward the engine and to pressurize the cockpit. Joe's voice sounded despairing as he made his reports, but he didn't recommend any abort—he seemed too eager to make the mission happen, even with low source pressures.

I went to lunch at the NASA cafeteria with Ed Cokeley, the head of the North American flight test facility at Edwards. We saw Joe Walker coming in alone, looking drawn and gloomy. We stopped to talk to him, and found him really down in the dumps. We both wished him good weather next week, and he scowled: "It won't be."

"How do you know?"

"Look at the weather I've had," he said, almost snarling it out.

I knew how desperately he wanted to make this speed mission a success, to break the speed record by a good margin. Right now, he was incorrigibly depressed.

Another depressing item is that NASA now doesn't plan the speed run until the end of next week, or maybe even the week after that.

I saw one cheering item, though, as I came into the North American engineering department at Edwards this morning before the mission began: looking down toward the hangar floor I saw technicians working over the slick long shape of Bird No. 3—and now I could see the Big Engine in a bird. This is the one that has already been static tested last week. It's going to be tested again today (it slipped from yesterday). Next to No. 3 was the No. 2 Bird, a group of men working around its tail. The engine has been removed and they are modifying the tail for the second Big Engine, which hasn't arrived yet but should be in this week.

Later, when the B-52 was taxiing out this morning toward the lake bed for take-off, the No. 3 Bird was moving slowly across the hard stand in the foreground, under tractor tow, heading for the North American engine test stand near the X-15 servicing area. It was good to see the big, single tuba horn of the rocket exhaust in the stern—a real missile-size exhaust. I would stay around for the test, but it's apt to drag on until tonight, or maybe tomorrow or the next day. That's the way with engine-test programs—they're finicky.

After today's NASA abort, Q. C. Harvey came in to the hangar from NASA Central Control and talked to Cokeley. I asked Q. C. when the No. 3 Bird with the Big Engine would be flying, and Q. C. Harvey said the eighteenth. "But the Big Missions won't be for a couple of years."

Cokeley nodded. "But once it's flying, every flight will break a record."

The Big Engine should be something sensational.

THURSDAY, JUNE 9. This morning early I heard a shocking radio news bulletin: "The experimental rocket ship X-15 was blown apart last night in a test of its new engine. The test pilot, Scott Crossfield, was uninjured."

I called Colonel Brown's office at Edwards Air Force Base to get the dope. This explosion could be anything from a bent tail pipe to a complete liquidation of the bird, and Brown was close to the horse's mouth.

He was cooperative and unruffled as usual: "The ammonia tank blew and the peroxide tank. The damage is in the section aft of the trailing edge of the wing."

I asked if there was anything left of this tail section.

"It's in pieces—lying on the lake bed. The front part is still in one piece. It blew forward about 20 feet."

"And Crossfield wasn't hurt?"

"Not a bit. He stayed in the cockpit while they put out the fire. That was S.O.P."

"Nobody else hurt?"

"Nope."

"Can they repair the bird?"

"North American says it's repairable—subject to rejigging. It's a rugged bird." He meant it could be rebuilt on the original factory jigs.

I jumped into my car and headed for Edwards. I knew getting a ride with one of the North American planes from Los Angeles International was improbable: there would be a backlog of engineers wanting to get up there. And besides, North American wouldn't be too keen on helping any outsiders to look at the smashed bird, at least in this early stage of excitement.

At Edwards, Colonel Brown and I drove across the taxiway to the high cyclone fence of the engine-test area: behind the fence hangar and shacks the usual long yellow fuel tanks and a big new concrete blockhouse. Beyond the blockhouse I could see the forward part of the X-15. It seemed untouched, except that there were shreds of bent metal attached at the rear end of this part. Beyond it, the engine and tail section were completely separated, bashed and bent, the vertical stabilizer torn. The part of the plane between the vertical stabilizer and the tail was gone. The explosion had been over two of the tall light poles ranged around the bird; a few hunks of metal were spotted on the desert floor.

The area seemed quiet, almost sleepy, in the baking desert sun, like a Mesopotamian tomb. A few men in sports shirts were scattered around the bird, apparently investigators measuring the distance to the various pieces of wreckage. They would make a map of every bit of wreckage out there in an attempt to isolate the cause of the explosion.

A rope had been set up so that it enclosed the big blockhouse, the bird, and the knobs of concrete marking the two small subterranean bunkers beyond it. A blue-uniformed company cop stood guard at an opening in the rope cordon.

I parked the car outside the fence and Colonel Brown and I walked down to the bird. We saw big Bill Berkowitz, the North American launch operator, and Dick Gompertz, one of Rocketdyne's missile men, also moving toward the ship. Gompertz, who works up on Rocket Ridge on the mammoth F-1 engine (the one-and-a-half-million pound job for the Nova space rocket) had come down to help out with the investigation.

Charlie Brown spoke to Berkowitz: "That's what you get for lighting matches."

Berkowitz grinned. "You gotta see if they work." He added: "It's not my system—my system's working fine. I'm just bringing Gompertz down here."

Charlie and I walked along the rope, where a sign said "Restricted Area—Authorized Personnel Only." But we could get a good look at the bird. The nose wheel was down, the strut slightly bent, and the front section of the plane turned toward our left. But the fuselage seemed undamaged for about 35 feet back from the nose. At that point there were some rumpled strips of metal bent toward the front. The rear tankage section was gone. We looked right into the curving pipes of the engine: the metal structure that would ordinarily lie between us and the engine had been blown into hunks or bent back as if a giant had been hammering the X-15 in a fit of pique, breaking apart and shredding the tail surfaces. The engine appeared to be relatively intact.

I asked Colonel Brown how the engine had stood up. I knew he had looked at it more closely last night.

"The engine looks pretty good—the combustion chamber looks fine. You can see—the tail is mangled, and the ammonia-tankage section is gone; though the lox tank didn't go." He pointed out the twisted scraps of metal scattered on the lake bed, where the North American engineers and three Air Force officers from Flying Safety were occupied.

The North American men in short-sleeved shirts were working with measuring tapes, the Air Force officers, in more formal dress, watching or talking.

"The North American people are doing the work," Charlie Brown explained. "We're doing what we call monitoring."

I asked Colonel Brown what he could see when he first got to the scene of the accident last night, about fifteen minutes after the explosion.

"A lot of people around talking. The fire was long since out. Q. C. [Harvey] was here and the men were preparing to unload the systems."

I inquired about the ammonia fumes at that time: "Pretty noticeable still."

We looked at the forward section of the plane and Brown pointed out that the few places where the side paneling was missing were not blown off. They had been taken off for access to the fuselage, before the engine test began.

We saw where the forward three quarters of the plane had broken away from the tail and jerked ahead 18 or 20 feet.

"He had a brief powered flight," Brown said, poker-faced. "He had a heck of a jolt."

On the way out we saw Ed Cokeley, the North American chief at Edwards, talking to Gompertz, who had made a brief survey.

As Cokeley walked out, I asked if the tail section could be rebuilt. "That's what General Wray wants."

General Wray is the dynamo who runs the Air Force's Wright-Patterson Air Development Center in Dayton, Ohio.

"He was in today?" Brown asked. It was quick action for Wray, but then he moves fast in his KC-135 jet tanker.

"He sure was," said Cokeley, and he and Brown laughed. Wray's penchant for quick movement and decisive action is apparently well known.

There were two questions I wanted to ask Cokeley: 1) Did he see the explosion? and 2) Would the explosion set back the research program and record flights of the NASA-Air Force bird with the Small Engine?

On the first point, he said he was not on the scene when the blowup came. He heard about it five minutes after it happened and came over. "It was about the same as it is now."

On the second question: "It doesn't look as if it will hold up the Small Engine flights now." He went on to say that the engine systems are different, and the Small Engine system has been pretty well tried and tested.

Colonel Brown was a little more guarded in his prediction of the effect on the Small Engine flight-test program.

"It's going to throw a delay into the program, until they find out what caused it—that's true of the 99 [Big] engine, anyhow. The North American people were talking about a three-month delay last night on the Big Engine. But what it does to the other program is something else. Nobody knows now."

I checked with Lynn Manley, the new public information man for NASA at Edwards (Stan Miller has been moved to the Santa Monica office) and found that the official NASA plan is to go ahead with the Small Engine flights. Joe Walker's speed-record flight is still set up for late next week or the following week.

I still hadn't talked to anyone who had seen the explosion and fire. I tried to reach the firemen who had been closest to the blast, who had sprayed water on the forward-three-quarter section of the fuselage, to keep the fire away from Scott. They were off duty, taking a well-earned rest. I finally located the fire chief, Howard P. Crews, who told me by phone:

"When I got there from my quarters, the fire was pretty much under control—the fire was out in about three minutes." Chief Crews must have practically flown over to the explosion site.

I asked him how he would describe the explosion and fire.

"It seems to have been a ball of fire, more than a regular explosion," he said in a pronounced deep-South drawl, "the way it was described to me. It was in the fuel area, and it was confined at once."

I asked how Crossfield got out. "After the boys washed the fuselage down with water, and washed the fire back, he was able to get out."

I still haven't been able to get to Crossfield. I called him tonight at his home and his wife said he wasn't home yet, and suggested I call him at the office tomorrow.

FRIDAY, JUNE 10. I reached Scott Crossfield by phone this morning, finally was able to talk to someone close to the heart of the explosion when it happened.

"It was the most violent thing I've ever experienced in my life," he said. "The loads were way beyond what anyone expected—approximately 50 gs up to 100 gs."

"How did you take all those forces without getting hurt?"

"They were in a direction that I was supported. As you know, it's an excellent restraint system."

I asked how the explosion sounded and felt.

"I've never experienced an explosion of this magnitude before. I never heard an explosion as loud. It was much louder than the explosion in the air—by several orders of magnitude. It seemed like a tremendous hammer blow.

"I was waiting for another one. As you know, you can't see back much from the cockpit. I didn't know whether the explosion was in the engine or not. I figured if it was in the engine the tanks might go. I knew I was better off in the cockpit, if it came."

Scott said he was much concerned about the three men in the south pillbox only about 20 feet from the explosion:

"I was trying to see if the bunker was still there. I could see it out of the corner of my eye."

That pillbox, I gathered from talking to Colonel Brown, and reading the fire report, had been momentarily enveloped in flames and after that inundated with a wave of ammonia gas. The three men had climbed out untouched, wearing gas masks. In the west pillbox, out of the direct blast of the explosion, was Art Simone, a North American fire safety man. He climbed out of his bunker and moved right over to the nose, while the fire was still burning in the tail area, and tried to help Scott out of the cockpit.

"Simone and a crew chief were trying to open my canopy. They were risking their necks. I would have sat there, but I didn't propose to sit and argue with them while they were standing out there in the open. So I got out."

Crossfield had a sobering thought: "Thank God for those pillboxes. Without 'em, everybody would have been wiped out. We just got 'em about a month ago." I believe he was right. Without those thick concrete walls to protect them, probably half of the score of men on hand for the test would have been killed or injured.

I asked Scott about the remark the newspapers quoted him as having made after he got out of the cockpit. The Los Angeles *Mirror-News* had it:

" 'Are you hurt?' he was asked.

" 'No,' said Crossfield, 'but those firemen soaked my trousers.' "

Here was Scott's account: "It was just a crack I made, when everybody—Charlie Brown, too—was asking if I was okay. I said the only thing that suffered was the press in my pants [he was wearing slacks and shirt], and Charlie gave it to the papers."

SATURDAY, JUNE 11. Today I got in touch with Q. C. Harvey by phone to the North American facility in Edwards.

Q. C. said he had been in the big main blockhouse, and I wanted to know what he had seen of the explosion.

"Nothing," he said. "The television went out as soon as the explosion happened, so we had no picture. The explosion made a loud noise and shook the ground. We put on masks and opened the front door to check the ammonia fumes. They weren't bad. When I opened the door and got out there, I thought we were through with any major explosion. The ammonia was gone, the peroxide was gone, at least the tail tank."

I asked him the vital question of the moment: did he think the Small Engine program would be held up by the explosion?

He said he didn't think so. "We've had a couple of hundred tests of the earlier configuration and this new program shouldn't affect it." That was cheering news.

MONDAY, JUNE 27. Planning a trip East to look into the publication of this book, I checked with NASA's Stan Miller at the Edwards installation to see when the next flight will be.

"If you can be back the week after the Fourth of July," he said, "you should be all right. Maybe the week after that, even."

I was glad to hear that I could make the trip. But it was a shock that the delay might be so long.

"Is it because of the blowup in the No. 3 Bird?" I asked.

"Yes. It'll be a little while before the No. 1 Bird gets airborne again. They're holding back a little."

"What are they checking? The plumbing? Does the explosion in the No. 3 Bird make them suspicious of the plumbing in No. 1?" I was anxious because it sounded to me as if the worst might be happening: maybe the whole X-15 program is being held up because of the Big-Engine explosion.

"I don't know exactly what they're checking," Miller answered. "I know they're checking some of the valve systems—and they're taking advantage of the opportunity to go over some of the other things that would need checking, too—like the cabin pressurization seals."

WEDNESDAY, JUNE 29. Alarmed about the schedule, I called Colonel Brown of the Air Force and Blount of North American to see if I could get any late word. Both men were tight-lipped.

I asked the question that is much on my mind these days: is the plumbing of the No. 1 Bird now suspect because of the explosion in No. 3?

"It [the cause of the explosion] could be anywhere," Colonel Brown said. "But they're getting close to a place where they're going to have a reason."

Blount was even less communicative: "Everybody's sworn to secrecy and they're not supposed to be talking to anybody."

THURSDAY, JULY 14. Back from Washington, I checked Miller to see what had happened to the X-15 schedule.

"There aren't any flights scheduled yet," he said. "The bird's still waitin' on the investigation of the No. 3 aircraft. . . . They're checking specifically into a lox regulator valve and the lox venting system. These parts are common to all [the birds], so they're going very slow."

This was what I'd been afraid of, that the whole program had stalled because of the explosion. I asked how long a delay was in sight.

"It could be a week, could be a month. It's a problem they're really going to have to iron out before they'll let anyone into it."

This seems to be the development everyone has feared. The No. 1 or NASA-Air Force Bird is grounded, even though its power-plant system is in many ways different from No. 3's.

WEDNESDAY, JULY 20. Good news today from Gordon Gray of the North American PRO office:

"We're expecting the speed flight next week or the week after."

That was a surprise. When I pressed for details, Gordon said:

"They [the engineer] concluded their investigation yesterday."

"What was the finding?"

"Can't say."

"What do you mean, you can't say?"

"We're not ready to release it yet. Earl [Blount] read it to us last night."

I asked if the fundamental cause had been a lox regulator, as Miller indicated to me a week ago.

"It's all in this goddamn engineering language," the forthright Gray answered. "It's dull. It'll have to be rewritten."

But aside from the cause—which we'll hear about soon, I'm sure—the salient fact is that the difficulty has been solved with the No. 1 Bird and the record flight is coming up at last.

WEDNESDAY, JULY 27. Blount this morning: the flight won't be this week. Maybe next week. One good thing: the engineers are concentrating on making changes on the No. 1 or NASA-Air Force Bird, so that this one will be cleared for flight before they tackle the changes on the No. 2 Bird—which will have the Big Engine. As usual, many of the engineers are putting in 60-hour weeks. The public statement of their findings about the explosion is still unreleased.

MONDAY, AUGUST 1. A pleasant surprise this morning. I heard from Portz that the speed flight in No. 1 Bird is scheduled for Thursday; and maybe only a week after that Bob White will take the bird and try for the world altitude record.

This afternoon, for the first time in nearly two months, the bird was run up in a ground test. With the new valves and regulators, it performed without a hitch.

And this morning I got from the Air Force X-15 power-plant engineer at Edwards, Bob Nagel, the first definitive account I'd heard of the cause of the explosion in No. 3 Bird. Now at last information on the blast is loosened up somewhat.

Nagel, a young civilian engineer who looks, thinks, and talks the part of what I'd call the typical double-dome space engineer—he's slim, intense, high-browed, with a lean, intelligent face—phrased the explanation in rapid technical gobbledegook. It was too technical for me, but I could see that it was precise:

"An ammonia regulator valve failed in open position. It [the valve] just sat there and modulated. Also the GSE [ground service equipment] imposed about 68 pounds more of back pressure. And the fuel-tank pressure gauge was 43 pounds off. The pressure was rising and Crossfield had no indication of what was going on.

"The pressure built up until it reached possibly 170 psi. Then the ammonia tank failed structurally. The core failed, bending it in an aft direction, and struck the hydrogen-peroxide tank behind it. The peroxide-tank explosion was the initial explosion. The ammonia-tank explosion was a result."

After I went over this explanation several times with Nagel so that it began to make sense to me, I would venture the following free translation:

A valve controlling the flow of ammonia, the fuel, was supposed to shut itself off but it didn't. So fuel pressure built up in the ammonia tank. A vent hose on the other end of the tank wasn't designed right so it caused back pressure. And Crossfield didn't know this was happening because his gauge was reading low. Then—kerblamm!

"It took two malfunctions and a design error to kill it [cause the explosion]," Nagel summed up.

Making the same changes in the next Big-Engine bird, the No. 2, will take a month or so, Nagel said. That Big Engine for No. 2 has arrived at Edwards and is already being run up at the test stand. Each of the ten Big Engines so far built at Reaction Motors is worth $6 million, he added parenthetically, since the cost of the Big-Engine contract is $60 million.

I asked about the possibility of rebuilding the exploded No. 3 Bird, which, except for the fuel tank, tail, and engine, is in pretty good shape. Nagel said this hadn't yet been decided by the Air Force, but the repair job, according to the North American people, would run to at least $5 million—plus, of course, $6 million more for a new engine.

THURSDAY, AUGUST 4. I arrived at the Edwards North American hangar—my window on the flights for the last few missions—at seven-thirty this morning. This, I knew and everybody in the building seemed to know, was supposed to be the day for the decisive breaking of the world speed record. But there had been three such days before which had ended in aborts—three days on which Joe Walker had been cussing and fuming as he climbed out of his silver suit after the drop from the B-52 had been canceled. The last two times the aborts had been extra exasperating to Joe because they were respectively two and a half and four minutes before drop—close enough so that the ship is all set to go on its own and Joe is also psychologically keyed to the maximum. Then, with all the mechanical and physical tensions screwed up tight and just about at the breaking point, came the abort.

The thing that was different today was that it'd been almost two months since the last try, with the explosion of the Big-Engine bird intervening. More than ever now Joe was geared up to go and make the all-out effort to break the record by a decisive margin.

As I checked in with the cop at the North American hangar, I saw Mel Beach, the chief engineer of maintenance at the company installation. I walked down the hall with Beach toward the tower stairs.

I commented that I heard the X-15 had a new pressure gauge so everything was going to be all right.

"Yeah," he said. "We got everything fixed again."

I spoke about the fact that at the time of the explosion Scott was sitting there in the cockpit not knowing what was going on because his fuel-pressure gauge was off.

Mel said as we started up the stairs, "If he had, he'd have started counting his beads."

Scott is a Roman Catholic, and the principle would have been sound—that is, after he'd shut off his fuel supply.

As Beach and I came into the glass-walled tower room we found one person on deck already: Fred Underhill, a service engineer, sitting at the radio desk.

Others entered quickly: three men with a tape-recorder mechanism to make electronic notes of the flight, and Elmer Jezek, an instrumentation engineer, who began to fiddle with the desk radio. Underhill took a seat at the long table with me. There was an air of constrained eagerness—as if everyone hoped this would be the big day, but scarcely dared to hope for it. I would have bet that over at the NASA control tower, the Master Control or Monitor Console, off limits to newsmen, the atmosphere would be the same, one of hopeful nervousness.

In our North American tower room the radio was strangely silent, and the silence seemed to increase the tension. Mel Beach took his place at the radio table, opposite Elmer Jezek.

Elmer broke the silence. He asked Beach with attempted casualness, "When is the first engine run?" He meant the first ground run of the newly-arrived Big Engine at the test stand.

"The first engine run will be the week of the fifteenth." Beach's formality was the measure of this strangely tense moment.

Suddenly Joe Walker's voice crackled on the radio: "Data . . . calibrate." It startled us. Then he read his gauges aloud, the routine of preparation for take-off.

The time was seven fifty-nine. That moment, we saw the big, rake-tailed B-52 moving along the taxi strip, with its train of vehicles, an ambulance, a suitcase-shaped fire truck, a small crane, and a couple of pickup trucks scuttling along behind, and the red-and-silver Air Force rescue helicopter thrumming overhead, hovering. The cavalcade disappeared behind another hangar as it headed for the end of the runway.

At eight-one we heard Joe Walker say:

"All set."

"Right, Joe." The other voice was Captain John Allavie's, who would be flying the B-52 today. Everyone seemed to be sparing with verbiage today.

The B-52 came back in the other direction, taxiing down the runway to head into the wind, the black, slick X-15 infant tucked under one drooping wing. We all watched, and one of the tape-recorder boys called out:

"Rots of ruck!"

Joe read his gauges aloud, once more: helium sources, nitrogen sources, cabin-pressure source, the hydraulic pressures on the APUs' (auxiliary power units).

The seconds dragged, and then Allavie's voice, "Take-off countdown—three, two, one—*release.*"

In a moment we saw the long spear shape of the B-52, its wide wings now upangled in the flight position, climbing into the sky, a thin trail of water-injection smoke behind it, a wheel of the landing gear still about halfway up.

"And away she goes!" shouted Beach.

The B-52 was edging up into the bright eastern sky.

"Fifteen minutes late," someone said as we watched the glinting wing climb over Rocket Ridge to the east. The take-off schedule was 0800. The weather appeared to be perfect for a flight.

Joe was saying as the plane climbed, at eight-sixteen:

"Blowers off. Ram air's open."

At eight-seventeen a radio voice, either at NASA Ground Control or in the B-52, offered a conversational try: "Nice day, Joe." There was no answer. Joe was evidently concentrating hard and didn't want to be bothered with chitchat.

The B-52 was only a dot in the east. Jack Allavie, the B-52 pilot, announced:

"At 10,500 now. Two-sixty."

We heard a smudgy series of transmissions from Jack Russell, today's launch operator, a NASA technician. They were garbled, but he was concerned mainly with reporting on lox top-off, reading the number of gallons as he kept the X-15 lox tank filled, replacing the evaporation.

Next came another routine check as the big bomber ascended:

"Joe—Jack here," Allavie called. "We're ready for an SAS check."

The stability augmentation system, the system of control dampers on the X-15, had to be checked while the bird was still a captive of the B-52.

"Okay—ready," said Joe. And in a few moments: "Checked out fine." Joe, I reflected, is beginning to sound as if an X-15 flight is routine. This, if it comes to a launch today, will be his third powered flight.

The rest of the routine went as perfectly as everything else today.

NASA Ground Control relayed the wind reports from their weather ship, a C-130 flying over the area where the launch would be made. Joe checked the endless column of readings he had to make: hydraulic temperatures and pressures, nitrogen and helium pressures, the flow through the complicated tanks and pipes that, underneath the slick outer shell, make up the muscle structure of a rocket ship.

There were some new wrinkles about today's flight, though: first, the true space instruments, the inertial platform gadgets which would give absolute readings for speed and altitude anywhere in space, were connected today. Second, for the first time the B-52's position for the launch was going to be determined by a radar fix radioed to the B-52 pilots by NASA Central Control.

Allavie asked Joe how the inertial instruments were reading, and Joe reported: "We're running about 39 to 40,000 inertial altitude and 600 feet a second."

The reading for altitude checked out with the old-fashioned air-pressure gauge readings Allavie had just been giving on the radio, but Walker's velocity readings were way off. The figure of 600 feet per second was 682 miles an hour, while Allavie's speed reading from the conventional air-speed meter had been about 250 knots, or 288.8 miles an hour.

"Okay," Allavie acknowledged. His tone of voice was noncommittal; usually it takes time, perhaps twenty minutes or a half-hour, for the gyro mechanism of the stable-platform instruments to get into proper position, or, in engineering lingo, to be erected.

The second new bit of space business, the positioning of the B-52 by radar, was going better.

NASA Master Control called out the direction to the launch operator, Russell: "Russell, I presume you're set on zero north." Russell needed that radar bearing to help in setting up the stable-platform, or space, instruments.

"Right."

"Okay—that'll be the first one I'll give you." He meant that he would post the launch operator on the radar bearings as they were given.

Then Allavie told Master Control: "I'm starting the climb to 45,000." That was the launch altitude.

Things were going completely on schedule. At eight-forty Launch Operator Russell reported to Aircraft Commander Allavie:

"Twenty minutes to drop, approximately, sir."

And Pilot Allavie reported a few seconds later:

"Forty thousand three hundred—240 knots."

At eight forty-three the flight was still going smoothly as Russell said:

"Estimating sixteen minutes."

We in the tower squinted into the eastern high sky where the white comb of a broad contrail marked the progress of the B-52, with three other thin white streaks of the chase plans spaced out near it. The trails seemed to be heading down in the sky, but they had turned to get into launching position, and were coming west.

Our group in the tower had grown as the time for launch approached. Apparently all the engineers and technicians who had been working in the engineering department across the floor had drifted in, including Ed Cokeley, the head man, and a company cop. Now the room was full—maybe 20 people were in it now.

Beach, the handsome silver-haired chief of maintenance, crouched to look up into the glare of the eastern sky.

"They're headin' over toward the lake right now," he said nervously. "They won't make a circle, they'll just make a 180 turn."

"What's your inertial altitude?" A voice, probably Allavie, was asking Walker by radio.

"Reading about 44 and 700 feet per second." The inertial altitude meter in Joe's cockpit was evidently functioning pretty accurately as the B-52 approached launch altitude, but the inertial speed meter was still way off. However, Joe could still check his altitude and speed with the conventional air-pressure instruments in his ship during the speed run; and of course a really accurate speed reading would come from the radar instruments tracking the X-15 from NASA Master Control.

Russell was getting position readings from NASA Master Control. "Russell—setting at East 65."

"Roger, 65."

A lot would depend, on this or any other record run where maximum performance was sought, on perfect positioning for the launch. If Walker were released too far north or south, he might have to turn to get himself lined up for his glide landing at the end of his run and lose speed in his turn. Or he might have to cut short his run under power if he were released too close to Edwards. He dare not overshoot, because there might be no handy lake bed for the powerless landing.

I realized how much the speed run or any record run must depend on the pilots of the carrier airplane—and on the radar gadgets and crews that positioned it, and on the infinite detail work of the maintenance crews that prepared it, and the weather ship, and the master minds making the decisions at Ground Control. In a maximum performance effort like this, everyone has to be functioning at maximum efficiency.

The launch point for today's effort was to be over Silver Lake, a little town in the brown Sierra Mountains, a point 110 miles east of Edwards.

The plan for X-15, after launch, was to fly in a generally west-by-southwest direction from Silver Lake over Bicycle Lake, then Camp Irwin, then Three Sisters Lake, come coasting out to the east of Rogers Dry Lake (Edwards), and make a gentle turn there and glide in for a landing. From the launch altitude of 45,000 feet, which was about as high as the B-52 could conveniently drop him, Walker would light off full power, pull up to 77,000 feet where the air is thinner and higher speeds therefore possible, and level off for his run to an objective of 3.4 Mach, or at that altitude about 2,244 miles an hour.

At eight-fifty Russell called: "Nine-er minutes." The flight was going without a hitch or a hold.

Mel Beach said as he stared up into the glary, smudgy blue sky: "We might just be able to see it right from launch today."

The white comb of the B-52 and her covey of white streaks moved steadily toward us. Joe Walker was remarkably silent on the radio. No doubt he was keeping a hawk eye on his array of gauges up there in the dim X-15 cockpit, and willing the indicator needles to hold within normal limits.

There was sparse talk as Russell called off his lox top-off levels, doing his utmost to make sure that the evaporation losses should be replenished so that when the bird was dropped, the lox tank would be brim full. Without a full load of lox there might not be enough oxidizer to burn the last gallons of fuel.

We saw the wide contrail of the B-52 curve toward the south, lining up for release. But it was heading toward a bank of mist or hazy clouds lying on the horizon above Rocket Ridge.

Underhill, at the table next to me, was watching apprehensively. "It looks like it'll be hidden behind the clouds." The other engineers, technicians, and miscellaneous employees—all of them emotionally involved because this was their baby on one of her biggest days— edged around nervously watching the bird. This wasn't quite Graduation Day, but they still wanted to see. Graduation Day would come next week when the bird went up into space and broke the world's altitude record—that is, it would be next week or so if today's flight in quest of the world's speed record went okay.

"Oh three, in the turn," NASA Control called to the B-52 to keep the big bomber's position correct.

Then Joe Walker was reading his pressures, an edge of anxiety in his voice because if the needle readings fell the flight would be canceled again.

"Four minutes," Russell's sharp-toned voice called.

The contrail lines were curving north again, above the bank of mist in the east. It looked as if we were going to be able to see the launch and the flight—if it happened.

Joe was finishing his gauge reading: ". . . No. 2 APU thirty-five hundred." Then he made the announcement that was critical: "Power off. X-15 oxygen." This signaled that he was setting up the X-15 for launch—cutting off the supplies of oxygen and power which he had been receiving from the big carrier plane, and turning on the independent sources built into the X-15. Now there was no way to delay the moment of launch. It would either go or not go within three minutes. It would not be wise to put it off now because the X-15 supplies of power, oxygen, etc., are limited.

Russell said: "You got one minute and thirty seconds."

From NASA Master Control came the concerned voice of Stan Butchart, the director of the operation: "I show one minute fifteen seconds, please advise."

But there was no clarification of that slight time difference between the B-52 and NASA Control. The people in the B-52/X-15 combination were too busy checking off their long list of details which must synchronize into a good launch pattern.

Now I could sense the presence of more people squeezing into the room behind me, and I thought I could also sense their anxiety.

"Forty seconds," Russell called.

Someone wanted to make sure Joe heard it: "Forty seconds now, Joe."

"—now blossoming," Russell, the launch operator, was checking the prime trail of the X-15 rocket tubes. We lost the first word on the radio but we knew what it signified: Joe had cranked up his prime, readying his rocket tubes to go, with a clearing blast of lox.

"Ready-to-launch light on," Allavie called from the B-52 cockpit. "Fifteen seconds."

The launch could still be aborted, if a gauge reading suddenly went down. Once, on a company test flight, Crossfield had aborted at eight seconds. But it wasn't likely.

"Ten seconds." I looked at my watch: eight fifty-nine. "Five, four, three, two, one—*launch!*"

Looking up into the glary blue, we saw a new, fat white prong arching down from the contrail of the B-52, toward the white pencil mark of one of the chase planes: the X-15 was under power.

The chase planes were calling in: "Back here it looks good," said one, and I recognized the light-timbred voice of Bob White.

"Looks good here, Joe." Probably that would be Navy Commander Forrest Petersen in the chase plane down below.

The chase planes followed the procedure of calling in right after launch to advise the X-15 jockey that his engines were running well. Crossfield had once said the most critical time in an X-15 flight is the moment after launch—and of course that was the moment when he had his first explosion accident.

The fat white prong of the rocket under power was sweeping up sharply now, suddenly way ahead of the B-52 and the chase planes, forging faster and faster up—very sharply up. The white arrow of the rocket was dividing the high blue into halves, then curving over somewhat, although from this distance and angle it appeared still to be climbing. And, as usual, the broad rocket trail was visibly accelerating, even at that distance of a hundred miles.

But at that speed the hundred miles was rapidly being annihilated.

"Heading the Three Sisters area," Ground Control called.

"Roger." Joe's voice sounded calm, but we knew he was nursing that black baby along with every nerve, every reflex, and every brain cell he could command.

Joe's rocket trail was so long now that the tail end had grown ragged and smeary as the winds of high altitude took it, only seconds old but already 50 miles behind.

"Ninety thousand now—700 feet a second," Joe was reading his inertial-platform instruments, but these newfangled space instruments were evidently still agley. The 90,000-foot reading could be pretty close to accurate, but the 700 feet per second was way off—only 489 miles an hour when he must be going at least four times that fast. The old-fashioned Mach meter on his instrument panel would give him a better indication, and of course the radar reading from the ground would eventually give him the true speed.

"You're in Cuddeback area, Joe."

"Roger." Cuddeback was practically home. The time was a little after nine-two, meaning that Joe had covered about 90 miles in something under three minutes. The fractions and milliseconds would determine how much faster than 30 miles a minute (1,800 miles an hour) he had been traveling.

"Edwards area, Joe."

"Roger." That call had come only a few seconds after the last. The end of the line was coming fast. Now we could see the contrail of the X-15 closer, thinner now because the rocket had burned out. Ahead of the contrail we could see the dot of the black rocket ship, gleaming like a steel point as it caught the sun.

Joe said: "Left turn." The dot of the X-15 was veering slightly to the south.

"Yeah," said Butchart at Master Control. "You're a little off the track."

We knew Joe must be pulling gs even in that gentle curve as he tried to get the ship into position for his landing approach. He was coasting without power but his momentum was probably more than 2,000 miles an hour and any turn would pull plenty of g-forces.

The time was nine-four and some seconds, and in the immensity of the sky the steel point of the X-15 had disappeared, though the plump trail of the B-52 still chugged along far to the east, and in between the thin white line of one of the chase planes trying to catch up, angling down sharply. The chase planes would want to be right with Joe as he glided in for his landing at Edwards.

Joe was coming down, somewhere in the blue. I heard it even if I couldn't see him, since his rocket trail had disappeared after burn-out.

"Goin' down to about 400 knots." A minute later: "I'm quoting a pulse." He meant that the telemetering people should stand by to receive data (pulse) sent by the X-15. And then:

"Comin' up on 40,000—pulse." A telemetering check. Now Joe was really getting down. "I'll start slowin' down toward 221." He evidently felt his speed was too fast for the gliding approach so he was pulling up somewhat to slow his speed.

Now he announced he was switching off the pitch damper of the stability augmentation system to test the reaction in control—a reminder that this was still a research flight, though temporarily dedicated to a speed record.

"You're approaching the west edge of the lake," Ground Control told him.

"Yeah, I got it."

The time was nine-seven. I still hadn't found the approaching dot. Ground Control was checking to see by radio that the jettisonable tail was ready to be dropped—the now-familiar routine of an X-15 landing. "It's armed," Joe reported.

The exceptional part of the flight—the record or lack of it—was done now and the relatively slow routine landing still had to be accomplished.

At nine-nine I looked toward the lake bed where a thin purple cloud of smoke eddied beyond a fire truck. That would be a landing marker to guide Joe in.

The wedge-shaped X-15 suddenly appeared above the northern edge of the lake bed, moving slowly, with two chase planes stacked in the sky right over it, holding there miraculously despite the slow speed.

The three planes disappeared behind the GE hangar next to us. The crowd in the tower room around me craned to watch the ship.

"We'll have to move that hangar," someone complained. It did block the view. In a second the X-15 appeared on the lake bed beyond the hangar—boiling up the usual wedge of brown dust behind it.

And Joe Walker yelled on the radio: "Yipp-ee!"

In our room someone shouted: "There they are."

The X-15 skated along the lake bed, came to a quick stop—and the two chase planes zoomed off while the fluttering rescue helicopter came in and quickly sat down beside the rocket.

The X-15 was at a stop, the dust settling behind it, but new streams of dust churning up in all directions as vehicles dashed toward it. We heard Joe Walker reading the instruments as he shut down the bird—and as he read the inexpressive figures—like "temperature is about 50 on each APU"—you could hear the excitement in his voice.

He was reading fast: ". . . the altitude ball reads 17. The inertial velocity says—it says—holy mackerel, it's up on velocity and down on altitude—meter says 3.43." He raced on: "Cabin source is twenty-three hundred—APU switches are comin' off."

That was all: a flight that went perfectly, although we didn't know yet whether Joe had cracked the speed record. We would know when we had the radar readings.

Cokeley and I briefly discussed what Joe had said about his Mach meter reading: Did he say 3.43 or 3 point 3 plus? The radio transmission had been blotty.

The crowds were leaving the room now, a good flight over. Elmer Jezek got up from behind the radio. "Real fine," he summed up. "No holds—no nothing."

I jumped into my car to drive over to the NASA headquarters, where there was to be a press briefing. A contingent from the press had been taken out to the edge of the lake bed to view the flight, but the public information people had provided no way for the newsmen to hear the radio calls. That was why I had promoted a chance to listen in at the North American tower.

Back at the big NASA conference room I found a dozen or so newsmen. This flight had been lightly covered, considering that it was an attempt to break the absolute world's speed record of four years' standing.

Paul Bikle, the NASA head man, was standing by to tell us what had happened—and to wait with the rest of us for the appearance of Joe Walker.

Matt Portz, the PIO for NASA, had already announced to the newsmen that Walker had broken the world record, and had hit at least 3.3 Mach—at least 2,150 mph. Bikle was saying now in his quiet way that 3.3 Mach was a conservative figure "judging from what Joe said in the cockpit."

While we were waiting for Joe Walker to arrive, the newsmen took advantage of the chance to ask Bikle about plans for the future X-15 flights. There was interest especially in the next mission, scheduled to be the much-discussed assault on the world altitude record.

"What are you planning for on altitude?" Ralph Dighton, the AP regular assigned to X-15, wanted to know.

"Much as we can get," Bikle replied.

"How much?"

Bikle knows that Dighton is familiar with the subject and now he answered exactly:

"One hundred and thirty-five thousand."

We trooped out to the front lawn of the NASA installation where the TV cameras had been set up in the bright, hot sun for the interview with Walker.

Walker was in shirt sleeves and slacks and beaming. Matt Portz introduced him in florid tones:

"Ladies and gentlemen—here's the fastest man in the world, Joe Walker!"

First question:

"How do you feel about it, Joe?"

"Fine." That would have been an exact enough answer ordinarily, but this was an exceptional occasion, so he added:

"I'm sittin' up there watchin' the needle go and I'm sayin' 'Go! Go!'" He went on to explain that he meant the needle of his Mach meter; he was really concentrating, trying to squeeze maximum performance out of the bird.

"I don't remember looking out of the window until I started lookin' around for the lake."

Another question: "When you landed you said 'Yippee!' "

"I sure did."

"What was that conversation?" The questioner wanted that radio call clarified.

"It was sheer exuberance." What a wonderful mixture of the intellectual and the rural is the speech of Joe Walker!

"When did you know you'd broken the speed record?"

"When I saw the Mach meter go on past the mark, I hit my best time."

The newsmen and newswomen pressed him for his sensations during the run. Joe gave us a good honest answer:

"You're so busy in there the sense of speed is when you watch the Mach meter climb to another number." I remembered that Walker had told me that flying the X-15 was like flying the simulator: you fly it by the instruments and you usually don't look out of the cockpit until you're lining up for the landing.

What sensations did he feel the moment he hit his top speed, someone asked.

"You've watched the ballplayer break away at a football game," he said, "when somebody's catching up to him—and you start yelling 'Go! Go! Go!' That was me."

Some of us, like Dighton and Stan Hall of the UPI, had been up here for Walker's three previous aborted attempts at the speed record and knew with what grim vigor that inner voice must have been shouting "Go!" inside him today, all day. And we knew how much he felt was at stake, after the long delay because of the explosion, and how much he and many other people in the Air Force, NASA, and North American wanted to make this flight a success, to vindicate the bird.

There were questions about the future of speed: "What do you think will be the next big jump in speed?"

"I dunno: on the order of three to five hundred miles an hour—because of the way we approach it, by small steps." He went on to say that when the Big Engine was flying, it would be worked up to maximum speed by these gradual steps, since that is the method of a research program.

The newsmen clung to speed, a fascinating subject. "At what point did you reach maximum speed?"

"If you watched the vapor trail—the trail behind—it was at the point where it cut off. It was only for a second—like that!" He snapped his fingers.

"Any heating problems today—because of the speed?"

"We weren't up at that speed long enough to feel it. There might be some paint smeared on the side." He said that the bright decorative paint on the tail—the yellow NASA banner—isn't as heat resistant as the black paint on the rest of the ship.

How fast will men be flying in our lifetime? someone asked.

"We'll be up to escape velocity from the earth in my lifetime—25,000 miles an hour."

"What was your goal this morning?"

"To make it go as fast as it could go."

"What did you think of as you climbed up?"

"That everything was real fine. Then we came out over a big cloud and I said, 'Oh, no, not again.' "

Those of us who had been around before knew how much trouble the murky weather had caused at launch time on Joe's most recent attempts to make the bird go.

"Now that you're the fastest man alive, what are you going to do about it?"

Joe grinned, liking the question. "I'll just keep struggling along."

I asked what Mrs. Walker had fed him the night before this flight.

"My wife's been on the defensive since I had sausage the time before the last flight." I remembered that he had mentioned sausages and potatoes as his dinner the night before that mission. "So last night we had roast duck."

"What did your wife say to you when you left the house this morning?"

"She said: 'Remember your lessons.' " Which, to my way of thinking, was touching, and also appropriate for Grace Walker, a former schoolteacher.

Joe good-naturedly went through the introduction by Matt Portz again, twice, for the movie cameras, coming into camera view after Portz said, "Ladies and gentlemen, Joe Walker, the fastest man alive."

After the session was over and he was hurrying off for the debriefing session with the engineers, someone shouted one last question after Joe:

"What insurance do you have?"

"Just the regular," he answered over his shoulder—apparently meaning the regular $10,000 policy carried over from his Air Force days. That would be in keeping with a man of such regular-guy good nature and unassuming skill as Joe Walker.

Tonight the newspapers carried banner headlines about the flight, billing it as 2,150 miles an hour, although it will probably be revised upward in the next day or two. Most of the papers and broadcasts mentioned the fact that the speed flight presages a record flight to altitude: "ROCKET SHIP X-15 FLIES 2,150 MPH—WARM-UP HOP FOR SPACE ASSAULT," was the line in the Los Angeles *Herald-Express*. And if today's flight was dangerous, the next should be more so, and in many ways much more significant.

FRIDAY, AUGUST 5. The speed mark was revised upward as expected. Portz gave me the new figure of 2,196 miles per hour, a good 100 miles an hour faster than Milburn Apt's record of 1956. The new figure was determined after NASA engineers checked over radar instruments. Portz also told me the altitude flight, with Bob White at the controls, is scheduled for next Thursday. That will be fast work, if it goes on schedule.

SATURDAY, AUGUST 6. Joe Walker's phone was busy pretty steadily this morning, but I finally got through to him with some questions I'd wanted to ask about his record flight and its aftermath.

I said Portz had told me that all the TV producers in the vicinity were after him to make personal appearances since the flight.

Joe said Portz had been screening the people who got through to him, but:

"It's a real rat race. I'd hate to pay the phone bill of all the people that've been calling me."

I wanted to know what had happened after Thursday's flight— what had Grace said when he got home?

Joe answered: "She wasn't there. I called her on the telephone." He didn't elaborate on that conversation, but he added: "She and the kids have been callin' me 'Flash' since [the flight]."

"Whose idea was that?"

"Tommy's." It sounded as impish as Tommy could be.

"What did Grace say when you called her?"

"She said she'd heard all about it on the radio." He paused, and I wondered if she had said something special and endearing which he didn't want to repeat. "I don't remember exactly what she said."

"But she was excited, is that right?"

"Yeah, she was excited, because for some reason she thought we were going to back off on the speed run this time. She didn't know we were going to crack right through with it."

The newsmen who had questioned Joe about his sensations on the flight had failed to ask him about acceleration and deceleration, the phases of the speed run where he would really feel the speed—had he felt it at those times?

"Sure did. You know it didn't take much to build up the gs when I built up the angle of attack [at the start]. I pulled about four gs when I pulled up and a steady three gs in the turn [at the end]. I was ridin' the shoulder harness."

"What was the effect in your head—and body?"

"Just what I usually get." Again, as when I asked him about Grace's first words, after the flight, he was reticent. But everyone knows about the sudden draining of the blood from the head—despite the silver suit's cushioning effect—that comes with a 4-g pull-up force or a 3-g turn at those great speeds. Even with the suit holding you and your own body tensing to avoid the g-strain, you are racked by a feeling of being drained away—a gray-out.

I asked if the flight represented maximum performance for the Small-Engine bird.

"Just about. I burned out all the WALC [water alcohol fuel]."

"Was it a perfect flight?"

"Best I ever had. Both engines chopped off clean as a whistle [at burnout]. No blurp-blurp—just a solid clunk."

I asked Joe what he had done to celebrate, that night. He said he'd had to go to a local water-board meeting (he is one of the five citizens on the board), but "I begged off early for a general gathering of the clan at my house—the people involved in the X-15.

"I didn't realize the house was so small—until all those people were there. But everybody wasn't there. It wasn't a full-bore blast—a lot of the crew were on the night shift."

To append a moral to the interview, I would like to point out that it's only when he's trying to entertain the X-15–NASA crew that Joe Walker suddenly finds his house too small. Otherwise, he wouldn't complain.

THURSDAY, AUGUST 11. I hauled up to Edwards this morning and joined the North American engineering crew in their tower to watch what should have been Bob White's flight to break the world's altitude record.

All the preparations followed the habitual pattern—frequent reading of the gauges across the board (this time from the X-15, White's voice, lighter in timbre and more clipped and formal than Walker's); the checkout of stable-platform (space) instruments (which again were slow to warm up); the struggle by the same B-52 pilots as last time—Fulton and Allavie—to get into precise position for the drop; the painstaking lox top-off by Russell, the launch operator in the B-52; the wind reports from the weather ship; the minute-by-minute countdown before launch—up into the critical last five minutes when White called "power off" and we knew there couldn't be much delay in launch because the X-15 was set up with its own power and oxygen systems.

After the four-minute call, Bob said: "Let me know when, Russ." He was asking for the word the moment the lox top-off was completed.

"Okay—top-off is complete," said Russell.

"Three minutes."

"Steady at 48 to 50."

"Ready to go." Bob was busy with his array of switches and his constant checking of gauges. "Data." Bob alerted the ground for a data (telemetering) burst.

Again, the North American tower room was filling up with people as the moment for drop approached.

"Is your vertical armed, Bob?"

Then came the reading that killed the mission: "N_2 is down to twenty-one hundred." That meant that his nitrogen source was dropping. If it fell farther he probably wouldn't have power to run his controls or pressurize his cabin for the flight.

"Source is down to eighteen hundred." Things were turning very bad and Neil Armstrong, running Ground Control at NASA today, reacted quickly—with thirty-five seconds to go:

"Aborted launch, Fitz [Fulton]."

Armstrong, at NASA Control, instructed White with palpable regret in his voice:

"Bob, we'd better jettison, I guess—peroxide first."

Bob, in the same dismal mood, was reporting on his rapidly-diminishing nitrogen pressure:

"Source down to 450."

Someone in our room opined: "Must have blown something."

And Bill Berkowitz, the North American technician who had been sitting next to me in the tower, cracked: "Send the N_2 tanker up."

So the X-15's first try at the world altitude record and penetration into space ended in anticlimax. We don't know when the next attempt will be—maybe next week.

But I heard one bit of good news: the new Big Engine has been tested once on the stand and will probably be run again tonight. By next year, it may be making record runs.

Tonight I had a good word about the Small Engine, too. The NASA-Air Force Bird No. 1, with Bob White at the controls, will try again for the altitude record tomorrow. The crews are keeping the bird mated with the B-52 overnight, and barring bad weather or an accident will start servicing and fueling at 4 A.M. for eight o'clock take-off.

FRIDAY, AUGUST 12. When I got up to the North American tower this morning, about seven-thirty, Fred Underhill, the service engineer, was very much on deck. He's been listening to the radio calls, which indicated that everything was going fine today; servicing was just about done down in the mating area.

"They're finishing the lox top-off [on the ground] and they'll be ready to go," he said.

Elmer Jezek, Bob Field, the tape-recorder men, and other regulars here at the tower room showed up, while the last-minute groundwork at the mating area went smoothly. The distinctive, light-toned voice of Bob White, from the X-15 cockpit, was cool and efficient as he read his gauges. At seven-fifty, ten minutes before scheduled take-off, the long shape of the B-52 was moving along the taxiway, her usual train of land vehicles hurrying after her.

The B-52 taxied behind a hangar at seven fifty-one and was out of sight when we heard White's distinctive voice reading his instrument panel, ending ". . . plus 30 and plus 30 . . . source 3,500."

We heard the call of Chase One as he made ready for take-off: "Chase One-726-taxiing." That would be Captain Bob Rushworth, Bob White's back-up pilot, today his first chase in an F-104.

And the weather report from NASA: "Surface wind running five to ten knots out of the north."

It wasn't eight o'clock yet and everything was clicking nicely. Ed Cokeley, the North American head man here at Edwards, came stiffly in at seven fifty-nine, immaculately white-shirted as usual, and demanded:

"Did they have any troubles this morning?"

"Not that I know of," Jezek answered.

A few seconds later the B-52 pilot, Major Fitzhugh Fulton, was calling his take-off countdown: "Five, four, three, two, one."

At eight-one, almost exactly on schedule, we saw the big Momma Bomber airborne, appearing from behind the Air Force hangar to the south, lumbering toward the northeast, her landing gear going up into the fuselage, a faint smoke trail from maximum-power water injection fading behind. She passed behind another hangar, the long airplane body sloping up, and appeared beyond the hangar climbing rapidly now into the eastern sky, the sun glinting on the top of the fuselage.

And it wasn't eight-two yet; all the 80-odd Eager Beavers on the B-52/X-15 team were sharp today: the pilots in the B-52 and the chases and the X-15, the B-52 launch operator, the servicing technicians, and maintenance engineers working for NASA and the Air Force; the instrumentation, power plant, telemetering engineers and technicians, the crews of the emergency fire trucks and ambulances and the crane, the cameramen and the crews of the rescue chopper and the C-130 weather ship, the radar crews on the NASA range where the flight will be made, and Neil Armstrong, the ground director at the NASA Master Control in the tower, and all the specialized engineers standing by him there. All these must have been much on the ball for everything to go so promptly like a good railroad, this morning. And I knew why the intense effort and precision: this flight today was the biggest, the biggest that had happened to the X-15 since the first captive flight back there on March 10, 1959. What was supposed to be happening today was the thing for which the X-15 had been designed, built, and refined: flight into space. Even the world-record speed flight of a week ago was only a step in this direction. Later flights with the bigger engine, some time in the future, will go higher, everybody hopes, but today's flight is a reality, a reality with a bird in being, a tested bird and engine that can do it, can break the world's altitude record and go into the dark edge of the ocean of space, the Wild Black Yonder beyond atmosphere.

I thought of the thousands of people who had contributed to this flight in previous efforts, starting with the Chinese rocket militia at Pien-King in the thirteenth century, with heroic Wan Hu in the sixteenth, and Colonel Congreve of the British Artillery, and Hyder Ali of Mysore in the nineteenth, and Ziolkovsky and Oberth, Von Braun and Goddard, Max Valier and Opel and Wyld and Shesta, Kincheloe and Apt, all the people stretching back in time and across the band of nationalities, who had worked to make this moment possible today. It was only one of many moments in space history, and there would be greater moments as men reached farther under rocket power, but if it worked today it was going to be a great moment for all the dead pioneers and all the living and working ones like Q. C. Harvey, Feltz, Robinson, Benner, Butchart, Armstrong, Welker—all who had sweated to design and build and test this bird, this powerful blackbird representing for now, for the moment, the culmination of all men could do to put a man beyond the new frontier—such a close frontier, not as far away from us here as White Plains is from the Battery or Fontainebleau from Paris, 24 miles away, no distance at all as earthly distances go, except that this distance is straight up, the unknown for men.

"NASA 1—Winds at Las Vegas and Edwards are 23 at 7 knots." The NASA Master Control was giving that weather bulletin to guide the B-52 launch plane on its upward course. Fitz Fulton reported how it was going in the concise language of the airman: "20,000—two-six-zero."

Fred Underhill, sitting next to me in the tower room, was looking at a photographic portrait of Bob White among my papers on the table: White, a handsome, healthy, vigorous man with luminous, intelligent eyes. The picture showed him in his silver suit, smiling, his hair tousled, the photograph evidently having been taken just after he had returned from a mission. Like Joe Walker, White is the archtype of the best American pilot-engineer in physical and mental prime, willing and able to go where it is demanded he go.

Underhill studied the photograph and put it down. "A helluva nice fella—quiet-spoken, easy-goin', very polite."

Only the most talented and trained we can offer, I thought.

Eight-ten: "Twenty-five thousand—two-six-one." Altitude and speed from Fulton.

"Bob, this is Blackbird Two." That would be Mobile Control, the yellow truck wagon with the anemometer on top, out on the lake bed. "Could you give us your hydraulic temperatures?"

"No. 1 minus 50, No. 2 minus 50," White answered quickly. Was this better, I wondered, than an automatic instrument reading sent from an unmanned missile by the finicky and primitive mechanism of telemetry? It became instantaneously apparent that it was better when Bob White went on to volunteer pertinent and related data: "To go across the board: No. 1 source is thirty-five fifty, No. 2 source is thirty-four hundred, APU source is thirty-seven fifty . . ."

Even for an apparently mechanical function like reading a spread of dials, the human brain can offer the advantages of penetrating selection, voluntary action, and decision—and go beyond what the largest collection of thought machines can do, as of right now anyhow. The brain, ninety cubic inches of precise and practically unlimited power, four pounds of convoluted gray matter summing up all that men have been able to do, are, and will be able to do, in the future. If the Martians sent a space ship to land in Times Square, how much better for them to have one human brain to observe, report, and evaluate there for ten minutes, than an Empire State Building full of IBM 709s functioning for a month. Someday scientists will train a thought machine to do solid geometry problems, but will they ever really teach it to make a decision or change its mind as a changing situation dictates? I shudder to think of the many times before this we would have lost the X-15 if a machine had been reporting from up there instead of a man, and how many times the destruct officer would have pressed his button on the basis of reports from an accurate but unadaptable mechanical brain.

Now Bob was working over his Stability Augmentation System, checking out the pitch and yaw dampers in preparation for free flight:

"Check—on roll and yaw—reset."

The sky in the east looked dazzling bright and still, hazy here and there but with scarcely a cloud. In the northeast corner of our big window we could see the wide three-pronged contrail of the B-52, with the little white zips of the chase planes following it, heading generally toward the bulging brown mass of the Sierras beyond the Mojave Desert, and the pinpoint called Silver Lake in the brown mountains 110 miles away, near which, at 45,000 feet, the launch would occur.

The positioning for the drop from the B-52 was starting now. Soon Neil Armstrong, an X-15 back-up pilot for NASA who was running the show at Master Control in the NASA tower this morning, would begin to give radar bearings to the B-52 so that it would be set in the most advantageous spot in the sky for maximum performance in the arc into space, so that Bob White could follow the trajectory curve which the engineers had figured out, and come out at the end of it conveniently positioned to glide in to a safe landing on the lake bed.

But now the radio was silent. The group of North American engineers and technicians—and the company cop and other miscellaneous employees who also wanted to see the Black Baby perform —stirred restively in the quiet.

In the empty time someone mentioned the successful recovery of an orbiting space capsule by Air Force search planes over the Pacific yesterday: the capsule from Discoverer XIII.

"It's about like trying to catch an eagle with a butterfly net," commented Cokeley. And this led to a brief discussion about eagles, led by a gray-haired technician, Rocky Mast, sitting at the radio desk. Mast told about a young eagle he and his friends once captured: ". . . it was about so high—not old enough to fly—it ate a full-grown rabbit a day—" Then Cokeley shushed the conversation and everybody leaned to hear, because something was coming on the radio. It was the high-toned but very clear voice of Neil Armstrong from NASA tower:

"Okay, Russell. Mark it."

In a few seconds Russell gave the first call for the countdown to drop: "About sixteen minutes."

Armstrong's clear voice was calling White to check on the space instruments which by now should be erected or warmed up enough to give a reading:

"Give us your inertial altitude, Bob."

That youthful voice made it easy to picture the boyish, blond, crew-cut Armstrong running today's show from NASA Monitor Console. He is the youngest of the X-15 pilots, just turned thirty a week ago, but he has the mature concentration and responsibility you sense in all of them.

"Forty-three thousand," Bob White reported. It sounded as if the instrument reading must be about right, considering where the B-52 was now in the sky. The routine for today's flight was for Armstrong to call off the X-15's altitude as measured by radar while it arched in rocket flight up into the sky—and for White to compare these readings with the height he was showing on his inertial-altitude indicator. Above 90,000 feet the old-fashioned altimeter also on his dial would be almost useless, since it works on air pressure and there is almost no air pressure above 90,000.

Armstrong was calling radar position: "Okay, Fitz. It looks as if the initial point will be zero zero eight." This drop had to be engineered with all the precision of a wartime aircraft lining up to plaster a target; except for the A-bombs on Hiroshima and Nagasaki, this was probably the most important single load ever let loose by a bomber.

Information on winds was relayed from the C-130 weather ship: "Winds at Silver Lake remain at five to ten knots."

Fitz Fulton reported: "We're at 44—200." Altitude and speed.

Weather reports were continuing; giving barometric pressure over Silver Lake so the altimeters could be set accurately, and a report on clouds: "Cirrus at 40,000 very, very thin."

"At 45,000—accelerating," Fulton reported with a detectable ring of excitement and somebody, probably a Chase, enthused:

"Looks real good."

We saw the fat white trail of the B-52 heading more directly east, almost fading into the high screen of blue haze. At eight thirty-five Russell warned: "Just past ten minutes to launch."

And Armstrong was pursuing the radar positioning: "Russell, let's take the next setting—eight zero east—and go to stand by when you're ready. . . . Okay, Russell, mark it. . . . And the next setting will be 60 north—six zero north . . . make the next setting 65 north if you didn't read that last message." Russell had to know the exact position so he could help set the gyro of the space instruments.

"Sixty-five north," Russell acknowledged to set Armstrong's nerves more nearly at ease.

Silence on the radio as the white rake of the B-52 contrails plugged eastward into the thin blue haze.

"Seven minutes . . . seven minutes," Russell's voice burst out.

Bob White was reading his pressure gauges aloud, but the dispatch was smudgy. Ground asked for a repeat.

"Okay, starting the run," Fitz Fulton interrupted.

White was reading his gauges again: ". . . source pressure thirty-seven hundred, No. 1, thirty-five hundred, No. 2 oil pressure, thirty-two fifty, running chamber temperature plus 40 and plus 30." It sounded as if White were priming engines now, and to the engineers here in the North American tower room the figures from the pressure gauges sounded just fine.

"Pretty good," Cokeley said—and for him that was enthusiasm.

Underhill was more lavish: "Sounds like they just got through servicing." Everything was going perfectly.

"Four minutes . . . four minutes," Russell called, and now time was very short. It was eight twenty-nine.

Bob White called tensely: "Pressures are up on all eight chambers."

"Three minutes . . . three minutes."

"Top-off looks good—just right," Russell reported. Lox was going fine.

"Okay. Tank pressures are holding pretty well." This from White.

"Two minutes . . . two minutes." I felt the pressure of a thickening crowd behind me in the tower room.

Armstrong called from NASA Control, anxious to get performance information via telemetering: "Check your data on, please, Bob." "Roger. Data is on."

"Got a minute and five seconds," Russell called. "One minute." Time was getting almost too scarce now to abort.

Then came the rush of calls as the drop was only seconds away, several voices on top of each other:

"Twenty seconds—the master comin' on—temperature plus 40 and 30" (White). . . . "The launch light on" (Fulton). . . . "All set" (White). . . . "Rog" (Fulton). . . . "Ten seconds . . . five, four, three, two, one—*release!*"

The flight was on. We squinted into the sky.

"You look good," the first Chase reported promptly to Bob. "You're heading just a little south of Three Sisters."

A new-blooming white trail, fat and thick as rockets make, was angling sharply up in front of the plodding B-52; already the fledgling was shooting higher than the mother plane, moving so fast that the lower end of the rocket trail, down below the mother, was already smudged by the wind.

The high, clear voice of Armstrong, as the rocket ship went up: "Okay, Bob—we have you coming at 60." Sixty thousand feet—the radar trackers had a grip on the flight, or at least the altitude of the X-15.

To altitude: the white streak was shooting up faster—almost straight up, it seemed. The angle appeared to be increasing in steepness.

Armstrong: "Okay—seven, Bob . . . okay, we don't have any Mach number for you." Seventy thousand feet, that is, and no speed reading. The plan had been to get speed readings for White from radar at NASA Ground Control as he went up. His speed would be a critical matter as he arced up into space. He was going to rely on speed to give him pressure on his earth-bound conventional control surfaces—control up there where there is practically no air for the surfaces to bite on. He had to depend on conventional controls today because his space or rocket controls were not functioning—the bugs had not been ironed out of them.

Bob had said he was going to hope for speed above Mach 2 (1,320 mph) for better control as the ship soared into the virtual vacuum at the top of its ballistic trajectory. He would have to depend on radar plot, on the ground, to know what his speed was. His own old-fashioned Mach meter wouldn't help up there where there is no air—and his space speed meter, connected to the inertial platform gyro, wasn't working today. Like the inertial altimeter and the space controls, the X-15 space-velocity meter is still beset by mechanical difficulties.

Anyhow, Bob's speed would be determined by the sharpness of the angle he assumed as he started his climb, and would be largely beyond his control. The arc of his flight, the distance he would go into the edge of space, and the angle and speed he would follow as he came down on the other side were dependent on his initial angle and how far and fast the rocket engines boosted him before burnout. Today, rocket burnout should be about 120,000 feet, and the engineers hoped the boost would carry him up another three miles or so before he started coming down. This was only a rehearsal, in a way, for the future flights with the Big Engine, which would burn out at about the same altitude, but with four times the thrust, shoot the X-15 many times higher in its trajectory. But today's was still a record flight, and a dangerous one—in some ways more dangerous than the later flights will be, because for this one the space controls were not connected. Later, they will be. Today, Bob wouldn't have any real control over the top of his arc. He could trim the ship as it went over, could keep it in the right attitude, he hoped, with his conventional controls. That's what he had told me, and I hoped he was right as he zoomed toward what he calls "The Murk."

"Eight!" Neil Armstrong called: 80,000 feet only a second, it seemed, after he had called seven.

"Your angle looks good, Bob."

"We're goin' up!" Bob sounded breathless.

"Comin' up on 10 now." The tens of thousands of feet were clicking like seconds. The white tail of the X-15 was still fat and healthy—the ship still very much under power. The white streak stood high in the sky now and it was growing taller fast, although its lower stage was smeared and torn by wind.

The ship was nearing record height now. Everyone around me in the room seemed to be reaching for it.

"Going through 11 now with no Mach number," Armstrong was saying. "Coming up on 12 now! . . . got 12.6!" Armstrong knew this was the significant figure—the record height of 126,200 feet which Kincheloe had set up four years ago.

And White was still going up—although his rocket trail had truncated abruptly and he was invisible up there. He had burned out, but he would keep on going.

"Thirteen!"

". . . very sensitive." Bob's voice was smudgy and far away. His controls were giving him trouble. He was hitting the dangerous top of the curve, his control down to minimum. Now was the time he could have real difficulty.

"You look good here—still good," Armstrong told him.

Bob's radio transmission was still smudgy. He seemed to be saying something about "14.2 inertial height" and "fantastic up here."

Then we couldn't see him but we knew he was coming down on the other side of his curve.

"Twelve point five coming down now," Armstrong said. The eyes of his radar were tracking the invisible X-15 on its return to earth.

The record was broken, but another difficult time was coming up in seconds—the moment of re-entry. It was not so critical this time, with a flight only 25 miles up or so. But later, when the Big Engine arches up to four times as high and comes back twice as fast, the aerodynamic heating will be a great problem. On today's record flight the speed of re-entry into atmosphere shouldn't be higher than Mach 2.5 (1,650 mph).

Armstrong called: "Now 12."

"Rog."

"We got you about ten point five now." The X-15 was down to 100,500 feet, and it would be falling faster and faster from here: not too fast, if that initial angle had been correctly chosen—and if Bob White had been able to keep the X-15 in correct trim over the top of the ballistic arc, and hadn't lost control so that he would be re-entering upside down or end for end. We couldn't see him, but if he were in trouble, tumbling like a pinwheel in inertia coupling, we would probably have heard some indication of distress on his radio or the NASA radar.

The seconds were long, long seconds full of thought about what had happened to White, the record, and what would happen when the diving X-15 would hit the thicker air at 60,000 to 50,000 feet.

"Speed and angle's good . . . okay, eight . . . okay, we got you on seven now." Armstrong sounded as if he were coaxing the X-15 down.

And now we had pretty good proof that White was all right. "I'm showin' eight," he said clearly, indicating that he was functioning, and was comparing his inertial altimeter reading with that which Armstrong had just given him from the radar.

"How about Mach meter?" Armstrong asked.

"Got two point two." White had progressed into air thick enough so he could get a reading on his conventional Mach meter: 2.2 would be 1,452 mph.

Bob was calling his altitude in thousands: "55-54-52 . . . speed's about 1.95." The ship was slowing nicely.

"Okay," Armstrong called, "I got 45. You're right south of the lake bed . . . 44 . . . got you at 41."

Now the flight was nearing an end and White was still okay.

"Chamber switches are off," he reported. "Anybody picked up a jettison yet?" He was dumping his excess lox preparatory to the landing.

Bob was calling speed and altitude: "270 [knots] . . . twenty-four point five now." Then suddenly a garbled, strange transmission: "Ask Bert Rowan what happens if I'd lift up this face mask."

It was a weird message and one could almost sense in the air a wondering if the X-15 pilot had suddenly blown his top. Armstrong asked him to say it again, and Bob repeated:

"Ask Bert Rowan what happens if I'd lift up this face mask."

There was no answer on the air as the NASA crew tried to decipher the message. Bert Rowan is an Air Force flight surgeon White knows, and the question sounded as if he were having trouble with anoxia and it was making him lightheaded: his question didn't make sense unless he was running out of oxygen and requesting instructions.

Armstrong had evidently figured what might be wrong. "Your oxygen okay, Bob?—or your face mask?"

But Armstrong's fears were not grounded. White answered: "Yeah, I got oxygen."

Another possible calamity which could have overtaken White just before landing had not occurred. (Later, Bob said he'd had a stoppage in one ear and was making a joke when he'd asked about lifting his face mask. But there must have been some considerable pain or the well-disciplined White probably wouldn't have brought up the matter—certainly not as a joke.)

Now the small X-15 cigar shape appeared over the northern edge of the lake bed, two chase planes just over it, the broken-bandana rescue chopper hovering near, while the purple smoke of a landing marker eddied up from the lake bed. The X-15 scooted behind a hangar and when we saw it again on the other side it was tailing a cone of tan dust, on the ground again, and slowing rapidly to a stop.

"He's down!" one of the rubbernecks in our tower yelled.

And from Armstrong at NASA monitor console the somewhat

pukka salutation: "Good show, Bob. . . . Attention, all stations: post flight briefing at ten-thirty."

Bob sounded similarly nonchalant: "I'll run through my close-out check." And he read calmly, in the usual monotone, as if it were a school lesson: "Uh . . . stable platform is off . . . thirty-two fifty No. 1 . . . bearing temperature plus 60 on No. 1—60 on No. 2 . . . source pressure No. 1 400, No. 2 400 also . . . showing 58,000 on inertial height, inertial velocity zero. . . . Are you ready for me to turn off the APU switches?"

White was not making with any "Yippees" as Walker did after the world-record speed run and I was reminded what Charlie Brown had said about White after his first flight in the X-15, when he had never before flown a rocket ship: "A cool young man."

"Okay, Bob," Armstrong responded to White's question about his APU switches, and the great mission was over, and in the tower room where I sat the crowd was breaking up. Cokeley was going out, too, with a half-smile on his face, quite a smile for Cokeley, and as he walked by, he permitted himself a good deal of enthusiasm for Cokeley. He slapped me on the shoulder and said: "Looks like we got it."

There was a press conference at the ASA briefing room, as there had been after the Joe Walker speed flight. The old standbys of the news services, Stan Hall and Ralph Dighton, were there—and so were the local press of the Edwards-Lancaster vicinity.

Matt Portz of the NASA PIO came into the conference room where the pressmen and ladies were ranged at a long table and began: "Here's the dope." He went over the facts as known that moment: White went to 131,000 feet, a conservative figure that might be revised upward later on. Portz went over the time of take-off and drop, burnout and landing, and repeated the quote from Bob at the top of his trajectory as Portz had picked it up: "This is fantastic."

While we waited for Major White to appear, Portz asked us jokingly: "What can we call Bob?—not the highest man in the world."

"The tallest man in the world," suggested Stan Hall.

It was nine-thirty when Bob came in, wearing a summer Air Force uniform, and Matt introduced him simply: "Ladies and gentlemen, Major White."

Bob sat down at the long table with us, and the personality difference between Joe Walker and the Air Force major soon became apparent to the correspondents. Like Walker, White is modest, but he has none of Walker's racy homespun humor or dash. White is well disciplined, careful, thoughtful, and polite. He speaks with a certain polish and fondness for polysyllables which sometimes makes what he says sound ponderous, like an official military report.

First question:

"You said at altitude, 'It's really fantastic up here.' Would you tell us what it looked like—what the sky looked like, what the earth looked like from up there?"

With characteristic earnestness White answered: "I hope I can give you what you want. People asked about it the last time, when I went up to 107,000 feet.

"This time I took a look out. I was impressed very greatly with the altitude.

"It seems that you usually take in 100 miles in a sweep across the horizon. This time you would take in ten times the horizon. But I didn't see anything like the picture you see taken from the missiles."

Bob got to the question which he knew the reporters were very curious about: Was the sky black up there? Did he see the Wild Black Yonder?

He said: "After my last flight I didn't care to comment on any darkness. However, this time it wasn't exactly night but there was a very strong contrast between the sky—and the lower bands. . . . It appeared there was a band of light, of brighter sunlight, at about 50,000 or 60,000 feet. Above this there seems to be a much deeper and bluer sky.

"Realizing that I was pretty busy in my cross-checking in the cockpit—[Bob left the participle dangling and charged on with all the earnestness of Eisenhower at a press conference]—I didn't try to pick out Candlestick Park in San Francisco. . . . However, shortly after coming back for re-entry I could take in the whole Antelope Valley [the wide Mojave Desert area]."

"Could you see the curvature of the earth?"

"If you could see a picture you could probably see the curvature." He was evidently trying to communicate that curvature was not instantly noticeable at that height, but that in a photograph it would show—and that he hadn't had too much time to look out.

"Were you at the absolute altitude limit of the X-15?"

"I think this is fairly close, with this power plant. Could be, with a little longer burnout, we might be able to go a little higher."

"What was your sensation when you were climbing up?"

"It felt as if I was going just about straight up. But my pitch angle was about 50 degrees."

I asked Bob what he did last night—did he go to bed early?

"Ten minutes to ten," he said, and hastened to add further details: "I read a *Saturday Evening Post*—about three weeks old—an article in the 'Adventures of the Mind' series, by a Rand mathematician."

I asked if the article was any use or if he had thought of it during the flight.

"No."

"What did your wife say when you left home this morning?"

" 'Good luck, honey.' That was all."

"What are your plans for tonight—are you going to celebrate?"

"I think I'll sit down at a friend's house and talk about the past, present, and future." (He told me later that the friend was Colonel Rowan, the flight surgeon. Others there were Captain Bob Rushworth, his back up, and Major Harry Andonian who had been the copilot in the B-52 today.)

"What were your emotions during the flight?"

The interview had turned toward subjective matters and White shied away as Walker had after the speed flight.

"I'm just greatly pleased at this . . ." He paused and went on even less expressively (but with determination): "The research objective was to explore maximum performance at low dynamic pressure."

"Did you wish you had reaction controls?" The questioner was AP reporter Ralph Dighton, an old hand at covering the X-15 and wise in the ins and outs of the space world.

Dighton knew that it had taken monumental courage for White to venture into the unknown of space, where no man had ever been, without workable reaction or space controls.

Bob had known he was taking a risk when he zoomed up into the sky 25 miles where there is only a cupful of air per cubic mile. He had counted on speed, the velocity of his rocket-powered climb, to make that piddling little quantity of air give him some control with his conventional airplane-type control surfaces, as he went over the top of his trajectory.

But White, being the kind of duty-bound, devoted Air Force officer he is, would be the last to emphasize the risk he took today. I knew he had relied heavily on other Air Force and NASA engineers to help him plot a pitch-up angle on his climb which would take him to maximum altitude without going too slowly, lest he lose control as he went over the top. If he had chosen to angle up at 65 degrees instead of 50 when he started his climb, he might have gone another 5,000 feet high, but he would have been going much more slowly, and might thus have lost control and started tumbling as Kinch had tumbled in the X-2. And he would have re-entered earth's atmosphere more steeply on the other side and had a greater re-entry heat. These will be the running problems of this research vehicle as, with the Big Engine in the future, it probes higher and higher.

Now, today, Bob White had known the risk he was taking, and depended on his own calculations and the calculations of the engineers who work with him—and also, as I had found out at the time of his first rocket flight, on his strong Roman Catholic faith.

And White wasn't going to admit that he had any doubt about flying out there into emptiness without his reaction controls or Ballistic Control System. He answered Dighton's question as Dighton and I might have expected:

"I was just getting into the area where I might have used them [the reaction controls]—but I might not have used them if I'd had them; because I wouldn't know the degree of control I could get from them." In other words, he was into the edge of space so briefly and needed his reaction controls for such a short time that he might have been chary about using such an unknown quantity for that short interval.

The control situation—White's flying up there without his BCS or reaction controls—intrigued me. When Bob went out to the NASA front lawn to pose for the movie cameras, I followed him and noted that Harrison "Stormy" Storms, the great engineering brain who had built the X-15 for North American, had the same question on his mind.

While the reporters asked White about weightlessness on today's flight—he had been weightless on the ballistic arc for one minute, longer than any man before, and was little affected by the experience —Stormy waited on the side lines and when the interview was over he asked White the question about control at the top of the arc. I heard White answering, as one engineer to another:

"It started to get a little soft on pitch." Even that opinion delivered to another engineer, though, was probably a massive understatement of the hours of calculation, worry, and courage—and faith—that went into the planning of the control factor in today's great mission and its successful completion.

Now White was hurrying off to the engineering debriefing to be held at the NASA conference room. He would sit for an hour with NASA, Air Force, and North American engineers to help them evaluate today's mission in terms of research, and to help them plan the next X-15 research flight for next week, a flight at 70,000 feet and Mach 3 to study aerodynamic heating at high speeds. To the research types, today's flight, whatever dangerous unknowns were involved, was only another step in the research stairway that leads to space. They can have their dry opinion: I will join the millions everywhere who will honor Bob White as a brave pioneer and explorer of the unknown.

MONDAY, AUGUST 15. Last week was a good one for the United States in space: the Discoverer XIII capsule was recovered by the Air Force in the Pacific after orbit, presaging the day when men will orbit and be picked up; the 100-foot silver-colored communications balloon called Echo was sent into orbit by NASA and was circling the earth like a star; and it would be there to serve its function as a communications booster for many days to come. There were two successful missile firings—a Navy Polaris shooting 2,000 miles, an Atlas flying 5,000. And there was the bit about the X-15 having flown higher than a man had ever been before, the black rocket ship working its way up the ladder of space.

Today NASA announced that its first estimate of the altitude Bob White had hit was low—low by nearly a mile. He had reached 136,-500 feet, nearly 26 miles up. Matt Portz of NASA told me about the new finding, and told me also about the next mission of the X-15, scheduled for Thursday: it will be the aerodynamic heating flight, to about 1,980 miles an hour at relatively low altitude, 70,000 feet. It wasn't long ago that 70,000 feet was high, and 1,980 miles an hour was a speed record. That's the way the world of space travel is progressing these days.

I told Matt I was surprised to see an X-15 mission scheduled so soon after the recent triumph. He said: "You don't expect us to sit and rest on our laurels, do you? We've got a bunch of tigers up there."

And he was right.

Index